CHILDREN
OF THE
FUR TRADE

CHILDREN
OF THE
FUR TRADE

FORGOTTEN MÉTIS OF THE PACIFIC NORTHWEST

John C. Jackson

Mountain Press Publishing Company
Missoula, Montana, 1995

Cover art: "Indian Women in Tent,"
by Peter Rindisbacher. Courtesy
West Point Museum Collections, U.S. Military Academy

Library of Congress Cataloging-in-Publication Data

Jackson, John C., 1931-
    Children of the fur trade : forgotten Métis of the Pacific
Northwest / John C. Jackson.
        p.   cm.
    Includes bibliographical references (p.   ) and index.
    ISBN 0-87842-329-X (cloth : alk. paper) — ISBN 0-87842-
339-7 (pbk. : alk. paper)
        1. Métis—History. 2. Métis—Hunting.   3. Métis—Commerce.
    4. Fur trade—Northwest, Pacific—History.   5. Oregon—History—
    To 1859.   I. Title.
    E99.M47J33   1995   95-42976
    979.5'00497—dc20   CIP

Printed in the U.S.A.

Mountain Press Publishing Company
P.O. Box 2399
Missoula, Montana 59806

For my daughters,
Apryl and Maria

Contents

PREFACE

The mixed bloods of the Pacific Northwest were marginal people who finally reached their farthest boundary, the Pacific Coast. For forty years they influenced the development of the Oregon country, a vast area bounded on the east by the crest of the Rocky Mountains, on the south by the Spanish territories running along 42 degrees north latitude, and on the west by the shore of the Pacific Ocean. The northern boundary, which was disputed by Great Britain and the United States, might fall as far south as the Columbia River or as far north as Russian America (Alaska). The region included areas of lush river valleys, semideserts, and high mountains in three parallel north–south environments: coastal, rain shadow, and piedmont. Fir forests towered west of the Cascade Range and pine trees spread across the semiarid east. It was a rugged land still being shaped by volcanic activity and vigorous rivers—a youthful world looking forward rather than backward.

The native cultures of this geographical capsule included coastal fishermen, woodland hunter-gatherers, plains rangers, and desert dwellers. For most, the Northwest was a relatively easy place to live. Along the coast, tribes rose above the subsistence level and developed spectacular cultures. Until the late eighteenth century, the Northwest remained isolated from nonnatives. Then ship traders began probing the coastal bays and rivers. By the turn of the century, fur trappers were working their way southwest from the Canadian Northwest and west from the Missouri River.

During the first four decades of the calamitous nineteenth century, Indians and intruders found ways to accommodate mutual interests and live together without serious conflict. Often the cushion between cultures in collision was a handful of fur trappers who crossed the mountains early and mixed their complex bloodlines with the western tribes.

The Pacific Northwest mixed bloods were the children of European or Canadian fathers and native American mothers. In the Canadian woodlands or prairies they were called Métis. For almost half of the nineteenth century the Métis enjoyed a unique subculture built around hunting and mobility. The sometimes dangerous contest for beaver resources taught them to hang together for mutual support and fostered a tribal identity that was reinforced through intermarriage.

Some Métis congregated around the trading posts, where they were employed as laborers, packers, or boatmen. Most traveled with the trapping brigades in a loose business environment that took authority lightly and fostered a sense of independence. There is an ironic reflection of their status in the trader's term "western freemen." When the mountain hunt declined, a few French-speaking Catholics settled in western Oregon or the lower Puget Sound area. The three main areas of Métis concentration were the French Prairie of the lower Willamette Valley, the north Tualatin plains, and the open prairies along the Cowlitz River. Lesser communities grew in the Walla Walla Valley, in the Flathead country of western Montana, and around the old fur trade depot of Fort Colvile. By mid-century many Métis were already in retreat to less developed places or to the recently established Indian reservations.

The initial isolation of the Pacific Northwest from contingent frontier development makes it a unique laboratory for the study of cultures in collision. Unlike their eastern kinsmen, the Northwest Métis did not develop a distinct material culture. Theirs were the habits of the hunting trail, the transport brigade, and the camp. Those patterns, which flared with the first kindling of campfires, fell into ashes only after being scattered by the winds of change.

This is an informal, and admittedly incomplete, survey of the marginal people of the Pacific Northwest. Their neglected record is occasionally found as vague footnotes to mercantile, mission-ary, or political history. The trappers who carried the frontier thesis in a soggy parfleche, and found manifest destiny in a pack of beaver pelts, were significant beyond their actual number. Their families of mixed ancestry left a lasting imprint on the region. Without pretending to scientific detachment, this book is meant as a celebration of a life force; it lets the mixed bloods, in their vitality, misery, joy, and disappointment, speak for them-selves.

The term *Métis* is used in a broad, nontechnical sense as a convenient, concise designation for people of mixed Native American and British or French ancestry. Similarly, the historically common designation *half-breed*, when used, is meant as an identification rather than a social judgment.

A word on the correct spelling of Indian and Métis names: there isn't any. At best, transcriptions of native and French names heard by an Anglophone ear were phonetic compromises in a time that tolerated wide latitude in spelling. The best I have been able to do is keep the variations to a minimum and allow the reader the opportunity for imaginative interpretation.

A Northwest freeman was beholden to no one, but an author muddling in shadows accumulates inescapable debts. Fred Lockley, "the Journal Man" as he liked to call himself, had the foresight to search out and interview the pioneers while they still lived, as well as the wisdom to let them speak in their own voices. Through her careful translation and insightful annotation of the Catholic church records of the Pacific Northwest, Harriet Duncan Munnick baked the campfire bannock dough into a fine Scotch scone and single-handedly created a body of data that is a rich lode for future historians. No reputable western library should be without a reference set of her works. Readers interested in the humanity of this last Eden will find wonderful stories in those seven volumes. Taking up the challenge of Métis history in the Pacific Northwest with infectious enthusiasm, Juliet Pollard has completed the first detailed analysis of that unique life experience. Several of the threads of family history, which are the warp and woof of this homespun fabric, were spun by the Canadian researchers T. R. (Pat) McCloy, Charles Denny, and C. A. Kipling. Joe Meek's great-granddaughter, Judy Goldman, has helped keep the memories alive and the cemeteries presentable. James Ronda, with his usual grace, suggested important eleventh hour improvements. As a faithful editor and better friend, Dan Greer herded this work through the press. Undoubtedly, there are errors and oversights, and they are mine alone.

The danger of unintentional oversight precludes naming the many western family historians who generously contributed to the Métis panorama. But I cannot overlook Maria Brooks. My hunger to know more about the forgotten forebears came from the pioneer stories of a Métisse grandmother peeling apples in the gathering twilight.

∽ 1 ∽

PARENTS OF THE MIXED BLOODS

By 1799 traders from Montreal and London were hard against the barrier of the "Stoney Mountains." Most of the tribes they dogged in search of valuable beaver pelts were buffalo-running plainsmen, whose equestrian pride precluded dismounting to dig rodents from the cutbanks of prairie rivers. The Saskatchewan traders relied on the trapping habits of Strong Wood Cree and Assiniboin, or on the Pikuni and Inuksik Blackfeet bands, who made use of the natural resources of the upper Missouri River.

In the autumn of 1800, the North West Company traders at Rocky Mountain House on the upper Saskatchewan River were delighted to receive twenty-seven apprehensive Kutenai Indians from the west side of the mountains. The Westerners had come at considerable risk, having had to evade the Siksika and Kainah Blackfeet middlemen who usually levied a duty on furs from distant places and discouraged direct exchanges.

After completing their business, the Kutenai agreed to take two North West Company engagés to winter with them on the western drainage. Sending men to live with Indians was an old economy on the Saskatchewan that cut down on subsistence expenses, ensured the repayment of Indian debts, and spread the use of the relatively new steel-trapping technique.

One of the men who crossed the mountains was Charles La Gasse. He spent the next fourteen years on the Pacific drainage. His companion during the winter of 1800–1801 appears to have been the "country son" of the former lower Saskatchewan River trader Francois Le Blanc *dit* Franceway and a native woman. The father had been the human link between the old French trade and the British expansion after the conquest of 1760. After killing an Indian, Franceway had to flee the country in 1779, leav-

3

Descending McGillivray's (Kootenay) River. —Pencil sketch by H. J. Warre, National Archives of Canada, C-058144.

ing his son behind. A genuine son of the Saskatchewan fur trade, young Pierre Le Blanc represented the next link in that mercantile continuity.

Many of the men crowding the mountains came from distant places, such as Kaskaskia, Prairie du Chien, or Michilimackinac. Others were bred in the commercial cauldron of Montreal. Many were already identified as children of European fathers and American Indian mothers. They were the human by-products of discovery, commerce, and colonization. Those who melted into the tribes anonymously diluted proud Indian bloodlines.[1]

Soon after the temporary Atlantic coastal fishing, whaling, and trading stations developed into the colonial settlements of New France, coureurs de bois (French or French-Indian trappers) were coursing the distant lakes and rivers in competitive searches for Indian beaver robes. Those travelers *en derouine* (drumming up trade) made the long winters in Indian camps tolerable by arranging temporary domestic alliances, or country marriages. The children of these pairings were known as country sons and daughters.

By the middle of the seventeenth century, French fur traders had infiltrated the Indian world beyond the Great Lakes. After New France yielded to old England, and Louisiana passed to the new American republic, the Indian trade stood ready to cross the Rocky Mountains in the moccasins of a unique people.

What we know about the mixed bloods comes from the pens of their fathers. Those self-interested fur traders wrote the business records and letters of the mercantile conquest of North America. Some kept journals to record daily events and occasionally mentioned their families. Those brown, water-stained lines sometimes reveal fathers caught in uneasy marital situations, giving serious thought to the future of their mixed-blood children. Country families were unlikely to fit into the world where traders hoped to retire.

By the beginning of the nineteenth century, an observer in the Canadian Northwest estimated that one workman out of every four had formed a country union. With as many as 1,500 dependents attached to their operations, the partners of the North West Company began seeing families as a burden.[2] The 1804 merger of rival Canadian trade interests resulted in an excess of personnel. Two years later, the usually indulgent Nor'westers passed a resolution.

> No Partner, Clerk, or Engagee, belonging to the Concern shall henceforth take or suffer to be taken under any pretense what-

soever, any woman or maid from any of the tribes of Indians now known or who may hereafter become known in this Country, to live with him within the Company's Houses or Forts and be maintained at the Expense of the Concern.

The fine, fixed at £100 Halifax currency, was leavened by the pragmatic afterthought of concerned fathers. "It is however understood that taking the Daughter of a white man after the fashion of the Country shall be considered no violation of this resolve."[3]

By then many freemen were already adrift in the West, creating problems for the traders on the Red, Assiniboine, and Saskatchewan rivers. They were also beginning to drift across the overland connections to the middle Missouri River, where they came in contact with their counterparts from the United States.

Coastal trading ships began to enter the bays and river mouths of the Pacific shore to barter with local tribes for sea otter skins. They left behind evidence of their visits. The first identified mixed blood in the Pacific Northwest came out of the dripping coastal salal to greet the Lewis and Clark party in 1805. Apparently a Chinook Indian in dress and habit, he had red hair, freckles, and the name "Jack Ramsey" tattooed on his left arm. Later observers, who described Ramsey as the "offspring of a ship," apparently extracted the tribal memory of his father, a sailor wrecked or marooned on the coast about thirty years before. During the

Jack Ramsey, right, and his one-eyed brother, George. –copied from Charles Wilkes, *Narrative of the United States Exploring Expedition During the Years 1838, 1839, 1840, 1841, 1842,* vol. 5 (Philadelphia: Lea & Blanchard, 1845).

ten years of his exile, the older Ramsey spawned several children. In a final desperate attempt to perpetuate his identity, Ramsey tattooed his name on the boy's arm.[4]

Jack's brother George was less conspicuous in appearance and it is uncertain if his head had been flattened. He was in Gray's Harbor in 1811 when Americans from the Pacific Fur Company took him aboard the *Tonquin* for an ill-fated trading voyage to the north. Nootka visitors from Wickininish brought the news that most of the ship's crew had been killed by Indians. "Lamosoi" returned with the only first-hand account of the massacre. Nor'westers, Hudson's Bay Company shipmasters, and American naval officers knew George (Qua–luk) as a trustworthy pilot for the next thirty years. Lieutenant Charles Wilkes of the United States Exploring Expedition sketched the brothers in 1841. If Jack and George were truly mixed bloods, then their father's ship must have been among the first to visit the area, which would cast some doubt on the discovery claims to the Columbia River. Neither the American Captain John Gray nor the British naval officer George Vancouver left a crewman behind.[5] Surely the Ramseys were the stuff of legend.[6]

Three Métis arrived in the Pacific Northwest with the Lewis and Clark party in 1805. The most conspicuous was George Drouillard, descended from a significant Detroit coureur-de-bois family and a Delaware-Shawnee mother. Soon after the end of the American Revolution, Drouillard's Métis father accompanied a Wyandot delegation to the United States Congress to petition for assistance to visit France. Representative of an old tradition of interpreters and intermediaries, and witness to the negative experience of the Ohio Indian dispossession, the son lived near Cape Girardeau on the Spanish side of the Mississippi River. George Drouillard was part of the dispossessed community known as the Absentee Shawnee when the American explorers Lewis and Clark enlisted him for their Corps of Discovery.[7] George Drouillard never made it back to the Pacific drainage after the Lewis and Clark expedition. In spring 1810, the Bloods called in the debt he owed for introducing direct traders to the Three Forks of the Missouri River.[8]

Nearsighted Pierre Crouzette was an unlikely western visionary. He was a part-Omaha mixed blood who returned to St. Louis in 1806 and may have hurried back up the Missouri to join the forty-two Americans who discomforted the British traders the next year. Probably recruited from the boatmen of St. Charles or St. Louis, Crouzette and Francois La Biche were as much sons of the Missouri as Le Blanc and Jacco Finlay were connections to the Saskatchewan. Drouillard symbolized the retreating mixed bloods of the Ohio Valley, but Crouzette and La Biche represented the early Missouri River Indian trade.[9]

The name Charbonneau threads into the fabric of the fur trade from an early origin on the St. Lawrence River. At the beginning of the nineteenth century, Charbonneaus were living in the American Bottoms along the Mississippi River, and at the forks of the Red and Assiniboine rivers in the Canadian Northwest. Prim Captain Meriwether Lewis took exception to Toussaint Charbonneau's treatment of Sacagawea, his sixteen-year-old Shoshone country wife, and branded him a disrespectable, thoroughly feral Frenchman. But when the expedition prepared for the plunge into the mountains, old Charbonneau was the best candidate for a useful interpreter. The explorers also hoped that his bride might facilitate contact with her people. Sacagawea, carrying her newborn son in a cradleboard, was the only woman with the party.

The first crop of western Métis was probably delivered to Chinook mothers nine months after the United States Corps of Discovery wintered near the mouth of the Columbia River. Those anonymous babies disappeared into the tribal world.

Unidentified freeman trappers surely crossed to the western slope after La Gasse and Le Blanc reported the prospects of taking beaver in the Kutenai country. There are indications that aggressive Iroquois hunters were there before autumn 1806, when the North West Company partner John McDonald of Garth told his Métis clerk to take a crew and improve the Kutenai trail into a useful pack road across the mountains.

Jacques (Jacco) Raphael Finlay was the country son of the pioneer British fur trader James Finlay. The elder Finlay wintered with Franceway on the lower Saskatchewan in 1768–69, so it is possible that young Jacco and young Le Blanc had known each other as children.[10] Later they were fellow Nor'westers, but Jacco enjoyed the influence of a wealthy father who could afford to educate his son to work as a North West Company clerk.

When the first North West Company outfit tried to follow Jacco's trail in spring 1807, David Thompson was disappointed in the poorly slashed road and he chastised the builder. By late summer Thompson had his men at work building a post on the lake near the head of the Columbia River. On 13 August he was astonished to receive a letter from an American party that indicated that as many as forty-two American trappers were already in the lower end of the Bitterroot Valley. A United States army officer sternly warned against British intrusion into American territory. The contest for the Oregon country had begun.

The forty-two Americans accurately counted by the Salish Indians came from the upper Missouri River. After breasting 2,000 miles of unrelenting river currents, they had crossed passes only recently described by the Corps of Discovery. But who were they?

At least five of the boatmen who rowed, poled, and towed the boats of the explorers to the Mandan winter camp of 1804–5 did not return downstream. Crossing overland to the Assiniboine River, they traded with the British and were again in the Mandan towns in 1807. One boatman, who returned from St. Louis on a mysterious errand, can be identified with reasonable certainty.

Francois Rivet returned from St. Louis in late 1805 with his trapping partner, Phillipe Degie. It is likely that they were the small party that the governor of Upper Louisiana equipped from his "private means" to trap on the Yellowstone River during the winter of 1805–6. The returning Corps of Discovery met "Reevea and Greinyea" above the Arikara villages the morning of 21 August 1806. Recognizing Rivet, the explorers gave the trappers some ammunition so they could return upstream to recover their traps from the Mandan villages.[11]

Rivet was one of the forty-two men who was in the Bitterroot Valley by September 1807.[12] From the evidence of the returning explorers, the party of the former captain of artillery John McClellan included a clerk, an interpreter, a black body servant, and fifteen hands. Rivet and Degie met and joined them later somewhere on the river. At the Mandan villages they recruited about thirty Canadian freemen who were eager to try trapping on the Yellowstone.

The trappers were former British engagés cast adrift after the merger of rival firms in 1805. Some came from the trading houses on the Assiniboine River, others from the Red River Department, or perhaps from the Fond du Lac trading region. Victims of underemployment, they risked following a relatively untried leader, counting on there being safety in numbers.[13]

The party may have included several men in the employ of a middle Missouri River trader, Charles Courtin. He came from the River Raisin area just south of Detroit, and two of his men, Michel Bourdeaux and Registre Bellaire, appear to have been brothers-in-law from the same vicinity.[14]

Coming up the Missouri River with a cargo of trading goods intended for Santa Fe, McClellan heard about Meriwether Lewis's concern about British intrusion on the upper Missouri. After unforeseen developments deflected him from his original intention, McClellan proceeded to the Yellowstone, where he wrote a letter warning British traders away from the upper Missouri. After meeting Salish buffalo hunters from the West, McClellan and his forty-two pioneers followed them into the Flathead country.

Whatever motives were behind the letters that McClellan fired at David Thompson, the party represented a significant American presence in the Rocky Mountains within a year of the return of the Corps of Discovery. By the time the shock waves of their presence reached the North West Company headquarters on Lake Superior, McClellan and eight of his men had been killed by Blackfoot or Gros Ventre warriors.

Some survivors probably joined the Missouri Fur Company at the mouth of the Big Horn River, but others remained in the mountains, living and hunting with the Salish Indians. When David Thompson expanded operations into the Flathead country in fall 1809, he found about twenty Métis freemen operating there. Some were Saskatchewan River hunters or Iroquois steel trappers, but several were Americans left over from the McClellan and Courtin parties. Most of them were still around in early 1810, when the Nor'westers distributed the property of the slain Courtin. Receiving payment for their services to the deceased were Michel Bourdeaux *dit* Bourdon, Michel Kinville, Francois

Free Hunter, by Father Nicholas Point. –Historical Photograph Collections, Washington State University Libraries, 537.7.29-48.

*Comcomley's grave overlooking Astoria and
Young's Bay.* –Collection of Patricia Jo Kern-Bowers.

Sans Facon, Francois Gregoire, Pierre Grignon, and Francois
Rivet.[15]

After Courtin's death, Michel Bourdon was associated with the
North West Company as a freeman trapper. Later that summer,
Bourdon, Jean Baptiste Bouche, and the North West Company
clerk Finan McDonald accompanied Salish buffalo hunters east
of the Rockies. When the ever-vigilant Pikuni gamekeepers at-
tacked the poachers, they were surprised to find their western
enemies armed with twenty North West Company trade guns.
Worse, the three Nor'westers supported the Flatheads in a fight
that was an unforgivable disaster for the plainsmen.

The following spring, Bourdon was in the boat party that
Thompson took to the mouth of the Columbia River, only to find
that the Pacific Fur Company had been in residence there for
almost two months. Primacy went to an American venture, and
inland Indians were already coming down to check out the new
market.

Nor was the availability of an alternate market lost upon the
men who accompanied Thompson. The returning party was

obliged to leave one of the boatmen, Boulard, who was too weak to make the upstream trip. Thompson took an Owyhee (Hawaiian) called Cox to paddle in his place. By 5 October 1811 the mountain freeman Registre Bruguier appeared at Astoria with some returning Astorians; he stayed to try trapping on the Cowlitz River.

Organized in New York by John Jacob Astor, a fur merchant, the Pacific Fur Company depended on a field management and work force largely recruited from the traditional voyageur labor pools of Montreal and Michilimackinac, augmented by hunters from around the Missouri. One of the Astorians, Gabriel Franchere, recognized Bruguier as a respectable Iroquois trader who had lost his outfit on the Saskatchewan and was forced into the life of a trapper. Bruguier's extensive knowledge of the upper reaches of the Columbia River was something the amateurs in Astor's company could use.[16]

The brief appearance of Michel Bourdon suggests an interesting ambiguity. He was, at least technically, a U.S. citizen.[17] Years later, Thompson in his dotage was concerned about downplaying his failure to press British pretensions to the Oregon country. He recalled that Bourdon and a trapping companion, Michel Kinville, were killed by the Blackfeet in 1812 and used the story of their deaths as a homily on the elimination of incautious American hunters. But Thompson was wrong—"young" Michel Bourdon was still hunting in 1823. After fourteen years with a Blackfoot death warrant hanging over his head, Bourdon was finally killed on the Salmon River while traveling with the Snake Hunting Brigade of the Hudson's Bay Company.[18]

Registre Bellaire, whose relationship to Bourdon stretched back to the Detroit area, was called a "half freeman" in 1808 when Thompson engaged him to help carry the Salish House returns across the mountains. During the winter of 1813-14, Bellaire worked on the Willamette River as a free trapper in company with the Astorians Alex Carson, John Day, and William Cannon. On New Year's Day 1814, he agreed to pay 180 pounds of beaver for the services of four Hawaiian trappers. Bellaire and his family traveled up the Columbia River in the boat brigade of 1814 but dropped off at the mouth of the Walla Walla River to hunt in the Snake country.[19]

That part of the mountains safely south of resentful Blackfeet had been trapped during the winter of 1810-11 by the Missouri Fur Company hunters who followed Andrew Henry. Some of them met the overland party of Astorians coming up the Missouri River and returned to the upper Snake Valley for a second year of trapping.

One of the overland Astorians was young Pierre Dorion, a second-generation Westerner from a French and Sioux family, who brought along his pregnant Iowa wife and two children. After a long association with the Teton Sioux, the Dorions were reasonably safe passports through the territory of those not-always-understanding tribesmen. The depth of Astor's purse convinced young Dorion to travel with the capitalist's mixed bag of voyageurs, long hunters, greenhorns, and entrepreneurs with high expectations.[20]

Canadians were hired as boatmen, while beaver trapping was left to men from the long hunter tradition of the Ohio Valley. French names camouflaged Métis bloodlines from the Great Lakes and Mississippi drainage.[21] Names from the Montreal vicinity included Beauchemin, Brazeau, Delorme, Dufrene, LaBousin, Papin, Perrault, Picotte, Robillard, and Turcotte. From Mackinac came Boucher, Brugiere, Gervais, LaBonte, Landry, Lucier, Marcial, Ouvre, Perrault, Pillon, Plante, Provost, and Saint Ament. The St. Louis melting pot contributed Carson, Day, Delaunay, Dorion, Gardipie, and Valle.[22] About thirteen men were left to trap in the Snake River Valley.[23]

For a few years the freeman hunters enjoyed the advantage of competition between rival companies, but in 1813 the precipitous sale of the Pacific Fur Company to the Nor'westers repeated the excess manpower situation of 1804. Some of the Astorians returned home, but others stayed on, and by spring 1814 agreed to work as free trappers on shares with the British.

Had they known the fate of the trappers John Reed took into the Snake country, they might have made other arrangements. Reed was a mature, apparently sensible Irishman who was backed up by the experienced interpreter Dorion. During the fall of 1813, when they went to work the streams above the Snake River gorge, Dorion took his family along. Only a few months later, trapping parties didn't enjoy such safety.

As the 1814 boat brigade neared the mouth of the Umatilla River, it was hailed from shore by Madame Dorion and her two children, the only survivors of the Snake hunting party. After all the men were slain, Madame Dorion fled on a horse, which she later killed to feed herself and her two boys. Her sons grew up in Oregon, adding Sioux and Iowa to the growing list of transplanted tribesmen.[24]

~2~

THE STEEL TRAPPERS

A common historical misconception is that pioneers invaded and overwhelmed the Indian Northwest. But the initial dispossession was through infiltration and assimilation—by Indians as well as whites. The blending of northeastern and northwestern Indian cultures was neither racial nor racist; it was economic.

By 1800 intimate associations on the Saskatchewan River had blurred matters until it was difficult to draw clear distinctions in the fur trade between people of authentic European origin and native Americans. Engagés with French names were often descended from ancestors who had crossed the ethnic border several generations previously. Many of the steel-trapper Iroquois were actually Métis. Others, like the Algonquian-speaking Pacquin brothers, were Nipissing. An unnamed Ottawa and at least two Cree mixed bloods were soon operating on the western slope.[25] When Alexander Ross of the Hudson's Bay Company (HBC) led the Snake Brigade of 1824, he was bemused to find himself in command of twelve Iroquois, two Abenaki, two Nipissing, one Saulteur Ojibwa, and two Crees.

Americans coming up the Missouri River also introduced eastern tribesmen to the Mountain West. Foremost was the Shawnee mixed-blood George Drouillard and at least five of his tribesmen. The Bloods killed several members of the party, but a hunter called Placota and two Kaskaskia Shawnee survived to descend the Yellowstone in summer 1810.[26] Algonquian-speaking Delawares came west in later years, as did Iroquoian-speaking Wyandot who ended up among the Flatheads.[27] Tribal distinctions were never quite as impeccable as generalization would have it, and the powwow circuit is nothing new.

Baptiste, Iroquois Bowman, 1845.
—Pencil sketch by H. J. Warre, National Archives of Canada, C-55333.

Conspicuous among the westward migrating tribesmen were descendants of the Iroquois Five Nations. The ancient Longhouse influenced the frontier history of New France, New England, and New York for more than 170 years. Mohawk, Oneida, Onondaga, Cayuga, and Seneca middlemen controlled the trade of their neighbors, and their beaver hunters ranged into Canada and the Ohio Valley. After the American Revolution, those hunters were forced to travel beyond the Great Lakes.[28] By the end of the century, Iroquois contract trappers became a significant factor in the greater Northwest.

Indian hunters usually sniped at unwary beavers, or tore the roofs off dens and clubbed the animals. But on the western plains, few proud horsemen were willing to dismount and dig out bankside dens. By 1793 Ottawa and Ojibwa hunters from the Great Lakes appeared on the lower Assiniboine River with steel traps.[29] In the next year, David Thompson noticed three Iroquois trappers on the lower Saskatchewan and wrote:

> The Nepissings, the Algonquins and the Iroquois Indians, having exhausted their own countries, now spread themselves over these countries [the Swan River area of Manitoba and Saskatchewan], and as they destroyed the Beaver, moved forwards to the northward and westward; the Natives, the Nathathaways [Cree], did not in the least molest them; the Chippaways and other tribes made use of Traps of Steel; and of the Castorium. For several years all these Indians were rich, the Women and Children, as well as the Men, were covered with silver brooches, Ear Rings, Wampum, Beads and other trinkets. Their mantles were of fine scarlet cloth, and all was finery and dress. The Canoes of the Furr Traders were loaded with packs of Beaver, and the abundance of the article lowered the London prices. Every intelligent Man saw the poverty that would follow the destruction of the Beaver, but there was no Chiefs to controul it; all was perfect liberty and equality. Four years afterward almost the whole of these extensive countries were denuded of Beaver, the natives were poor, and with difficulty procured the first necessaries of life, and in this state they remain, and probably for ever. A worn out field may be manured, and again made fertile; but the Beaver, once destroyed cannot be replaced: they were the gold coin of the country, with which the necessaries of life were purchased.[30]

Because they traditionally traveled afar to hunt, Iroquois attracted the attention of Montreal recruiters shopping for skilled voyageurs, or beaver trappers. Brought to the greater Northwest under fur company auspices, Iroquois hunters soon spread over the beaver streams. They became the missionaries of the new gospel of the steel trap and the communion of castoreum baiting.[31] The impact of that technology set Indian against Indian.

Iroquois and Cree hunters found different paths between worlds in collision. The Cree stayed close to the basal exchange, a skin for a skin. The Iroquois were searching for something more.

The first HBC Edmonton House Journal of 1796–97 noted a credit to an Iroquois hunter who brought in seventy-five beaver skins. At the end of outfit 1797–98, a Mohawk gave in fifty skins. By spring 1798, HBC men counted 250 "Bungee, Tawau, Mischelemacana [and] Eroquee Indians" (Ojibwa, Ottawa, Michilimackinac, and Iroquois), who were accompanied by six women.[32]

The HBC journalist was concerned because the Iroquois were causing trouble with the local tribes. Seventy-five of the new-comers went to the Red Deer River to gamble with the Gros Ventre; a third of them were killed in an inevitable quarrel. Falling back to the North West Company Fort Augustus, the survivors tried to rally 120 warriors for retaliation until the wiser Cree dissuaded them.[33]

By summer 1801, the Montreal-based North West Company and XY Company had 300 "Eroquees or Mohawk Indians" engaged on three-year contracts swarming over the Saskatchewan. They were so efficient in cleaning out beaver that Hudson's Bay Company returns were reduced by half.[34] The "General Return of the Departments and Posts" of the North West Company for 1802 listed 1,058 Nor'westers, and went on, "Exclusive of the above number of Partners, regular Clerks and Servants who winter, there are 80 to 100 Canadians and Iroquois Hunters with whom the North West Company have Contracts, but who are not considered Servants of the Company, ranging free over the Country wherever they find it convenient to Hunt."[35]

One of the reasons Duncan McGillivray and David Thompson visited the Piegan winter camps on the upper Bow River in autumn 1800 was to obtain assurances of safety for contract hunters who were beginning to work the south branch of the Saskatchewan.[36] Thompson claimed to have met a favorable response, but fourteen Iroquois and two Canadian trappers who entered the area were killed in March 1802 by the Gros Ventre.[37]

At least one intruder got the message to leave the region. In 1804, a Mohawk named Daniel Green returned after spending two years in the northwestern part of Louisiana. He told a Moravian missionary that in the West he had seen white bears (grizzly) and goats that climbed mountains.[38]

Men with tin ears, like David Thompson and Alex Henry, gave up trying to spell Iroquois names and referred to Pierre Iroquois, Joseph Iroquois, Thomas Iroquois, or Charles Iroquois. Most were contract trappers who crossed the mountains to exploit the Kutenai and Salish country. As freeman hunters or part-time workmen called "half-freemen," they were not the full responsibility of the Nor'westers.

Individuals were soon being recognized. Registre Bruguier, who later appeared at Astoria, was a former Saskatchewan trader from a respectable Montreal Iroquois family who lost his outfit and was reduced to hunting.[39]

Thomas Grey of St. Regis was accompanied by his wife, Marie Nipissing. Their son Joseph was born at Jasper's House on the

Athabaska portage in 1809.[40] The Edmonton House Iroquois who descended from brothers Michel and Baptiste Callihoo, of Caughnawaga, became known as Michel's band. Other hunters pushing across the northern Rocky Mountains took their name from Pierre Hatsination (sometimes Hathawiton), an Iroquois also known as Tête Jaune (Yellow Head) because of his light hair.[41]

By 1817 both the North West Company and its rival, the Hudson's Bay Company, were engaging St. Lawrence River Iroquois. Most of the HBC Iroquois seem to have been sent into the Athabaska and Peace River country as provision hunters. On 3 October 1817, Ignace Giasson agreed to lead Iroquois hired on two-year contracts into the Peace River country as provision hunters.[42] Giasson and twenty-six Iroquois arrived at the north end of Lake Winnipeg on 19 June 1818, where Chief Factor James Bird was obliged to return "a list of sums which several Iroquois have been told their wives and other friends in Montreal shall receive on their accounts."[43] Bird's lack of enthusiasm came out when he wrote, "It appears that the Iroquois are not approved of, they cannot be depended on at the Posts, and the Country is too poor to admit them doing much as hunters."[44]

The trader Daniel Harmon described the Iroquois hunters in New Caledonia in October 1818. "The natives of the Country consider them intruders. As they are mere rovers they do not feel the same interest as they who permanently reside here, in keeping the stock of animals good, and therefor they make great havock among the game, destroying alike the animals which are young and old."[45] An Iroquois who ignored the warning of the Stuart's Lake Carrier Indians was killed along with his wife and two children. Harmon hoped the deaths would discourage others from coming into the region. But the redoubtable Giasson came to the Peace River in February 1819, ready to lead his hunters in New Caledonia. A year later, HBC records show that four of the Iroquois were dead, six had deserted, and Charles Tayurhesere had gone to the Columbia.[46]

Of the eleven Iroquois who assisted David Thompson in the expansion of the Kutenai and Flathead trade, six were at Salish House in 1810, helping to build canoes. Two descended the Columbia the following spring, where their skill as boatmen was more valuable than their trapping.[47]

Alexander Henry was not entirely pleased to find several Iroquois engagés at Fort George on the Columbia River in 1813.[48] The North West Company list of ninety-two Nor'westers on the Columbia for winter 1813–14 names Pierre Cawanarde, Thomas

Ocanasawaret, Jacques Ostiserico, Etienne Owayaissa, Jacques Shatackoani, Ignace Salioheni, and George Teewhattahowie.[49] J. B. Saganakei was called "the old Nipissing," and Henry knew M. Manicque as a Wyandot (Huron) Indian.[50] Francois Eno *dit* Canada, Nicolas Montour, Andre Piccard, and Maurice Piccard had northeastern tribal roots. St. Regis and Caughnawaga Iroquois like Thomas Pembrook or Registre Bruguier were disguised by English or French names.[51]

The lighthearted Irishman Ross Cox learned about professional pride when he tried to tell the six-foot-tall boatman George Teewhattahowie how to conduct his canoe. The insulted expert got drunk at Fort George and came looking to avenge the insult. In the resulting knife fight, Teewhattahowie was cut several times before he was subdued and bound. But when he sobered, the repentant boatman forgave everyone and vowed to flatten any who spoke against his friend Cox.[52]

The imported Indians felt little loyalty to the trading companies. Two Bungees (Ojibwa) passed along an invitation from their brother-in-law, Jacco Finlay, to bring an HBC trading outfit west of the mountains. In March 1814, several Nor'wester Iroquois gave useful business intelligence to the Edmonton House factor, James Bird. They told him that they had hunted as far south as the mouth of the Snake River but found that trail overly long, and the food short.[53]

Those insights gave Bird the opportunity to evaluate the boasts of his North West Company opponent, James Hughes, who flourished a letter from the Columbia River outlining his partnership's expectations. If each of the 100 freeman and Iroquois trappers made three ninety-pound packs, the Columbia would yield significant profits.[54] Bird countered in October by sending a black man, Joseph Lewis, and an Iroquois, Tommo, to hunt with the Sarcees.

Nor'wester dreams apparently failed as the former Astorian Donald McKenzie returned to the Columbia River in 1816 to develop an efficient Snake River hunting brigade. The unenthusiastic Fort George officers' council assigned him a "medley of savages, Iroquois, Abanakees and Owhyhees" as trappers. The following year, when the retiring Astorian Cox met Joseph Larocque at Rainy Lake, the Nor'wester was headed west with a reinforcement of forty men, mostly Iroquois Indians from Canada.[55] That party gave McKenzie the manpower he needed to push into the dangerous Snake country.

In the escalating struggle for the northwestern trade, the North West Company augmented its Oregon hunters with a second

Fort George, formerly Astoria, 1845. —H. J. Warre. National Archives of Canada, C-001626.

Iroquois party, which seems to have included wives and families.[56] Single men took companions from the local tribes, but such relationships were no guarantee against conflict.

The Iroquois hunters frustrated McKenzie. After warning against private trafficking in horses with the Nez Perce, he had to deal with a dispute between Grand Pierre and an Indian over a horse. Asked to mediate, "Big Donald" solved the problem by shooting the animal.[57] McKenzie's downstream anchor, Alex Ross, was also skeptical about the Iroquois:

> Among the people employed in this trade are a set of civilized Indians from the neighborhood of Montreal. They are chiefly of the Iroquois nation, at this period they form nearly a third of the number of men employed by the Company on the Columbia.
>
> They are expert voyageurs but especially so in the rapids and dangerous runs in the inland waters, which they either stem or shoot with the utmost skill. The object of introducing them into the service of the traders was to make them act in the double capacity of canoe men and trappers.
>
> They are not esteemed equal to the ablest trappers, nor the best calculated for the voyage. They are not so inoffensive as the Owhyhees, or to be trusted as the Canadians. They are brought up to religion, it is true, and sing hymns oftener than paddling songs; but those who came here, and we are of course speaking of none else, retain none of its precepts. They are sullen, indolent, fickle, cowardly and treacherous. And an Iroquois arrived at manhood is still as wayward and extravagant as a lad of other nations at the age of fifteen. Iroquois have been found uniformly to deceive without fail.[58]

McKenzie detached twenty-five Iroquois in September 1818 to hunt along Indian Creek. Instead they traded their horses, guns, and traps for women, and abandoned themselves to debauchery. When McKenzie returned from the interior in the spring, he found them dispersed among the local tribes, gambling, fighting, and womanizing.[59]

Other Columbia Department officers were also troubled by unmanageable Iroquois. John Haldane equipped fifty or more Iroquois at Spokane House in early September 1820. They were supposed to hunt in the Flathead country but proved a disappointment. The local situation was complicated because Jacco Finlay, anticipating a corporate reorganization, had induced other freemen to come over from the Saskatchewan and compete in the hunt.[60]

Iroquois were the undoing of the pioneer trapper Michel Bourdon, who inherited the command of the Snake Hunting

Brigade in 1822. Refusing to carry their returns through areas raided by the Blackfeet, his Iroquois hunters cached their packs at the east end of the Snake River Valley. Before going off on their own, the dissidents promised to return to Fort Nez Perces. But when they were free of supervision, the fourteen trappers and their families doubled back east toward the Big Horn post of the Missouri Fur Company, where they meant to compare fur prices.

Those refusing to come out of the Snake country in fall 1822 included Pierre Cassawasa, Thomas Nakarsheta, Ignace Solihonie and his stepson, Francois Frenetorosue, Lazard Teycaleyecourigi, and Ignace Tahekeurate.

Iroquois who dutifully returned to Spokane House with Bourdon were Ignace Dehodionwasse, Ignace Hatchiorauquasha (the half Iroquois also known as John Grey), Louis Kanota, Louis Konitogen, Lazard Hayaiguarelita, Martin Miaquin, Fran Sasanirie, Baptiste Sowenge, Pierre Tennotiessen, Jacques Thatarackton, Laurent Karowtowhaw, Jacques Ostiserico, Pierre Tevanitagon, and Tevanitagon's two sons. Another trapper who returned, Sauteau St. Germain, may have been Ojibwa.[61] They returned to trap in the southern part of the Snake drainage and, after Bourdon was killed, pressed down the Missouri River as far as the Great Falls.

When Alexander Ross took the Snake Brigade from Flathead Post in 1824, the loyal Iroquois listened to the dissident ringleaders, Old Pierre Trevanigan and John Grey. In the end, Ross had to let them go out and hunt on their own with the promise of reuniting in the fall. But they returned with seven American trappers in tow. The Iroquois had been hanging around Bear Valley waiting for the return of the delegation that went east the previous year; they were pleased to run into Americans instead.

The incident meant that the decline of British monopoly was not going to be reversed by the presence of the deputy governor of the newly reorganized Hudson's Bay Company. When Governor George Simpson crossed the Athabaska portage in fall 1824, his party met Iroquois hunters who had been working beaver on the Canoe River, Cranberry Lake, Moose Lake, and the north branch of Thompson's River. Most were married to Carrier women and supported their large families by trading with Francis Antoine Larocque at the Athabaska-Miette River outpost.[62] But as Simpson descended the Columbia, he heard reports of Iroquois misbehavior, and by the time he reached Fort George had made up his mind that "old favorite Canadian Servants and useless Iroquois" hanging about would have to be sent back to Canada next spring.

As the governor returned east next spring, he began taking out his anger on Iroquois miscreants. "The Iroquois who caused trouble last year and are now here on way across and will be given iron bracelets, to be handcuffed tomorrow in presence of the whole company as example to the Columbia District."[63] One of them, Isaac, whom he called "the Iroquois chief and leader of the mutinous dogs," was banished from the Columbia for life. When the boat brigade ascending the Columbia River was beyond the possibility of escape, the governor's iron authority was unleashed. As he hiked across the Athabaska portage in disgrace, Isaac had nothing to lose by knocking in the head of a liquor keg. That started a party that got half a dozen men so drunk they could not continue. Seizing a stick, the enraged Simpson beat Isaac.[64]

Unaware of the appearance of Americans with the dissident Iroquois, Simpson had already reassigned the Snake Brigade to the former Nor'wester bully Peter Skene Ogden. It was early April of the following year before Iroquois "disloyalty" affected the Snake Brigade. Between 22 and 24 May 1825 Ogden came face-to-face with Americans just east of the Great Salt Lake. The appalled HBC man watched his Iroquois freemen move their packs of furs to the opposition camp. By mid-summer Ogden had lost two-thirds of his trapping force.

Mistreatment was a problem, but the western Iroquois went over to the Americans for strictly business reasons. After the coalition of 1821 created a western monopoly, the HBC reduced the price for beaver to less than two dollars a skin and jacked up the cost of outfits. Wasting no time in seeking a better market, the Columbia freemen were pleased to find American trapper/traders who were willing to pay three dollars a pound, or five dollars a skin.[65]

At the first great mountain rendezvous of 1825, on Henry's Fork of the Green River, Old Pierre Tevanitagon converted his furs into venture capital. In cooperation with the American trapper Johnson Gardner, the Tevanitagon clan invested in a trading outfit, and headed north to seduce their Flathead friends.

Old Pierre was still operating in the Flathead country during the 1827–28 hunt. He traveled with the Smith, Jackson & Sublette (SJ&S) brigade conducted by Robert Campbell, which bumped into a war party of Piegan Blackfeet. During the resulting fight, Old Pierre became excited and ran from cover to get a better shot. Instead he was killed, and his body captured by the enemy. Only his feet could be recognized when the mutilated remains were recovered. He gained immortality with the naming of Pierre's Hole on the west side of the Teton Range. The less-than-grief-stricken HBC men consoled themselves that Old Pierre's debts were secured by a mortgage on his property in eastern Canada. On the books of SJ&S, the widow enjoyed a credit of nearly $800.

Godin is a name known in such widely separated places as New France, Pennsylvania, Fort Coulougne on the Ottawa River, and the old coureur-de-bois settlements of Illinois. Thierry Godin, a voyageur for the North West Company on the upper Red River in 1804, was probably related to Antoine and Louis Godin, who later received pensions under the Voyageurs Fund. Thierry trapped west of the mountains with his grown son Antoine, and Godin's River was the name attached for a time to the Big Lost River on the north side of the Snake Valley.

By 1828, Thierry Godin had enough credit with the American traders to consider retirement. Blackfeet killed him before he could leave the country. Four years later, Antoine avenged his father by killing a Gros Ventre chief, thus precipitating the infamous battle of Pierre's Hole. The feud finally ended in 1836, when Piegans accompanied by an HBC "confidential servant" killed Antoine near Fort Hall.

Ignace Hatchiorauquasha was descended from William Grey, who at age seven was captured in New England by the Caughnawaga Mohawks. On reaching maturity, Grey refused to return to the white world and remained to become a spokesman and chief of the St. Regis Iroquois.[66] In the mountains, Ignace *dit* John Grey earned fame among the mountaineers for his horrendous encounters with grizzly bears. A consistent source of trouble for British brigade leaders, Grey was only slightly less bothersome to his American associates.[67] The name of Gray's Hole celebrates his reputation.

The Abenaki Joseph Portneuf and Joseph Loui accompanied the 1824 expedition to examine the Fraser River as a site for an HBC post. The next year, Portneuf was one of the few men who refused to leave Ogden's Snake Brigade. That loyalty was fatal five years later, when Portneuf worked the boat carrying the last Snake returns to Fort Vancouver. At The Dalles of the Columbia, the boat was sucked under, drowning Portneuf, his wife, and their two children. The Portneuf River in Idaho preserves his memory.[68]

When the American Fur Company trapper Paul Fraser was killed in September 1831, Warren Ferris noted that he came from St. Regis, Canada, could read and write in his own language, and

Top: Marianne Neketichou, wife of John Grey. —Nicholas Point, Historical Photograph Collections, Washington State University Libraries, 95-101.
Bottom: John Grey (Ignace Hatchiorauquasha), Iroquois trapper. —Nicholas Point, Historical Photograph Collections, Washington State University Libraries, 88-359.

had been roaming in the mountains for seventeen years. He left an Indian wife and several children.[69]

Another educated Iroquois was the skilled boatman Louis Oskanha *dit* Monique who came to the Northwest around 1813. Known as one of the "civilized Indians" from eastern Canada, he later signed the St. Paul church register in Iroquois.[70]

After 1807, western Iroquois and the interior Salish became closely associated. One of the first Iroquois to marry among the Flatheads was Pierre Michel. After accompanying two war expeditions during the winter of 1813–14, Michel felt entitled to claim the hand of a daughter of the hereditary peace chief. The sixteen-year-old bride was delivered to the North West Company post in a torchlight parade.[71] Another Spokane House trapper, Jacques Ostistericha, was with the Kutenai during the 1823 hunt. He and John Grey presented American trading overtures to the northern Indians in the fall of 1826.[72]

The Iroquois remembered the destruction of the ancient Longhouse heritage. The fur trade ended the dream of Indian unity, scattering natives like the ashes of the destroyed council fire. The Iroquois knew the fate of Indian America long before other nations. All that remained of those dreams was a transplanted religion.

The twenty-four or more Iroquois who settled with the Salish in what is now western Montana were responsible for the "Macedonian Cry" that planted the germ of Christianity in the mountains. By 1831 there was a community of retired Iroquois trappers and kinsmen living near the mouth of the Kaw (Kansas) River, where they enjoyed the attention of a Catholic priest from St. Louis.[73] That year a Nez Perce and Flathead delegation came from the mountains seeking teachers. Four years later, Ignace Shonomene *dit* Le Vieux Ignace La Mousse, who had lived with the Flatheads for eighteen years, took his sons Charles and Francois Xavier *dit* Saxa to St. Louis, where they were baptized on 2 December. They returned with a mountain-bound brigade in 1836.[74]

A garbled version of this religious deprivation was communicated to New England Protestant missionary societies by a mischievous half-blood Wyandot. Parties were soon on the trail west to rescue the misbegotten Flatheads from misconceived Popish beliefs.[75] One of the lay helpers sent by the American Board of Commissioners for Foreign Missions was coincidentally named William Henry Gray. Because his associates, Marcus Whitman and Henry Harmon Spalding, had already claimed the Cayuse and Nez Perce, Gray saw the Flatheads as targets for his proselytizing. After visiting their country in 1837, Gray joined Big Ignace La Mousse and several companions, who were preparing for another journey east. At Ash Hollow on the Platte River, they ran into belligerent Sioux buffalo hunters. Given the opportunity to step aside from the inevitable slaughter, Gray pusillanimously withdrew, leaving Ignace and his friends to their fate. Reports of Gray's cowardice caused the Protestant missionaries to lose face among the Flatheads and mountaineers.[76]

In the summer of 1839, two Iroquois, Pierre Gaucher and Young Ignace, made another trip to St. Louis, where they finally convinced the Jesuit Provincial Peter Joseph Verhaegan to send a Black Robe scout. While Gaucher carried the good news home, Young Ignace wintered on Bear River to meet the priest. When Father Pierre Jean De Smet arrived in 1840, it was the "creole" Gabriel Prudhomme who acted as his interpreter.[77] When a full mission party came the next summer, John Grey, the notorious grizzly bear fighter, returned as a hunter.[78]

After nine years of anticipation, the Indians did not receive De Smet as wholeheartedly as the priest later recalled. Among the tribesmen waiting at Pierre's Hole in July was a skeptical northeastern Métis named Tom Hill. Educated at Protestant Dartmouth University and familiar with the dispossession of the Delaware, Hill was unenthusiastic about a Catholic mission. De Smet's version of his welcome also differs from that of the Métisse Catharine Baptiste, who recalled:

> Some tribes were prepared by the Iroquois hunters and French Creoles to receive him. Other tribes heeded him not. The Shawnee warrior T. H. reject all evidences for favoring of religion, saying that the Parent Spirit was not to be found in dresses or bits of paper, pictures, or in yellow or red iron or beads, insisting that the sacred man that came so far must be a fool to preach some thing he did not know and for which the God Chief cared nothing, and told them it were better to ask that Spirit to give them health and buffalo and help them to scalp their enemies than listen to useless prayers that had no life but in the effort of them. His words were received by many of the leading Indians chiefly from their bold assertion and as he who spoke them was from the east and said to be a man in the battle with Black Hawk.[79]

Later at the Nez Perce Lapwai mission, Hill repeated his warnings of white intrusion, which the Iroquois Joseph Grey repeated to the Cayuse. Although condemned by the missionaries as godless misanthropes, Hill and Grey were trying to warn their friends about the reality of dispossession.[80]

After the decline of the fur trade, several Iroquois trappers followed their old friends to the Willamette Valley. The Tsetse, Tyikwarhi, and Tawakon families settled on the north side of the Yamhill River, about a mile north of present Dayton, Oregon, where their neighbor was Chief Factor John McLoughlin's part-Ojibwa son, Joseph.

Charlot Tsetse, who crossed the mountains with David Thompson in 1808–10, was still hunting with the Southern Brigade in April 1832 when he helped avenge the murders of Thomas Canasawarette and Pierre Kakawaquiron by Tillamook Indians. After the brigade disbanded, Tsetse retired to the French Prairie, where he used the name Carlo Chata on the petition asking for a Catholic priest. When overland pioneers began arriving in large numbers in 1844, Tsetse had 100 acres of land under cultivation near the Yamhill River. Four years later, he sold out to an American, James Martin.

Thomas and Jean Baptiste Tyikwarhi (*dit* Norwest) were in the Oregon country before their names appeared on the Snake Brigade rosters for 1826–27. On that trip, the twenty-eight-year-old J. B. Tyequariche (Tyikwarhi) acted as Ogden's cook. In the next outfit, Thomas Tewateon (Tawakon) from Caughnawaga was also listed. Jean Baptiste Tewateon, who married Marie Anne (Judith) Walla Walla before 1830, had a son, Thomas Jean Baptiste, who served with the volunteers avenging the Whitman massacre in 1847–48. The father died in 1855, but Thomas lived on a donation land claim until he moved to the Grande Ronde Indian Reservation with his brother Frank and his son Thomas. Francis Michel, the son of an Iroquois trapper and a lower Chinook mother, also retreated to the Grande Ronde.[81]

Thomas Tawakon was with the North West Company in 1820 when his son was born. A Chinook wife gave him two daughters. When he married Francaise Walla Walla on 8 July 1839, among the witnesses were his son Thomas and old friends Louis Monique, J. B. Tyikwarhi, Joe McLoughlin, and J. B. Jeaudoin. The son died at the nearby McLoughlin house on 7 May 1848, and the father was dead some time before 1854.[82]

The families of Etienne Aaniaessei and Michel Atenesse may have settled on the French Prairie near present Brooks as early as 1838. They disproved the stereotype of the transient half blood by staying there until 1860.

In their retention of a distinct identity, the Iroquois were not that much different from their trapper associates. The exotic Iroquois prospered or failed in the hunt, took wives from local tribes, and eventually found homes in Métis settlements or on Indian reservations. It was their stubborn sense of independence that created a negative, one-dimensional image. Their persistence shows how eastern Indians, or part Indians, were an undeniable part of the pioneer process. Beyond Catholic and Protestant sectarian disputes, the most significant Iroquois action was warning their Indian hosts of inevitable cultural defeat and territorial dispossession. The last broken links of the ancient Covenant Chain alliance that once united Iroquois and British colonies rust in unmarked and forgotten graves.

~3~

JACCO

The Columbia freemen were a unique body of adventurers intimately associated with the birth of society in a new land. Beyond a few geographical place names and a persistent image of unreliability, few have received the historical recognition they deserve. The name Finlay stands out because it spanned the entire history of the British North American fur trade. It was a lineage that stretched from the St. Lawrence and Saskatchewan rivers to the Columbia drainage.[83]

Jacques (Jacco) Raphael Finlay carried a name that grew from a pent imagination. It was the invention of his Scots father, who wintered in 1768 at bleak Nipowi on the middle Saskatchewan River. The baby's mother was an Ojibwa girl Finlay probably picked up at Saulte Ste. Marie or Grand Portage as a temporary winter housemate.[84] She was not much of a conversationalist, and James Finlay had time to think up an impressive name for the dark-eyed babe she nursed.

James Finlay was one of those Scots who found expression for their talents in the Northwest fur trade. In 1766 he came to the Saskatchewan River to trade with "Three Canewes" of merchandise, to the disappointment of the rival Hudson's Bay Company inland traveler William Pink.[85]

Finlay bought Montreal respectability with his profits from the fur trade and by 1773 was in partnership with John Gregory, satisfied to let others endure the hard winters in the unforgiving Northwest.[86] On his retirement in 1783, his eighteen-year-old son, James Jr., entered the upper country to continue the family business in the North West Company.

By then Jacques, known as Jacco, the sixteen-year-old country son, had been educated in some downstream school to qualify as a fur trade clerk. Nine years later, James was the partner stationed at Fort des Isles near the union of the two main branches of the Saskatchewan River. During outfit 1799–1800 Jacco served in the Upper Fort des Prairies Department under tough little John McDonald of Garth. Jacco's salary of £1,200 Grand Portage currency was the same wage received by men like James Hughes, James King, and David Thompson.[87] During the next outfit, the trader Archibald N. McLeod noticed Jacco at the lower Fort des Prairies, apparently well established in the business.[88]

Jacco's education did not qualify him for a higher station in the field management, which made all the difference as the business advanced toward the mountains. In the summer of 1806 at Rocky Mountain House, Jacco was associated with two other Métis clerks, Nicholas Montour and Jacques Quensel. McDonald of Garth selected him to prepare the road across the mountains that David Thompson would use the following year to enter the Kutenai country, "and follow the Columbia River to the Sea."[89]

After slashing a rough trace, Jacco and his family followed the Blaeberry River to the Columbia, where they constructed a canoe for Thompson's use. That put them on the Pacific slope in the same year that the American Corps of Discovery was returning from wintering at the mouth of the Columbia River. Primacy should have ensured Jacco's fame and reward, but Thompson was dissatisfied with his performance as a trail builder and administered a humiliating tongue-lashing coupled with a reduction in salary. Finlay's pride could not accept this, and he became one of the first western freemen, stripped of his place in the company that his family helped found.

Seeking a way to support his young family, Jacco turned to the rival Hudson's Bay Company. The Edmonton House master, James Bird, was delighted to include him in a sly industrial espionage system that penetrated the Nor'wester system. Jacco's crudely sketched contribution to the early understanding of western geography was preserved in the Edmonton journals and in the writings of Peter Fidler.

In October 1807 Jacco's Saulteur Indian brother-in-law came to Bird with the complaint that the North West Company would not pay the numerous Canadian freemen on the upper Saskatchewan in money unless they took their outfits from them. In his journal Bird mentioned another Canadian who had previously wintered in the "Cootnais" land. He had taken 600 beaver pelts the previous year, and he wanted to trade them at Edmonton or York Factory for a better price. The unidentified trapper promised to return across the mountains next summer for another hunt. Bird hoped that the arrangement would set an example for other free hunters.[90]

The identity of the dissident trapper is revealed by Bird's associate, Peter Fidler, who had a map that was "drawn by Jean Findley in 1806."[91] In conjunction with a diagram showing the wandering of two Iroquois free hunters during that year, Finlay described the upper parts of the Columbia River as far south as the Flat Bow Indian country. In addition to cutting the first trail into the upper Columbia drainage, Jacco was the first to map it.

Thompson came to realize his error in alienating Finlay. When the explorer descended the Kootenay River toward Lake Pend Oreille in August 1809, he was accompanied by Jacco, his country family, and his Saulteur kinsmen. At the recently established Salish House on the Clark Fork River in November, the Nor'wester "arranged and paid" Jacco before sending him to return some horses to another freeman. By then Jacco's son was old enough to hunt with his Saulteur uncles. The next February, a Saulteur from the South Saskatchewan passed the North West Company Fort Vermillion on his way to join his brother-in-law, J. F., at Rocky Mountain House.[92]

Jacco and the horseman Martin were camped on Camas Prairie near the Kutenai Indian camp in early March 1810 when Thompson prepared to go east on furlough. Finlay was reengaged in his former capacity as clerk and interpreter, but the big, red-haired clerk, Finan McDonald, was left in charge of Salish House.[93] Perhaps Thompson hoped that an experienced hand would steady the rambunctious young clerk.

McDonald and two of the slain Charles Courtin's former trappers could not resist following the Flathead hunters to the buffalo ranges or taking part in a fight with the Pikuni Blackfeet. The casualties inflicted by thirteen new North West Company trade guns sent the outraged Piegan north to blockade the mountain portage. A small party of Hudson's Bay men were permitted to winter with the Flatheads without being molested but were warned not to return.[94]

The brush with the Pikuni made Salish House dangerous, so McDonald and Finlay retreated beyond Lakes Pend Oreille and Coeur d'Alene. They built Spokane House in the sheltering shadow of the Greenwood Indians. For the next fourteen years, it was the inland supply depot for the Salish, Kutenai, and lakes trade. Few were more closely identified with that place than Jacco Finlay and his lodge of growing children.

Thompson was sent back to claim the Columbia River. "On the 14th [June 1811], we arrived at the Spokane House on the

River of that name, where I left a small assortment of Goods to continue the trade, with Jaco, a half-breed, as clerk." But at the mouth of the Columbia, Thompson found an American party (the Astorians) that had landed two months earlier. The disappointed trader returned to the mouth of the Snake River on 6 August and sent a message to Finlay to meet him with horses. Unfortunately they took different trails and missed each other until reunited at Spokane House on the 13th. Going on to Kullyspell and Salish Houses on 11 November, Thompson noted that he "Left Coxe & Paul the Iroquois with Jacque Finlay."[95]

After two competitive outfits, the Nor'westers swallowed the Astorians. In the list of people employed on the Columbia during winter 1813–14, "Jac Finlay" was listed as clerk and interpreter at Spokane House, assisted by his son Bonhomme, who was receiving the pay of a middleman and interpreter. Two other sons, Raphael Jr. and Thorburn, were serving downstream at Fort George as interpreters and hunters. In an Indian attack in the Cascades in January 1814, when the proprietor Stuart was struck by three arrows, it was young Finlay who shot the assailant.[96]

Jacco's associates were improving their positions in the Columbia drainage, but his dedication to the Nor'westers was still questionable. In November James Hughes flourished a letter from the Columbia that bragged that the Nor'westers were using 100 freeman and Iroquois trappers. If each worked three traps they could produce 600 ninety-pound packs of furs. Things were going so smoothly that Hughes was convinced that the United States would be forced back to the line of 1783 and the North West Company would soon establish trade on the upper Missouri River.[97]

The intended audience for Hughes's bragging was Finlay's HBC confidant, James Bird. Bird took the boasts with a grain of salt because two young Bungees (Ojibwa) had visited him in late October. They came from their brother-in-law, a Frenchman, long in the service of the North West Company but now dissatisfied and living as a freeman. This was Jacco Finlay, who now invited the HBC to cross the mountains. Bird and Joseph Howse considered Finlay a good man who had made sixty packs for the Nor'westers last year.[98] Was there something more than the Spokane House horse meat diet behind Jacco's dissatisfaction?

Jacco may have participated in Donald McKenzie's 1819 Snake country trapping expedition, but by then there were so many of his large family floating around the Oregon country that it is difficult to distinguish the activities of the father from those of the sons.[99]

After the coalition of rival British firms in 1821, Finlay was not listed among the former North West Company employees who were taken over by the Hudson's Bay Company. When the new governor, George Simpson, came to inspect the Columbia District in fall 1824, he was outraged to find Jacco Finlay and some other Columbia freemen hanging around the lower Canoe River. They meant to intercept Suswap Indians bringing their furs to the Company, trade them, and resell the pelts to the HBC for a tidy profit as middlemen. The disgusted Simpson wrote, "These freemen are a pest in this country, having much influence on the natives, which they exert to our disadvantage by inciting them against us." He instructed his officers to stop the nefarious traffic.[100]

When Simpson returned east the following spring, he ordered that Spokane House be replaced by a more convenient depot on the Columbia River. A year later the botanist David Douglas left Fort Colvile near the Kettle Falls, guided by two of Finlay's sons. They rode to the abandoned Spokane House, where Jacco and his family were living on a meager diet of camas and black pine lichen. When he presented his note of introduction from the Colvile trader, John Warren Dease, the botanist was surprised to find that the old man did not speak English.[101]

By August the food situation had improved, and another HBC man "found old Mr. Finlay, who gave us abundance of fine, fresh salmon from his barrior, placed in a small branch of the main river."[102]

William Kittson sent word to Fort Colvile that Jacco died about 20 May 1828. The deceased's Saulteur brother-in-law, Parsin (Pacquin?), carried the news to Edmonton by 8 October 1828.[103] Jacco's passing completed the cycle of exploration that had begun on the Saskatchewan thirty-two years earlier. David Thompson had retired to Canada to hone his reputation as a geographer and western explorer, and his trail builder was forgotten.

But the name Finlay prevailed. As one of the largest Pacific Northwest mixed-blood families, Jacco's sons and daughters were spread through the tribes. They were still active with the hunting brigades and transport system and in post operations. Keyackie Finlay, who hunted from Spokane House with Finan McDonald in spring 1823, accompanied the Snake Brigade of Alexander Ross under the misspelled name "Cadiac," and the four hunters in his lodge were probably his younger brothers. Keyackie was one of the freemen who deserted Peter Skene Ogden's Snake Brigade in May 1825, but Augustin, Miequim, and

Pinesta Finlay were with Ogden again in 1828–29. Augustin continued in the next outfit, and John Work's list of the 1830–31 hunters included Augustin, "Miquam," and Pinesta Finlay. After Snake Brigade operations closed down, the brothers were carried as trappers on the Fort Colvile outfit 1833, in association with other notable Westerners, such as Edward Berland, Nicholas Montour, Antoine Plante, and the educated Indian Spokane Garry. Keeping up the tradition, John Finlay rode to the Snake plains with Tom McKay's trading party in 1834, while brothers Augustin, Pinesta, and Miequm stayed around Colvile or assisted the Flathead trader Francis Ermatinger.

Settlement scattered the Finlay clan across the Pacific Northwest. The two Catholic missionaries who came west in 1838 baptized several of Jacco's descendants at Jasper's House on the Athabaska portage. Marie was the daughter of James Finlay and his Métisse wife, Bruyere. Sophie, Marie Anne, and possibly Rosalie were daughters of Pichina and his two wives, the Métisse Lisette and Marie Gaspar. Later marriage records show that Rose Finlay, the daughter of Jacques and a Pend d'Oreille woman, became the wife of Antoine Duquet. Josephte Finlay married her brother's Colvile associate, Alexander Guerette *dit* Dumond. Emelie became the wife of Pierre Bercier, and after his death married the Cowlitz settler Simon Plamondon. In 1841, after she had given birth to ten children, a visiting American naval officer described her as still "lovely."[104]

As nominal Catholics, the three Finlay brothers who lived along the trail between Colvile and old Spokane House (near present Chewelah, Washington) could be lumped as nameless half-breeds by the Tshimakain missionary Elkanah Walker. His description changed to freemen in mid-December 1847, when the Cayuse Indians rose against the Whitman mission and Walker's life depended on the Finlays' assistance.[105]

In the resulting incriminations over the killing of the missionaries, another brother, Nicholas Finlay, fell under suspicion. Nicholas had been living in a lodge a few hundred yards from the mission with a doubtful character named Joe Lewis. Although it was never proven that the Cayuse Indians planned the attack in his tent, Nicholas fled north to join his three brothers and married sister near present-day Chewelah, Washington.

During the hostilities that followed the massacre, the Finlays ranged freely through the Indian country, which created additional suspicion. They provided ready targets for Protestant attempts to fix blame on Catholics. Nicholas and Joe Lewis retreated to western Montana and settled among the Flatheads.[106] In the 1908 roll of Flathead families, the name Finlay occurred seventy-six times.[107]

The country–born Jacco was unable to match the career accomplishments of his two Montreal half brothers. Hampered by an imperfect education and unable to speak English, Jacco fell outside the British-dominated mainstream. It was bad luck that the 1804 combination of rival Montreal interests created a surplus of clerks and short-circuited his career. Mixed bloods were easiest to eliminate, although still useful as obligated free trappers.

Jacco's command of Indian languages began at the breast of his Ojibwa mother and became a valuable asset when he slipped into the role of interpreter. By taking a Saulteur wife, Jacco established a close and lasting relationship with her tribesmen. When the full span of Jacco's life is considered, his father's fur trade connections and his downstream education were less useful than the Indian advantages of his duality. His children continued those associations among the interior Salish.

Jacques Raphael Finlay was more than a good man buried in the wilderness. In a modest way, he contributed to the geographical understanding of the transmountain West when his sketches of the western country were incorporated into the maps drawn by the London cartographer Aaron Arrowsmith. In the establishment of Spokane House, Jacco located the logical site for a major northwestern city. But only the Jocko River and Jocko Valley of western Montana perpetuate his name.

～4～

New Ways to Play an Old Game

F ur traders east of the Rockies were never very successful in increasing beaver production through direct trapping. Because they were locked into the familiar symbiosis of hunter and trader, the Nor'westers were baffled by the Blackfeet and Gros Ventre, who disdained to hunt but obstinately denied other trappers access to their territory. Fortunately, the western Indians accepted direct trapping with better grace, and in early summer 1814 the Nor'westers were able to put to use the stranded Astorians they had inherited.

The turnover of Astoria left a number of independent but indebted hunters wandering the Pacific Northwest. Since coming into the country, they had acquired wives from local tribes and now had mixed-blood babies to dandle on their buckskin knees. Some hunted north toward Puget Sound while others went up the Willamette Valley and into the upper Umpqua country. Kinsmen by marriage trapped with Kutenai or Flathead indulgence.

But the pressure was on the Nor'westers, and such relaxed arrangements were as intolerable as the obstinacy of the plains tribes. In a few years the former Astorian Donald McKenzie returned to organize a Snake country hunting brigade. In 1818, bands of trappers began moving through the Snake River Valley as far east as the Green River. Those "leatherstocking" tribes with young families were the first true generation of "new people" in the Northwest. By 1822, when American traders and mountain men returned to the Rocky Mountains, the Columbia freemen were old hands at the skin games.

Salish and Blackfoot hunter-warriors continued fighting along the Continental Divide and near the Big Hole. Western Indians were as determined to continue harvesting buffalo east of the mountains as the plains tribes were to stop them. Those annual pilgrimages of buffalo hunters made excellent escorts for beaver hunters trying to break into the untrapped streams of the Missouri headwaters.

The Iroquois trappers living with the Kutenai and Flathead were now integrated among their wives' tribes. Nor'west recruiters looked for reinforcements among the single men and young couples from the reserves at Kahnawake, Oka, and Ahkwesahne near Montreal. Bringing a complex French or English heritage compounded by generations of captive adoptions, the Iroquois Métis relied on Salish hospitality for security, and they strengthened the bonds through complex layers of intermarriage. In return, the Iroquois taught their hosts how to use the steel-trap and castoreum method of trapping.

The new order that the western Métis helped create was centered around the trading posts—Kootenay House, Kullyspell House, Salish House—and Spokane House, the central depot. Later there were just seasonal posts among Flatheads and Kutenai.

The Nor'wester clerk Nicholas Montour was Métis to a glory and a fault. As a mixed blood of the fourth generation, he could recite an Algonquin, Iroquois, Delaware, Shawnee, Cree, and French heritage, including a father who was a founding partner of the North West Company and perhaps the wealthiest mixed

Dog train in the Rocky Mountains (meeting with Pere De Smet, 7 May 1846). –Pencil sketch by H. J. Warre, National Archives of Canada, C-058154.

blood of his time. After following Thompson across the mountains, Montour became the clerk in charge of the later Kootenay House below the Tobacco Plain. His Métisse wife traced an equally illustrious ancestry to the former HBC and North West Company pioneer Edward Umfreville. Her part-Cree sisters were the wives of promising young clerks, and their brother, Canote, was becoming famous as a Columbia River boatman.

Because they shared a tribal heritage, the Montours got along well with the serious-minded Kutenai. When Nicholas felt imposed upon by his Astorian competitor, Pillet, the neighbors marched down to the nearby meadow and exchanged shots. Ross Cox made light of the incident, but the bullets were real.

Thompson located his Salish House, later known as Flathead Post, near the traditional Flathead Indian winter pastures on the Horse plains. The place drew furs from as far east as the upper Missouri River. Lightly manned and vulnerable, the post was respected because it was a store where friend and foe could replenish their arsenals. The Astorians Ross Cox and Russell Farnham came to the Flathead country in November or December 1812. Like his incautious predecessor, Finan McDonald, Farnham could not resist traveling to the upper Missouri with the Flathead buffalo hunters.[108]

In 1814, Cox learned of the death of one of the most remarkable Flathead freemen. He believed that "Jacques" Houle was one of the French soldiers sent to Scotland in 1745 to support the Jacobite pretender and somehow survived the bloody mowing of the clans on Culloden Moor. In 1759 Houle faced redcoats again on the Plain of Abraham, where New France was lost to the British, and seventeen years later he helped defend British Quebec from American invaders. By then tranquility was beyond him, and Houle headed toward the western plains to be a buffalo hunter and beaver trapper.

Perhaps he was the Louis Jean Baptiste Hoole who accompanied David Thompson to the Mandan villages in 1797–98 and was still around ten years later, paddling a Lower Red River Department supply canoe with companions named Fleury, Suprennant, and Charbonneau. Whether he picked up an American trapping party headed up the Missouri River or came to the mountains via the Saskatchewan, Houle was a free trapper in the West who spent the last seven years of an eventful life among the Salish. The Blackfeet finally lifted his thin, gray scalp.[109] Seventeen individuals carried the name Houle on the Flathead agency roll of 1908.[110]

After Finan McDonald, Michel Bourdon, and Baptiste Buche managed to offend the Piegans in summer 1810, the Nor'westers fell back to a safer location at the junction of the Spokane and Little Spokane rivers. McDonald and Jacco Finlay built Spokane House, which became famous as a resort for lonely trappers.[111] When the Astorians trailed David Thompson into the inland empire, John Clark built a rival post. The accomplishment was celebrated with a grand ball that set the social tone for many years to come.[112]

In summer 1815, James McMillan, Nicholas Montour, Ross Cox, and others, who enjoyed "a fine kitchen garden," amused themselves by hunting deer on the Spokane plains.[113] Two years later, Alex Ross described the handsome establishment, which included a ballroom where there were "no females in the land so fair to look upon as the nymphs of Spokane. No damsels could dance so gracefully as they; none were so attractive."[114] For men like McDonald, the social relationships blossomed into more lasting attachments. Many of the mothers of Northwest Métis were Spokane brides.

The observant Ross Cox described a near marital disaster at Spokane. "One of the younger clerks, having become tired of celibacy, resolved to take a wife; and as none of the Columbian half-breeds had attained a sufficiently mature age, he was necessitated to make his selection from the Spokane tribe." When the buffalo hunters returned, it developed that the pretty seventeen-year-old girl was actually the wife of an absent Indian. The husband was bought off with a gun, 100 rounds of ammunition, a dagger, ten fathoms of tobacco, and some smaller articles.

One hundred and fifty miles down the Spokane and Columbia rivers, Okanogan Post was established on 1 September 1811 to draw trade from as far north as the Thompson River. In addition to taking in 1,550 beaver and other peltries worth £2,250 on the Canton market, Alexander Ross also acquired an Okanogan wife and a growing family of mixed-blood children.[115]

Six hundred miles downstream, clinging to a hillside overlooking the Columbia River, the former Pacific Fur Company post of Astoria was renamed Fort George. A fixed location and relatively permanent staff led to intimate relations with the local Chinook Indians, and it became a point of honor to trace one's Métis parentage to coastal aristocracy.[116]

Several randy traders at Fort George became the sons-in-law of the Chinook Chief Comcomly, whose demure daughters found husbands in Duncan McDougall, Thomas McKay, and Archibald

McDonald. As late as 1824, Comcomly approached the Hudson's Bay Company Governor George Simpson with a "buxom Damsel of 18 or 20 who has never seen daylight."[117] Simpson managed to slip the offer but continued to encourage his clerks to marry into the interior tribes as a means of gaining influence.

Working in pairs or small groups to discourage Indian opportunism, the Westerners hunted up the long Willamette Valley and over into the Umpqua River drainage. After some bloody lessons, the resident Kalapuya Indians learned to respect organized parties and tolerate the freeman trappers who sometimes married their daughters. The less complaisant Umpqua Indians became belligerent and gave the transplanted Ojibwa Métis, Tom McKay, an excuse to come down hard. The depot above the Willamette Falls, called Cantonment du Sable, later became known as Champoeg and was important in the Métis destiny.

Lower Columbia hunters trapped north on the Cowlitz River. That hunt was risky because the Nisqually Indians jealously guarded the southern lobe of Puget Sound, and the waters beyond were exposed to slave-raiding northern tribes coursing the inland sea in great cedar canoes.

When Catholic missionaries began legitimizing long-standing marital relationships in 1838, they made up names for the women from their tribal origin.[118] Sophie Tchinouk was the wife of Antoine Masta, Francois Gendron married Marguerite Walla Walla, Charlotte Okanogan became the wife of Jean Gingras, Marguerite des Chaudieres (Kettle Falls) was the bride of Antoine Felix, and Marie Pendoreil married J. B. Lajoie. Some of the Spokane wives were Isabelle, who married Charles Lafantasie; Marguerite, who married Francois Payette; and Therese, who wed Pierre Grenier. The wife of Peter Skene Ogden was called Julia Tête Plate although she had an Iroquois heritage and was Francois Rivet's stepdaughter.[119]

Finan McDonald's marriage to a Pend d'Oreille girl resulted in a daughter named Helene, who was born at Spokane House, raised on the brigade trail, and mothered a famous Montana dynasty. The life of Josephte Kanhopitsa des Chaudieres, the country wife of the Astorian John Clark, was less fortunate. After the Astorian collapse, Clark abandoned her to pursue a more promising career in the East. According to the custom of the country, Josephte was "set off" on a fifty-year-old interpreter, Jean Baptiste Boucher. After traveling the brigade trail until Boucher's death in 1824, Josephte was taken over by the Fort Colvile engagé Joachim Hubert.

John "The McKie Rouge" and his wife, Josephte (Clark) Boucher. –Collection of Patricia Jo Kern-Bowers.

Perhaps to express how she felt about Clark, his daughter took her stepfather's name. But she had not learned the danger of relationships with itinerant fur traders. When the Irishman Francis Heron became the resident trader at Fort Colvile, young Josephte yielded to his advances and bore a son. When he was transferred, Heron outraged his fellow traders by callously abandoning the young mother. There was a happy ending when the girl found a trustworthy husband in an upper river trader, John "the McKie Rouge." The family eventually retired to the Willamette Valley.[120]

Because the Indian mothers preferred to be near their tribesmen, interior posts usually supported a core of related families in addition to seasonal, floating populations of business travelers, transporters, and native shoppers. When the corporate interests of the Hudson's Bay Company required the transfer of servants to new duty stations, those Indian wives and children were forced into unfamiliar circumstances. Like corporate wives of a later time, the uprooted women developed webs of new relationships across the region, tying fur trade families together through shared experience and similar expectations.

Theirs was a society that followed the brigade trail and the dangerous river routes, diffusing community and never developing the distinct culture of their eastern kindred. The mixed

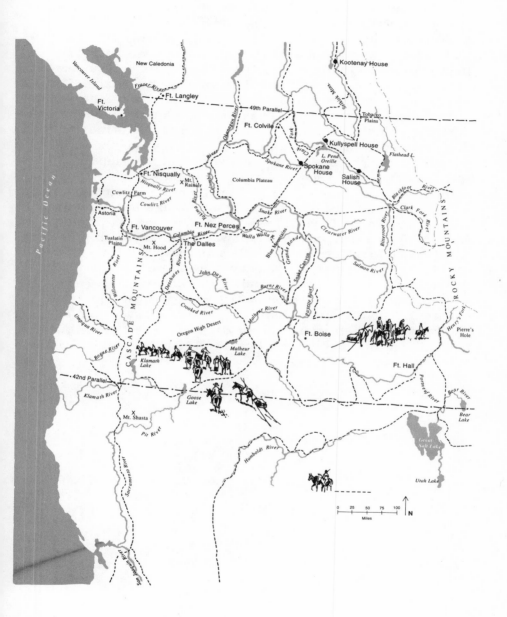

bloods who came from the East as workmen or freeman trappers were poor transporters of culture. During the first half of the nineteenth century, the most identifiable group of Métis were the small body of men and women who traveled with the Snake or Southern hunting brigades. That was a near-tribal structure that lasted for only about thirteen years. Like the workmen and their dependents living around the trading posts, the hunters were driven by commerce rather than community, and their Indian wives contributed tribal instead of Métis cultural patterns.

During the forty or fifty years of the Northwest beaver hunt, the habits of the western Métis reflected the demands of the trail, the boat brigade, and the hunting camp. Being nomads, the Métis were honed by practicality and efficiency, and their most conspicuous arts were horsemanship, packing, and camping.

In the absence of distinct cultural artifacts, the western Métis must be distinguished by their biological peculiarity. To refute the embarrassment of late nineteenth-century racism, present scholarship has attempted to shift away from the obvious biological baseline and emphasize the less controversial abstraction of cultural definition. But discretion does injustice to the very human, truly passionate, and proud relationships that these men and women found in each other, which were confirmed in their children. As herdsmen and hunters, they would have found no embarrassment in personal genetics; that was a fact of life. As true children of love, the Pacific Northwest Métis took a full measure of pride in their lineage.

⌒ 5 ⌒

SNAKE COUNTRY HUNTERS

The fur hunt was inescapably labor intensive, one beaver trapper against one furry rodent, both contesting for life in a frigid mountain stream. After 1821, although the inland management of the dominant Hudson's Bay Company was reluctant to admit it, the success of the western business depended on the relationship between the available trapping force and the officious institution. Small comfort for London gentlemen of business, or their overseas managers, that individualism was an early and lasting trait of Oregonians.

The international contest for the Columbia River fur trade seemed mooted in spring 1813 when the jubilant Nor'westers bought Astoria for a song. Among the party of free hunters who left the 1814 spring boat brigade at the mouth of the Walla Walla River was the former Astorian John Day. With some of his companions of the last three years, Day contracted to hunt on the Spanish River on half shares. By the time they learned that opportunistic Bannock Indians had slaughtered John Reed and nine trappers the previous winter, it was too late to back out honorably.

John Clark and Donald McKenzie carried news of the collapse of his plan to John Jacob Astor. In Montreal, the Hudson's Bay Company recruiter convinced Clark to enter the contest for distant Athabaska, but McKenzie saw his future on the Columbia River. He rejoined the North West Company, married Tom McKay's sister at Fort William, and left headquarters with a reinforcement of potential western beaver hunters. By fall of 1817 McKenzie was back at Fort George trying to convince his fellow officers to support a strong effort in the Snake country. All they gave him was an unsatisfactory collection of misfits.[121]

Leaving Alexander Ross to build a depot and base camp at the mouth of the Walla Walla River, McKenzie headed up the Snake

River in 1818 with a trapping brigade consisting of the remaining contract hunters, freemen with no obligation beyond trading their catch to the nearest source of supply, and the independent-minded Iroquois. The last soon broke off to operate on their own, which seriously weakened McKenzie's party as it entered the ranges of the dangerous Bannocks.

After overcoming some initial Bannock resistance, the brigade trapped along the Snake River to its sources, and probed the middle part of the Bear River. They may also have entered the Green River Valley. In 1818-19 the hunters wintered along the Snake River bottoms near the mouth of the Portneuf River, adjacent to Shoshone winter camps.

Ross portrayed "Big Donald" McKenzie as a reluctant writer who kept minimal accounts on a beaver skin. It was a personification that left Ross free to chronicle the history of those early Snake Brigades. But the correspondence that McKenzie kept up with a St. Louis friend, Wilson Price Hunt, and the letters concerning John Day's will and St. Louis estate reveal a gifted and humorous writer.

When the rival Canadian North West Company and English Hudson's Bay Company agreed to merge in 1821, McKenzie saw his prospects dimming. He stayed at Fort Nez Perces and turned the command of the next Snake Brigade over to "young" Michel Bourdon. Chiefs changed but the experienced trappers were a fixture.

Monopolies are not meant to benefit people. After almost two decades in the West, the Columbia freemen saw their earnings cut to the bone while prices soared. At the same time, other disillusioned Saskatchewan engagés shifted over the mountains to support their families by trapping. Everyone was sinking into debt bondage to the new Company, which ruthlessly exploited a captive production.

Michel Bourdon was a victim of reorganization.[122] After losing two men to Blackfoot raiders during the summer hunt, the trappers killed seven enemies and began thinking about alternatives. Indian friends told the pesky Iroquois that American traders had returned to the Yellowstone River and had a fort near the mouth of the Big Horn that offered attractive prices.

Before long, fourteen of Bourdon's hunters refused to carry their returns to Flathead Post. Bourdon was forced to cache 700 valuable pelts on the east end of the Snake plain.[123] The dissidents were Iroquois and leftover Astorians who ignored their promise to return to Fort Nez Perces and doubled back toward the Wind River Valley to winter with the hospitable Mountain Crows. Continuing east in the spring, they were intercepted and robbed of their packs and women by the River Crows. Veering east toward the Missouri River, the price shoppers had a fatal encounter with the Cheyenne Indians. Only six survivors reached Fort Atkinson in August 1823, but the impact of their description of Hudson's Bay Company parsimony revolutionized commercial politics west of the mountains.[124]

Losing fourteen valuable hunters pushed Bourdon back into his old role of assistant to Finan McDonald. After recovering the Snake plain caches, the 1832 brigade worked along the Salmon River, where lurking Blackfeet killed Bourdon and three companions.[125] After losing another hunter, McDonald cornered seventy Blackfeet in a narrow canyon, fired the brush, and mowed down the singed fugitives.[126] Shocked by this second lesson at the hands of the terrible McDonald, the Piegans sued for peace and allowed the brigade to cross Lemhi Pass and trap down the Missouri River as far as the Great Falls. That was a region that the Indians had denied to British hunters for twenty years, and that international law recognized as American domain.

In November 1824, Alexander Ross finally inherited command of the fifty-five hunters, including two Americans, seventeen Canadians, five half-bloods from east of the mountains, twelve Iroquois, two Abenaki, two Nipissing, one Saulteur (Ojibwa), two Cree, one Chinook, two Spokane, two Kutenai, three Flatheads, two Kalispell, one Palouse, and a Snake Indian slave. Twenty-five of the trappers were married, some with sons old enough to carry a gun. In addition, there were sixty-four Métis children. The brigade trailed away from Flathead Post packing their outfits on horses, or dragging travois like a band of Indians.[127]

Each hunter had a gun, six to ten steel traps, clothing, ammunition, and enough camp gear to require the use of two to four horses. The outfits were supplied by the Company on credit to be repaid in properly prepared beaver pelts. Although the traditional eastern credit system was generally discouraged in the West, it was now used to offset the impossible situation of low prices for furs and high costs of necessary goods. As they bucked their starving ponies through daunting snowdrifts to reach the trapping grounds, the western freemen must have realized that they could not earn enough during a trapping season to pay for the equipment they needed to support their dependents.[128]

Engagés and freemen were victims of the License of Exclusive Trade, which gave the HBC the monopoly on fur trade in British possessions. It was a tactic of a parsimonious British government to improve cheaply a claim of usage to the disputed Oregon country. Among the economies initiated by Governor George Simpson in 1824 was an order to reduce Columbia boat crews from eight to seven men—fewer hands to row larger bateaux carrying heavier cargoes, in a job where men were known to die of strangulated hernias.[129]

After receiving the dubious honor of conducting the Snake Brigade, Alex Ross experienced the usual difficulties of dealing with unreliable Iroquois and undependable Métis. Trapping west toward the Boise River, Ross yielded to Iroquois demands to be allowed to hunt on their own. The ringleaders, Old Pierre and John Grey, promised to rejoin the brigade in the fall. When they were out of sight, the Iroquois headed toward Bear Valley to meet their friends returning from the American market survey.

At the agreed rendezvous with Ross, the independents delivered a highly suspect story about quarreling with the Snake Indians and losing all of their packs. But the Iroquois came to the east side of the Snake plain accompanied by seven American trappers. These buckskin-clad hunters, who had been in the Green River Valley, were led by a lanky American whom Ross immediately pegged as a "sly Yankee." Jedediah Smith bragged that he had about the same number of furs in cache as the Iroquois claimed to have lost. Worse, the corporate hireling could not dissuade him from accompanying the Snake Brigade back to Flathead Post.

Bringing the competition to the heart of HBC operations was disquieting but that was not the reason that Governor Simpson replaced Ross. The arrangement had already been made that the former North West Company bully Peter Skene Ogden would lead the Snake Brigade. Tough Ogden could be expected to keep the troublesome trappers under his heavy hand. Early in 1825, the new broom took the brigade south toward Bear River and the Great Salt Lake, intending to sweep as many furs as possible from the American competitors.

By mid-May the Snake Brigade was camped in the mountains above Salt Lake. Three of the hunters missing since 1822 suddenly reappeared with a group of trappers from Mexican territory. Four of them had gone to Taos and joined a trapping party that intended to work on the Green River. The former Astorian Patrick O'Conner accompanied the leader, Etienne Provost, into the Salt Lake Valley, where he was killed by Snake Indians. When Francois Method, Jack McLeod, and Lazard Teycaleyecourigi rejoined their friends, they were the last of fourteen luckless non-conformists.

Ogden was pondering the curious reappearance of the three wanderers when a large band of pugnacious American mountain men rode into camp. They blustered about national sovereignty and cast around wild promises of better prices to the attentive freemen. The next morning eleven Iroquois free trappers led the exodus to the American camp, taking their families and their furs to an irresistible combination of better prices and cheaper goods. Before the desertions were over the Snake Brigade lost twenty-three invaluable hunters.

In their indignant letters and journals, the outraged HBC men howled disloyalty. British subjects were not supposed to enjoy a free man's right to self-interest. By exploiting the trapping and geographical experience of the Columbia roamers, the Ashley-Henry and Smith, Jackson & Sublette trading partnerships were able to dominate the mountain hunt for the next five years. Governor Simpson had to placate his London directorate with false claims of a fur desert created to keep the Americans at bay.

Although the HBC claimed otherwise, most of the men who defected at Mountain Green never returned to HBC service. Those who did had to be repurchased at considerable expense, which made Governor Simpson's Columbia Department economies

Peter Skene Ogden and an unidentified bowman.
—H. J. Warre, National Archives of Canada, C-027147.

penny-wise. Two attempts by him to field another trapping brigade recruited from Red River Métis also failed. The eastern peoples of mixed ancestry had not forgotten that the corporation turned them out after 1821 to improve profits.[130]

In 1830 the HBC Columbia District staff counted 138 Europeans, 218 Canadians, 55 Sandwich Islanders (Hawaiians), and 47 mixed bloods. Many of those identified as Canadian were probably Métis. Mixed bloods made up half of the only available labor force. Trapping with the Snake Brigade or the Southern Brigade that hunted into California, they were essential to western operations.

The Company rolls do not list those freemen who were floating around the Rocky Mountains with the Americans, with the Indians, or on their own. As the years of the bonanza hunt slipped by, they had to set their traps in the last productive streams, and sell their furs to the highest bidder.[131] But the resource was drying up, and hunters scrambled to find untouched or recovered streams.

After John Work led the last Snake Hunting Brigade in 1832, the Company decided to limit field operation to sending traders and outfit with Indian hunting bands. They intended to intercept pelts before they could be passed to Americans.

But freemen hanging around the trading posts were detrimental to efficient operations. The Hudson's Bay Company discouraged undesirables by requiring that discharged servants return to their place of enlistment. That corporate policy presented a hardship to the old hands who had made country marriages and produced half-breed families. The Fort Vancouver Chief Factor, John McLoughlin, occasionally evaded the rule by keeping favorite men on the roster, when they were actually settled in the Willamette Valley.[132]

Columbia River mixed bloods who had followed the brigade trail for a quarter century had little reason to return to nearly forgotten eastern homes. Having known each other since childhood and shared danger, discomfort, and grief, they had become a floating community, closer to each other than to distant kinsmen.

The decline of the beaver hunt left the mixed bloods without a profession. Those who tried to resettle their country families in the East found that returning to unfamiliar civilization was just too hard. One former clerk, John Dears, physically shanghaied his Indian wife when he left to retire at Sault Ste. Marie. When he died, she was stranded among unsympathetic strangers.

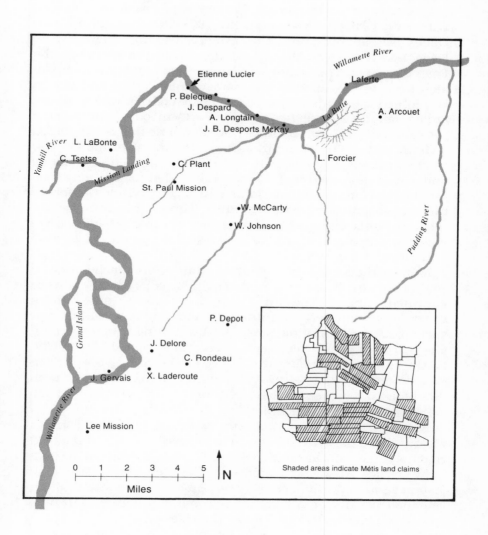

Willamette River

Etienne Lucier

Laferte

P. Beleque
J. Despard
A. Longtain
J. B. Desports McKay

La Butte

A. Arcouet

Yamhill River

L. LaBonte

C. Tsetse

Mission Landing

C. Plant

St. Paul Mission

L. Forcier

W. McCarty

W. Johnson

Pudding River

Grand Island

Willamette River

P. Depot

J. Delore

C. Rondeau

J. Gervais

X. Laderoute

Lee Mission

0 1 2 3 4 5

Miles

N

Shaded areas indicate Métis land claims

Ghosts shadowed the life of Nancy of The Dalles. She was the Indian wife of one of the western freemen who left the Snake Brigade to join the Americans. Her husband was one of the men with Sam Tullock who shared the 1827–28 winter camp with Ogden. Indians intercepted the Americans when they tried to leave, and Nancy's husband was killed near the mouth of the Portneuf River. The Dalles woman survived and was immediately taken over by an American named Archibald Goodrich, who had joined the British. Two years later, Goodrich was drowned at The Dalles. Nancy drifted down to Fort Vancouver and became the companion of Jean Baptiste Dobin. In time the couple staked a claim on the French Prairie. Under the terms of the Oregon provisional government, half of the holding was in her name, and a local story held that the cabin straddled the dividing line. Still wandering in tandem, Dobin and Nancy went to California during the gold rush, where he died. Three times widowed on the trail, Nancy managed to return to her Willamette Valley home, where she died on 3 May 1850 and was buried in the old St. Paul Cemetery.[133]

Many of the mixed-blood children around Fort Vancouver were sent to the post school established in 1832. Sons of officers were educated with the expectation that they would become a cadre of useful young men committed to Company service. But that was a hollow expectation, since most were unable to overcome Governor Simpson's deep-seated mistrust of mixed bloods. The institutional man preferred to bring in young English or Scottish apprentices who were totally committed to him. Such prejudice blocked several educated Westerners from achieving any significant level of responsibility.[134]

Between 1824 and 1837 the proven brigade leader Thomas McKay found his own career opportunities limited and realized that his three half-Chinook sons could not expect to rise in Company service. McKay arranged with the Methodist missionary Jason Lee to have them educated in American schools. William returned as a doctor. All worked in the Indian service, but Alex and Donal eventually retreated to the reservation.

McKay's stepfather, Chief Factor John McLoughlin, also sent his son outside for a proper education. Doctor John McLoughlin Jr. returned to Rupert's Land showing disturbing signs of political independence. Governor Simpson bought off the young gentleman with an unusually high salary, and shuffled him off to an out-of-the-way station at Fort Stikane. Inexperienced and burdened by loneliness, the young man was killed by some of his own men. Simpson's light-handed treatment of the murder offended the father and contributed to his withdrawal from Company service. After the evaporation of his father's influence, the other son, David McLoughlin, retreated into northern Idaho, where he married a Spokane woman and acted as a lawyer for the Kutenai. More indicative of the dilemma officers faced concerning their country children was the chief factor's neglect of his half-Ojibwa son by a prior marriage. Joseph McLoughlin never rose above the level of trapper. More at home among others of mixed ancestry than among whites, Joe settled near some of the Iroquois in the Willamette Valley.

If opportunities for officer's sons were so unpromising, what could the children of mere servants expect?

For many years the Company freely used the broad prairies of the lower Willamette Valley as horse pastures. In those open meadows, displaced trappers saw farms where a man could support his family. The first farms were along the Willamette River, near old Cantonment du Sable. It was a fine open bottom contained in a crook of the river. As settlements multiplied, the area was soon being called the French Prairie.

The Chinook sisterhood of their wives bonded the families of the former Astorians Etienne Lucier and Joseph Gervais, early settlers in the area. Soon after they established farms around 1828,

Celiast Clatsop, wife of Solomon H. Smith and sister of Mrs. LaBonte and Mrs. Gervais. –Helen Austin Collection.

the Timiskaming Métis Jean Baptiste Desports *dit* McKay joined them. Although reluctant to encourage settlement south of the Columbia River, and ignoring the standing orders to return men to their place of enlistment, McLoughlin allowed them to stay. They were required to post a bond of $50 for their good behavior, but McLoughlin saw that they were furnished a few tools, livestock, and seed on credit. The fur trade would absorb the crops of those small farms.

The success of the ground-breaking attracted others. Unlike the prior example of the Red River Selkirk settlement, which was competitively and politically inspired, the Willamette farms were spontaneous and self-generated.[135] The French Prairie was a community of circumstance.

Other pockets of Métis settlement developed north of the Columbia River. The locally famous Abenaki hunter Pierre Charles accompanied Archibald McDonald to the lower lobe of Puget Sound in May 1833 and helped build a supply depot on Sequalitchew Creek. In time the place developed into Fort Nisqually. Charles was still associated with the area as late as 1852.[136]

When the former Snake Brigade clerk and Kutenai Post trader William Kittson arrived to take charge of the fort on 18 May 1834,

John McLeod house on Muck Creek. Left to Right: Tristan Mounts, John M. Mounts, and Frank St. Germain. –Del McBride Collection.

64

the complement included Pierre Charles, William Ouvre, William Brown, the Iroquois Louis Sagohanenchta, Silvan Bourgeau, Anawescan McDonald, John McKee, and Tai and Simon Plamondon. Sagohanenchta, who was married to a Nisqually woman, had two children, Catharine and Ignace.

An HBC workman, Simon Plamondon, settled a bit to the south on the Cowlitz River, where the Company was expanding agricultural operations. Plamondon began farming in association with Francois Faignant as early as 1833. The families of Michel Cognoir and Joseph Rochbrunne joined them. When Catholic priests came in 1838, the little community returned to its neglected religion.[137]

As more former Snake Country hunters settled on the French Prairie, the growing community was still under the influence of the Hudson's Bay Company. Fortunately, John McLoughlin, the lord of the manor, was benevolent and a Catholic. But the Hudson's Bay Company realized that the disputed Oregon country south of the Columbia would inevitably fall under American control. The best line of division that it could hope for would run down the middle of the Columbia River, ensuring the right of navigation to its inland posts. A British colony north of the river would strengthen that argument.

Andre Longtain, whose donation land claim is now Champoeg State Park. This framed portrait hangs in the visitor center. –Helen Austin Collection.

To encourage the relocation of the retired trappers in the Willamette Valley, the corporation was willing to exploit their religion. Although it was nominally an Anglican institution, the HBC agreed to support a Catholic mission. The fathers were brought west with the understanding that they would use their influence to induce the Willamette settlers to move north of the river. With proof of settlement and effective usage, the Company could press for retaining the region and establishing the Columbia as the international border. When the priests failed to convince their parishioners to give up good farms for questionable relocations north, the Bishop of Quebec was tersely informed that additional missionaries would be required to pay for their passage on Company ships, and Father Blanchet's support from the Northern Council of Rupert's Land was dropped to a meager £100.[138]

On 10 October 1841, Francis Ermatinger started the last trapping brigade to California. One hundred colorful hunters trailed south but found poor trapping on the upper Sacramento River. Governor Simpson, who was at Monterey to inspect the California operations, ordered a halt to southern trapping. Chief Factor McLoughlin managed to slip in one more trip on the excuse that it was necessary to recover cached traps, but the free-ranging brigades were over. Another batch of displaced trappers who felt precious little loyalty to the corporation were turned loose.

6

Thomas McKay, Fur Trader

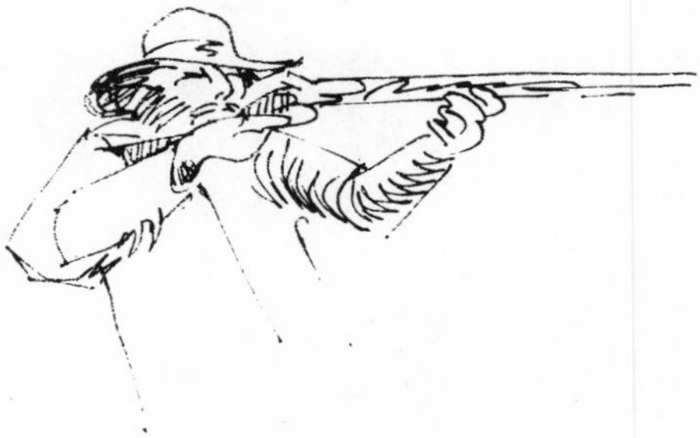

At the age of fourteen, Tom McKay was left an orphan on an alien shore. Leaving his son Tom with the Astorians building at the mouth of the Columbia River, Alexander McKay sailed north on the doomed ship *Tonquin*.

Pierre Gaultier de La Verendrye, Major Robert Rogers, Captain James Tute, and Peter Pond had tried to find a northwest passage by land to the Pacific Ocean. When that debatable honor was finally claimed by Alexander McKenzie in 1793, Alex McKay was with him on that barren rock at Bella Coola. Recognizing that there was no practical water route across the northern continent, McKay had the gumption to join John Jacob Astor's Pacific Fur Company and approach the western coast by sea. After leaving Tom with his partners, Alex sailed north to his fate. He hadn't been very bound as a husband and not that much more as a father.

Six weeks after construction of the depot began, David Thompson arrived from upriver with a couple of North West Company engagés, two Iroquois boatmen, and two American freemen. Nor'westers had been on the Columbia drainage for four years, and Thompson came expecting to connect with a nominally American company. But Astor was going to be a competitor instead of a partner in the Pacific trade, and Thompson headed back for the interior, trailed by the opposition. It is unlikely that the implications of international rivalry made much of an impression on young Tom, whose heritage was the fur trade.

Tom's maternal grandfather was the Swiss fur trader Jean Etienne Wadin, who took his Ojibwa country wife and daughter into the remote Athabaska country. Tom's mother was about seven years old when she saw the Nor'wester Peter Pond fatally wound her father.[139] The widow and girl returned to the Grand

Portage and Indian camps around Sault Ste. Marie, where Marguerite Wadin blossomed into an attractive Métisse who caught the attention of the promising young Nor'wester Alexander McKay. Thomas was born at Ile à la Crosse in 1797, and six years later carried to Lower Canada where he was baptized on 9 November 1804 in the Scotch Presbyterian church at Williamstown, Glengarry County.

After six years of schooling, Tom was engaged as a clerk in the Pacific Fur Company. His father extracted the generous salary of £100 per annum for a boy who had no practical experience. Alex McKay had left Marguerite and their daughters at Fort William. Madame McKay did not expect to see him again and had formed a new relationship with young Doctor John McLoughlin before the Indians of Clayquoit Sound killed her absent husband.

When north coast Indians reported the destruction of the *Tonquin*, young McKay had to reconcile his Ojibwa heritage to the hard truth that Indians had killed his father.[140] Dependent on the rough indulgence of sympathetic officers, Tom grew up fast. He learned his first lessons about the skin game in the Willamette Valley.[141]

In January 1814, Thomas McKay was assigned to assist Alexander Ross at the Okanogan Post and joined the boat brigade climbing the Columbia River. The party ran afoul of belligerent Indian fishermen who controlled The Dalles portage and expected to extract passage money. In the resulting fight, sixteen-year-old Tom killed his first man. Later, during a ride into the Yakima country, McKay fell from his horse and dislocated his hip. The injury left him lame for the rest of his life.

When Tom's engagement expired in 1815, he crossed the Rocky Mountains with the Fort William express to visit his mother at the Lake Superior depot. Madame McKay and his sisters were now living under the care of Dr. John McLoughlin. While he was at Fort William, Tom fell under the influence of Nor'westers who were outraged by the colony of displaced Scots that the Earl of Selkirk had settled at the forks of the Red and Assiniboine rivers. The Nor'westers saw that the Hudson's Bay Company intended to cut them off from the Indian-manufactured pemmican that was essential to their over-extended transportation system.

The Nor'westers resorted to a tactic as cynically conceived as the Earl's sly humanitarianism. McKay and several other young clerks were to use their mixed-blood heritage to convince the mostly Métis Red River freemen to resist the appropriation of their homeland. Riding behind a presumptuous standard that symbolized a new sense of Métis identity, a mixed-blood war party met the colony governor and his followers near the forks. In the resulting melee, McKay was seen killing a man who had fallen to his knees and was begging to surrender.

A Montreal grand jury found sufficient evidence to indict the young man for murder. With an embarrassing prosecution looming, McKay was shipped out of the country.[142] Tom returned to the Oregon country, a fugitive from justice and exile at the ripe age of nineteen.[143]

During the winter of 1819–20 McKay commanded sixty trappers hunting on the sources of the Willamette River. In the upper Umpqua Valley, Iroquois hunters bullied the inoffensive local tribesmen into a fight. Leaving fourteen dead Indians, the brigade was obliged to retreat to Fort George. Nevertheless, several trappers—Louis LaBonte, Joseph Gervais, Etienne Lucier, Louis Pichette *dit* Dupre, and Louis Kanota—continued to trap in the valley as freemen.

When McKay returned to the Willamette and Umpqua headwaters for the next trapping season, he had a reputation that potential troublemakers had to respect. Years later, on the Snake plains, opportunistic Indians demanded to know what he would pay for safe passage. After holding up one eloquent rifle ball, McKay was allowed to proceed unmolested. The courage that limping Tom displayed in those encounters confirmed his leadership of the Oregon mixed bloods.

In 1821 Thomas McKay passed into the service of his third fur-trading firm. The reorganization of the Columbia District required the transfer of Chief Factor John McLoughlin, and Tom went up the Columbia River to Jasper House on the Athabaska portage to greet his mother, and incidentally to meet the new governor, George Simpson.

Governor Simpson's first impression of the young half-breed was that he was "wild and thoughtless, useful only to accompany trappers." But now Simpson saw that he was "respected & feared by the Natives, resolute, an unerring marksman." By 1825 McKay was described as "a perfect dreadnaught on a service of danger who could live anywhere by his Gun." Tom stood near when the great little man christened Fort Vancouver by breaking a bottle of rum on the flagstaff. As the governor's boat rowed out of sight, the center of western operations belonged to McKay's stepfather, John McLoughlin.[144]

By now Americans were pressing into the Snake country and testing the Company hold on the western trapping force. Facing

71

Fort Vancouver, 1845. –H. J. Warre, National Archives of Canada, C-040845.

the seduction of the Columbia freemen, the Company strengthened the resolve of the field command by calling in tough nuts
like Peter Skene Ogden, Finan McDonald, and Tom McKay to keep
dissidents in line. In 1827 McKay led the northern arm of Ogden's
Snake River Brigade and wintered his detachment in the vicinity of the Salmon River. Only a short time before he was to rejoin
Ogden, Blackfoot raiders struck the Americans. The next autumn,
McKay accompanied the HBC Southern Brigade to recover the
property of the sixteen American trappers killed by Indians on
the lower Umpqua River.

McKay's value as a brigade clerk did not earn him promotion
to the rank of trader. Governor Simpson's impression dimmed
after he believed that Tom's "time [at Fort Walla Walla] was occupied in horse racing and shooting with Indians instead of watch-
ing [business]; Goods, provisions and Liquors were uselessly and
wastefully expended and the whole business of the Post neglected."[145] After his 1828–29 visit to the Columbia, the governor's
opinion of McKay further deteriorated:

> [McKay] has been employed on the most desperate service in
> the Columbia and the more desperate it is the better he likes it.
> He is known to every Indian in the Department and his name
> alone is a host of Strength carrying terror with it as he has sent
> many of them to their "long home"; quite a blood hound who
> must be kept under restraint.

The governor considered Tom "a necessary evil at such a place
as Vancouver" and felt "he had not a particle of feeling or humanity in his composition." According to Simpson, Tom was at
the height of his ambition and could not expect promotion because of his poor judgment and confirmed propensity for lying.[146]

Sensing how his career was headed after the governor's visit,
in 1831 Tom asked for a year's furlough. The following March he
told his stepfather that he wanted to retire to California. Later he
applied for permission to leave Company service and settle somewhere in the Oregon country. Clearly he was a very special man
at loose ends.

Before operations were shifted from Fort George, McKay en-
tered a country marriage with one of the daughters of Chinook
Chief Comcomly. His first son was born near Fort George on 18
March 1824 and named William Cameron McKay. Alexander and
John followed, as well as two daughters, before the mother died
in the early 1830s. Her death near Fort Hall was noted by the
Methodist missionary Jason Lee, who wrote, "Captain McKay who

Top left: James Birnie, HBC trader on lower Columbia River whose family settled at Cathlamet. Top right: Napoleon McGillivray, third generation son of the fur trade who settled near Fort Vancouver. Middle left: J. B. Gagnier, HBC trader at Fort Umpqua. —Elwood Evans, History of the Pacific Northwest: Oregon and Washington (Portland: North Pacific Publishing, 1889).

Bottom left: John Todd, fur trader in British Columbia, identified as a friend of Grandma McKay. Bottom right: Charlie Wren, Red River immigrant of 1841. —Buchtel & Stolze photo, Portland. Author's collection.

has buried one native companion last night took another to wife."[147]

The new Cayuse bride produced a son, Donald, and a daughter, Wenix. When the Reverend Gustavus Hines visited the Walla Walla Valley in 1843, he met an Indian woman who had lived with Thomas McKay for many years until she was put off so he could marry a younger woman.[148]

McLoughlin reclaimed his stepson for the fur trade in 1834 to get an HBC trading outfit to the American mountain rendezvous. Fearful of the reaction of Anglophobic trappers, the Company had previously outfitted a nefarious combination of an American trapper named Warren Ferris and the old Columbia freeman and trader Nicholas Montour. With his life savings held to secure the outfit, Montour was just a stalking horse. As it turned out, it was Ferris who absconded.

McLoughlin turned to his stepson because he was no longer directly tied to the Company and might pass as a free trader. Tom headed toward the east end of the Snake plains with a new outfit for the Ferris/Montour combination only to learn that the arrangement had fallen through. As Tom was returning, he discovered that the disgruntled New England entrepreneur Nathaniel Wyeth was building a trading post near the mouth of the Portneuf River. On his own initiative, Tom countered with a house on the Boise River, which led Governor Simpson, who never had a full grasp of Snake operations, to suspect that McKay was dabbling in private trade. On 25 June 1836, McLoughlin was instructed to restrict any future initiative to Company men. Tom was retained as a Snake country clerk.

McKay was also developing private interests on the Scappoose plains and near Champoeg in the Willamette Valley. In 1841, Lieutenant Charles Wilkes of the American Exploring Expedition found the fur-trader-turned-miller living on the Pudding River in a combination house and gristmill. The dusting of flour failed to disguise the tall, muscular middle-aged man whose energetic expressions sometimes inflated into large yawns. But beneath the projecting brows, deep-set, cold eyes were still enough to terrorize any Indian.[149]

At the manly gatherings in the Fort Vancouver bachelors hall, Tom's tall yarns continued to astonish and amuse visitors. One associate noted:

> Mackay has had many encounters with the bear & the best way,
> he says, when a wounded bear rushes at you, or perceives you,
> is to stand & reload & when he comes near, if your gun is un-

loaded, look at him steadily & he will not attack, but raised on his hind legs, will continue to return your gaze until tired of his position, when he takes himself quietly off.[150]

After more than a quarter of a century on the brigade trail, Tom was ready to settle down. The reign of the western nabobs began to slip when missionaries looked down their long Protestant noses at country marriage arrangements. Recognizing the inevitable, James Douglas authenticated his eight-year marriage to Nelia Connelly, and William Glen Rae legitimized his union with Maria McLoughlin. But when the officious HBC chaplain, Herbert Beaver, implied that John McLoughlin's marriage to Tom's mother was adulterous, he got cracked over the head with a cane. It was no more than he would have received in an English parish for insulting the squire, but the Company was scandalized. The humiliated chief factor was obliged to have Douglas perform a civil ceremony to authenticate his union.

A month after the Anglican was sent packing, a Catholic priest officiated at another marriage. Judging from the guest list of the New Year's Eve 1838 ceremony at Fort Vancouver, it was a considerable event. Tom married Isabelle, the Métisse daughter of Nicholas Montour. Those signing as witnesses to the union of a Protestant groom and a Catholic bride included John McLoughlin, James Douglas, William Glen Rae, John Todd, Charles Forest, George B. Roberts, William F. Tolmie, and the American Courtney M. Walker. Nicholas Montour, the father of the bride, had recently retired to the growing Métis community on the French Prairie, where the new couple also settled.[151]

In the fall of 1842 yet another combination of the sanctimonious and ambitious arrived in the person of the former missionary Elijah White. He presumed to lead a wagon train of overland immigrants, and arrived with the somewhat doubtful appointment as United States Indian subagent for Oregon. In December, he tried to apply this thin authority to the Cayuse Indians, with Tom McKay and Cornealius Rogers trailing along to keep him from creating too many problems.

White's eleven Cayuse laws imposed intrusive standards on warriors already disturbed by the Presbyterian mission in the Walla Walla Valley. If the subagent's bluster was accepted, it was because of the man standing behind him.[152] But even in the role of an intermediary, McKay compromised his standing among the plateau tribes.

A recognized Métis leader like Tom McKay should have found a place in the formation of the Oregon provisional government.

But he was too closely associated with the HBC. The most significant public service he came up with during those formative years was to suggest the construction of a better road into the Willamette Valley. Tom rode around the settlements collecting the marks of the old trappers on a petition to authorize him to build a wagon road across the Cascade Range and to collect tolls for two years.

An intimation of mortality caused Thomas McKay to draw up a holographic will on 23 February 1844. In disposing of eight cattle, two milk cows, two oxen, eighteen horses, and a number of pigs, the will named his children who were living at that time: William, John, Alexander, Mary, Maria, Thomas, Donal, and Louise. Corrections made to the will in the following year were witnessed by his father-in-law, Nicholas Montour, and brother-in-law George Montour. In a forecast of the drift of his religious affiliation, Tom struck out the name of Jason Lee as one of the three administrators and substituted that of Father Blanchet.

In addition to the homestead and mill on the Pudding River, McKay continued to hold a large horse farm on the Scappoose plains. That choice location fell under the land law of the provisional government, which limited land claims to 640 acres per family. However, no land-greedy settler dared challenge Tom's hold on the property until 1847, when he finally released the claim. Opening that choice holding generated a minor land rush that drew Tom's sons, William and Alex, and several of the Red River colonists away from their prior claims on the north Tualatin plains.[153]

In late 1847 McKay made an interesting demonstration against the growing anti-Catholic feeling by having himself rebaptized at St. Rose Mission in the Walla Walla Valley.

> October 29, 1847, we the priest undersigned baptized conditionally at Walla Walla Thomas McKay, aged 47 years, having first abjured the heresy and made public confession of the Catholic faith in the presence of many witnesses, and we named William McBean and Jane Boucher to act as godparents; we baptized him at once and gave absolution from censure. J. B. A. Brouillet, ptre.[154]

This was the second act performed by Jean Baptiste Abraham Brouillet after his arrival at Fort Walla Walla with an overland reinforcement of ten missionaries and lay workers led by Father A. M. A. Blanchet. It is uncertain what Tom was doing in the upper country at this time, but he must have been impressed enough by the bishop to renounce Anglicanism.[155] The next month, the local tribesmen fell on the Whitman mission.

In the rage that swept the Willamette settlement following the massacre, McKay's public value resurfaced. The Hudson's Bay Company arranged the ransom of the survivors, but the Willamette settlers were howling for revenge. As a punitive force formed, Tom got out his trail-worn buckskins and rode around the French Prairie to call out his old comrades. The other inexperienced militiamen rushed upriver to mill around The Dalles in confusion, while the mixed-blood company moved deliberately.

When the Cayuse confronted the circled wagons at Sand Hollow, the Métis stood behind their resolute captain. In an otherwise pointless little war without real action, the engagement was called a battle. The shaman Grey Eagle had bragged that he was invincible, a claim that McKay refuted by drilling him neatly between the eyes. When Chief Five Crows was pursued and wounded by Tom's second-in-command, Charles McKay, the Cayuse belligerence collapsed.

The war hero returned to another duty. McKay led a party of fifty wagons to the California gold rush over the trails he knew so well from his brigade days and a Puget Sound Agricultural Company cattle drive. In the mines, McKay enjoyed a certain fame among the goggling forty-niners, who saw him as the epitome of the unrelenting frontiersman who tolerated nothing from Indians:

> We saw this Mr. McKey in the California mountains and his appearance was beyond all others the most striking. Of middling height, and possessed of a square, athletic yet agile form, his continence bronzed by prairie sun and mountain breeze, the fire of youth blazed from his eagle eye, while its steady vigilance betokened the noon of life, and only the locks of iron grey foretold its later years. Of a respectable family and good education he nevertheless preferred the solitudes of the Rocky Mountains, every nook and corner of which he knew as well as the range of his rifle: and had been for many years an agent of the HBC. Fresh from this Cayuse War, and exasperated by the atrocities of the Indians, the mountaineers no sooner reached the head waters of the Sacramento Valley, there they avenged every theft of the California Indians by the rifle, which being retaliated as system of mutual murder has sprung up which men engage in who are called brave.[156]

In contrast to the admiring invention, Tom wrote a mundane letter to his son Billy from Sutter's Fort on 18 February 1849. "All my boys" had caught colds, from which most of them had recovered. But Tom was still afflicted when he rode home.[157] Some time in early 1850 he was buried on his old Scappoose horse ranch.

Few were so incautious, unless in carefully defined jest, to call Tom a half-breed to his face. Nor did he fit the stereotype. McKay was a charter member of the elitist clique of officers and gentlemen at Fort Vancouver and managed to assume some of the gentlemanly aura from his illustrious stepfather. The reciprocal respect came from a man who could not give as much to his own part-Ojibwa son, Joe McLoughlin.

But as a hard man in a hard business, McKay's real talent was operating in the world of Indians and half-Indians. Through a consistent demonstration of character and leadership, he earned and retained the loyalty of the rough men of the trapping brigades.

The legend was not a representative Métis. Less Indian than most, Tom was always closer to the white man's world. While other mixed bloods struggled with social adjustment, McKay was a fur trade aristocrat. In the political spotlight during the formation of the political government, his actions were open to public scrutiny and critical reaction. He avoided association with any faction. Backing off from his Scappoose land claim was a moderate's demonstration of acceptance of the new regime.

Jacco Finlay's clan survived in obscurity but Tom's sons were conspicuous. The three part-Chinook boys received a basic education at the Fort Vancouver school, but the Methodist missionary Jason Lee convinced Tom that they needed more to compete successfully in a complex American community. Billy McKay was sent to Marcus Whitman's old medical college, while his brothers, John and Alex, went to Jason Lee's alma mater.

Billy's medical training was completed before he was old enough to be certified as a doctor, and he returned home to become prominent in pioneer affairs, the upper country trade, treaty negotiations, and Indian supervision. Dr. McKay served as the secretary for the 1855 treaty meeting in the Walla Walla Valley, which brought the interior tribes into reluctant and grudging association with the United States. After the resulting Indian war, he moved east to become an Indian agent and agency doctor.

John and Alex's schooling failed to divert them from their frontier heritage. Alex and his Cayuse half-brother Donal served in several Indian campaigns. The frontiersman William Hamilton

William Cameron McKay, M.D., of Pendleton, Oregon, son of Thomas McKay. —Elwood Evans, History of the Pacific Northwest: Oregon and Washington (Portland: North Pacific Publishing, 1889).

wrote a vivid description of one-eyed Alex's war exploits with the Piegan Blackfeet. Donal was present at the first confrontation of the 1855–56 Yakima War and was a leader of scouts during the later Modoc campaign. In 1870 Emelie, the three-year-old daughter of Donal McKay and Susanne Warm Springs, was baptized at St. Ann Mission on the Umatilla Indian Reservation.

Like some children of self-made men, the sons of Thomas McKay were a bit overwhelmed by the responsibility of living up to an illustrious father. After struggling to earn the respect of the pioneer community, Billy resigned himself to a limited agency career and alcohol. After working as Indian fighters, scouts, and interpreters, Alex and Donal eventually retreated to the reservation, and Tom's daughters disappeared into the world of their Métis or white husbands.

Tom McKay grasped that his career expectations in the Hudson's Bay Company were limited. The North American–born officers in the Pacific Northwest were either descended from United Empire Loyalist families, like John McLoughlin and Peter Skene Ogden, or drawn from prior military service to empire, like Pierre Pambrun and William Kittson. Governor Simpson preferred to pack his field management with British- or European-born men who were dependent upon him and very much aware that they were on extended foreign service.

Native-born and environmentally conditioned, Thomas McKay was as much of an institutional man as the Oregon country was likely to see in a mixed blood. Like Jacco Finlay or Nicholas Montour, he began his career with important connections but unlike them managed to stay close to the action through his step-father, Chief Factor McLoughlin. But in the final reckoning, Tom McKay was still a marginal man.

～7～

THE OREGON QUESTION

In summer 1818 the Oregon question asked if the tribesmen who were assembled on a hill overlooking the mouth of the Walla Walla River were willing to tolerate beaver trapping in the Snake country. "Big Donald" McKenzie, former Astorian and present representative of the British empire, put the question to the chiefs of the Shamooinaugh, Ikamnaminaugh, Ispipewhamaugh, Insaspetsum, Palletopallas, Shawhaapten, Paluck, Cosispa, Necooimeigh, Wisscopan, Wisswham, Wayyampam, Lowhim Sawsaw, Umatilla, Cayuse, and Walla Wallas. Representatives from each group rose in turn to express a solemn opinion. In the end, they agreed to allow trappers in the area. It was the last time that the plateau and river Indians were consulted about the destiny of their world.

In the oak-paneled meeting rooms of Whitehall, American and British commissioners were also considering the question of distant Oregon. They met to arrange the long-overdue completion of the provision of the Treaty of Ghent, which called for a definite boundary between Upper Louisiana and British North America.

The Hudson's Bay Company claimed most of interior British North America through an ancient charter bestowed by an English king upon his cronies. The boundary along the 49th parallel was the Company's desperate invention, in a time long past, to block New France from Hudson's Bay. In 1719, the Company of Adventurers, trading near Hudson Bay, felt vulnerable to insidious coureurs de bois and encouraged the British diplomats to draw a deadline. The drainage divide between the bay and the Great Lakes was too complex, but the 49th parallel of north latitude was convenient. At the end of the American Revolution, United States treaty negotiators agreed to a water line as far west as Lake of the Woods midway between Lakes Superior and Winnipeg.

The northern bounds of Spanish Louisiana were uncertain, but over the next quarter-century, the 49th parallel enjoyed acceptance without gaining legal status. The northern plains lacked significant geography, which made the astronomical and mathematical precision of the abstraction appealing. The North West Company used its recently gained surveyor, David Thompson, to determine where 49 degrees passed through the overland Mandan Connection. In 1818, the commissioners formally agreed that the line should run from Lake of the Woods to the crest of the Rocky Mountains. However, no faction enjoyed a clear claim to the Pacific slope, and the Oregon country remained in dispute.

To resolve the issue, all the presumptuous paraphernalia of the age of discovery (or appropriation) was dusted off: first claim; operative possession; control of a river mouth, giving first rights to its drainage. The territory west of the Continental Divide remained disputed. Finally, the stalled diplomats agreed to leave that wilderness, and its benighted inhabitants, under the joint occupation of both the United States and Britain.

The American representatives agreed because most of the non-natives in the Oregon country appeared to be British subjects. Joint occupancy would have to be tolerated until "enterprising young men" from Missouri evened the balance. The Compromise of 1818 was sealed with elaborate impressions set in hot wax.

Meanwhile, the saddle diplomat Donald McKenzie extended the pax North West Company by resolving differences between the Nez Perce and the Snakes. After a successful council, everyone demonstrated sincerity by smoking a little dried horse manure.

The fur trade moved into the Snake River Valley with a small army of twenty-five Canadians, thirty-two Hawaiians, and thirty-eight Iroquois. As they stepped carefully through bankside willows to avoid offending a grizzly bear, those trappers were unaware that they were the object of distant deliberations. Time in this wide world was measured in traveling days, highways were Indian trails, and economics were rolled up in a prime beaver skin. The man who felt intolerably insulted shot the offending son-of-a-bitch. Wives occasionally obtained a divorce by the accidental discharge of hubby's gun. Hunched on a pitiless anvil of a sun-blasted plain or shivering as they crossed a snowy pass, the

Oregon Métis had no way of knowing that their trail was on a collision course with destiny.

Isolation was not political ignorance. There were gray-haired men among the Columbia freemen who had known the earliest American attempts to oppose British expansion. After 1821, everyone knew too well the impact of sellouts and heartless discharges. The red HBC flag, with the cross of St. George in the upper corner, came to mean niggardly prices, expensive goods, and snobbish disregard for ordinary people. The chances of falling into debt bondage were very real until competition evened the odds. The Company might brag that HBC meant "Here Before Christ," but not before Jacco Finlay or Francois Rivet, by damn.

Much of the information provided to the British diplomats was filtered through a corporate executive with little concern for his fellow man. Governor George Simpson was careful to avoid jeopardizing his standing with the London directors by revealing flaws in his management. The governing committee in England never quite understood why, less than a year after the achievement of the coalition, a delegation of disenchanted Iroquois went off looking for the Missouri Fur Company. Most of those dissidents died seeking economic deliverance.

In the ruthless harvesting of fur resources after 1818, the American hunters were not conservationists but they were at least working for themselves. Their British rivals were corporate men, directed to hunt out the country south of the Columbia, thus creating a cordon sanitaire for the HBC. While concentrating on the disputed area, the Company protected its downstream establishments and allowed its uncontested hunting preserves time to recover.

The Hudson's Bay Company entered the contest for the Oregon country with the large advantages of capital resources, an in-place trading organization, and a record of outlasting rivals. The weak link was the undependable freeman labor force, which was already alienated. Although the HBC could pour in additional workmen from the British Isles, it could not create skilled beaver trappers overnight.

Governor Simpson expected to use Columbia River trappers to create a fur desert in Oregon; their defection from Ogden in spring 1825 shocked him. Two attempts to recruit experienced trappers from the Red River settlement failed because the Métis distrusted Simpson. After 1825, the HBC was obliged to depend on hired trappers, taking care that the new workers did not get too close to beguiling Americans.

Politics intruded again before 1828, when the ten-year-old agreement of joint occupancy was due to expire. At that point, the fur desert was a mirage, and many pelts were traveling to St. Louis in the annual caravans of three poorly financed and patently inferior American traders. Although the London HBC officials were unaware that Simpson's strategy to dominate the region had not worked out, they were reluctant to make capital investments in a region that might be lost in a boundary decision.

American negotiators met their British counterparts to reconsider the Oregon boundary and agreed to the indefinite continuation of joint occupancy. The U.S. had seemed to enjoy a slight advantage in the region, since its fur trappers were attracting men away from the HBC. The American trappers who came over the mountains spoke of freedom, equality, and fair prices in terms that the western freemen could understand. However, the U.S. was content to leave the issue hanging in the limbo of joint usage. Although there was a provision that either party could withdraw from the agreement upon a year's notification, for the next nineteen years the boundary would be the thorn on the rose.

American suppliers of the mountaineers had to charge prices that allowed them to stay in business. Raising prices cut into their competitive advantage over the British and relieved the pressure on the imperial monopoly. Most of the American entrepreneurs who came into the mountains—the Missouri Fur Company; Ashley-Henry; Ashley-Smith; Smith, Jackson & Sublette; and the Rocky Mountain Fur Company—were poorly capitalized examples of free enterprise. They depended on returns to meet their bills, but as the bonanza trapping depleted resources, it became increasingly difficult to break even. After Smith, Jackson & Sublette withdrew in 1830, the pickings were left to too many new interests, and the firm advocacy of American interests degenerated into partisanship. When the American Fur Company emerged as the dominant corporation, the demand for beaver fiber had fallen off to the point that Astor's old firm was obliged to shift to the buffalo robe trade. Only then could the Hudson's Bay Company truthfully claim that it was the major force in the West.

Most of the returns that went to St. Louis were produced by the floating community of western trappers left adrift when the peltry market declined. Wandering in small parties and trapping in obscure places, they were increasingly vulnerable to Indian resentment. The mountaineers who assembled in Pierre's Hole and Green River in 1840 traveled far into the Southwest to find what had once been considered inferior beaver pelts.[158] Most of those trying to hang on to the old way must have realized that the chance of making a fast fortune in the skin game and retiring to the life of a country squire, or a tribal elder, had vanished up the smoke hole. They would have to settle for a little farm that would not demand too much of their rheumatic joints.

Several former Astorians led the way by starting farms in the Willamette Valley. Joseph Gervais, Etienne Lucier, and Jean Baptiste Desports *dit* McKay received some support from the sympathetic Fort Vancouver chief factor, John McLoughlin, but the loan of implements and seed was not entirely philanthropic. The Columbia Department saw opportunity for an alternative business in supplying foodstuffs to Russian Alaska. Although London officials might not agree with the policy initially, judiciously applied magnanimity encouraged old hunters to settle on the French Prairie and become productive agriculturalists.

Those officers also began thinking of agricultural alternatives to benefit themselves. The open meadows of the Willamette Valley and the grassy plains between Fort Vancouver and Puget Sound offered attractive opportunities for experiments in farming and ranching. Husbandry as the means of improving the imperial claim to the Oregon country occurred to Governor Simpson in spring 1829, and the Fort Vancouver officers took the hint and contributed to his joint stock firm, sometimes reluctantly. At Fort Colvile, Simpson extorted £75 for three shares of a cattle-raising scheme from the unenthusiastic Francis Ermatinger, who grasped that he could not refuse to cooperate and still expect promotion.[159] What began as a private adventure eventually caught the interest of London management, and corporate farming was encouraged on a grander scale. Farms were developed around Fort Vancouver, on the Cowlitz River plains, and around Fort Colvile. Tom McKay went to California to drive cattle and sheep north to stock ranches at Sauvies Island, the Tualatin plains, and the northern posts. The company shipped its wheat, and that purchased from the French Prairie settlers, to Russian Alaska.[160]

One of the first true corporate men, willing to devote his life to business, Governor Simpson never quite grasped why others were not so dedicated. Surrounding himself with a select coterie of acquiescent officers, Simpson exercised baronial authority over the Red River settlement of former Company servants. Corporate supremacy in Rupert's Land gave the HBC director more power than most appointed or elected officers of a real government.[161]

Willamette Valley, based on a drawing by Paul Kane, as it might have looked during the early 1800s.

Willamette Valley, from above Champoeg area, as it looks today.

Simpson regarded Lord Selkirk's colony of Assiniboia as the ill-conceived dream of a dilettante social reformer, whose death left it as a burden on the business. After the coalition of 1821, he made the Red River settlement into a company town subject to his opinions, fixations, and prejudices. Self-interest was interpreted as disloyalty.

However, Simpson could not control everyone. There was a class of half-blood buffalo hunters who produced pemmican to fuel the inland transport system. They traveled the plains to locate and run the herds. They enjoyed the freedom of crossing the border, and in their summer hunting camps they practiced a tribal democracy that owed as much to the example of Indian elders as it did to English monarchs or corporate directors.

In 1826 and 1827, Simpson attempted to recruit a second Snake trapping brigade from the Red River Métis. He was frustrated both times because they understood the risks in offending Indians and wanted to be commensurately compensated. Simpson groused that the half-breed community was becoming too resistant to "management."[162]

The HBC's License of Exclusive Trade was due to expire in 1842, leading the Company to begin to seek renewal in 1837. Governor Pelly of the HBC forwarded Simpson's statements that the Company had transformed the Oregon country from "a scene of violence and outrage" to "a state of the most perfect tranquility." As a glowing example of commercial colonization, the HBC intended to extend cultivation, establish an export trade in agricultural commodities, and induce retired servants and "other emigrants under their protection" to settle in the Pacific Northwest.[163] Whitehall bought it and on 30 May 1838 extended the privilege for twenty-one years, but with the provision that the Company fulfill its promises and settle British subjects to offset American intentions.

That fall, U.S. Senator Lewis F. Linn of Missouri introduced a bill calling for the expansion of territorial government west of the Rocky Mountains and north of the Mexican border. About the same time, Governor Simpson and Columbia District Chief Factor John McLoughlin met with the governor, deputy governor, and committee of the HBC in London to discuss the expansion of agriculture in the Pacific Northwest.

John McLoughlin, who had been behind the initial private cattle venture, had become pessimistic about Company expectations. Nevertheless a joint stock company was formed. The Puget Sound Agricultural Company (PSAC) was capitalized with an initial ten percent deposit on a total of £200,000. Again, it was the HBC officers who were called upon to invest in an essentially corporate scheme.[164]

Soon farm laborers were as much in demand as beaver trappers. For twenty years the Columbia District had tried to keep its manpower at the lowest level necessary to supply the interior trade and keep the posts self-sufficient. Now, during the labor-intensive times of planting or harvesting, there were not enough men available. Indian laborers were undependable and expensive.

The HBC already had a few skilled agricultural workers, some with English wives, brought in to work on the dairies associated with the coastal posts. The PSAC also had a few skilled herdsmen and shepherds. All that was missing to recreate a bit of old England was a resident peasantry. But efforts to recruit colonists in the old country were blocked by concern over the ultimate possession of the real estate. The Company could provide no guarantees until the boundary was decided.

In 1839, Chief Trader James Douglas counted fifty-one adult males living in the Willamette Valley, of whom twenty-three were Canadians considered to be friendly to the HBC. Eighteen were American settlers who could be pacified by fair treatment, if the ten Protestant missionaries restrained their bothersome inclination to meddle in politics as well as religion.

When their nominal Catholicism was challenged by intrusive envoys of New England Protestantism, the retired mixed bloods sent petitions to the See of Red River. In response, the Company provided transportation and support for two priests who came west with its express brigade. The corporation hoped to convince the retired trappers to remove north of the Columbia River, where a British community would strengthen chances for a boundary drawn down the middle of that obvious division. Fathers Blanchet and Demers made their first visit beyond Fort Vancouver to the Cowlitz settlement rather than to the larger congregation on the French Prairie.

Governor Simpson was passing through New York on his way to London in October 1839 when he learned that the Methodists intended to send a reinforcement of 200 permanent settlers to the Willamette mission. The damnable Senator Linn was encouraging a territorial takeover. By 15 November 1839 Simpson wrote Chief Factor Duncan Finlayson at Red River to begin recruiting "steady, respectable half breed and other settlers" to go to the Columbia.[165] He thought that the initial emigration should be limited to fifty respectable families.[166] Later, Simpson became more specific without altering the basic concept:

> You may therefore inform such people that allotments will be made each family, of at least 100 acres of land, besides the use of common or pasture lands, part thereof broken up, with the necessary buildings erected for them, and live stock advanced to each family, of a Bull and ten or more cows, 50 to 100 Ewes, with a sufficient number of rams, hogs, Oxen for agricultural purposes and a few horses; in short, as many of those different stocks as they may be equal to the management of; all valued at low money prices, the expenses of erecting the buildings being a charge upon the farm; the cattle valued at £2 a head, the sheep at 10/ [shillings]-a head, horses at 40/ [shillings]-each, and other stock in proportion; a credit given them each year for their increase, produce or returns at such fair prices as the state of the markets may afford.[167]

Governor Simpson wanted "good subjects: i.e. tractable, well-disposed, industrious people," and the London committee wanted to see fifteen or twenty families going out each year after the initial settlement. Duncan Finlayson, who had served on the Pacific coast, knew that the fertile Willamette Valley was far superior to the stony Nisqually plains. Upon approaching likely prospects in Red River, the governor encountered the same difficulties that discouraged Company recruiters in the British Isles. Neither impoverished British farmers nor discontented Red River Métis were willing to lease land without the expectation of eventual ownership.

On 15 April 1840 Simpson was still convinced that the offer was "greatly superior" to others meant to attract colonists to Australia or New Zealand. Two months later, Finlayson had to admit that the Red River folk were balking over the land ownership problem and were unwilling to enter into a farming agreement on halves, unless they would eventually come into full ownership of their improvements. That was impossible to guarantee because the HBC had no way of knowing how the boundary decision would come out. If the country failed to fall under English control, the HBC might have sold something it did not own. On 1 May 1841 Finlayson explained how he had altered the arrangement:

> The other point on which I found it necessary to deviate is the period of holding the farms on halves, which is by no means a popular measure. I have promised that as soon as the boundary line should be determined, and that part of the country on which

they are to be located, became British territory, land would be sold to them, and the system of halves abolished, otherwise not a single family of respectability would embrace the terms offered.[168]

Finlayson expected as many as fifty families to accept the proposal, but by spring 1841 only seventeen families representing eighty-five individuals were lined up. Still optimistic, he hoped that the total would grow to twenty or twenty-two when the prospective colonists signed the formal agreement on 31 May.[169] Of the 121 immigrants in twenty-two families who joined the party, 77 were children.

An Edinburgh-educated son of the country, James Sinclair, was engaged as conductor, although he had never been over the route or west of the mountains. The reason for his selection had more to do with the elimination of a troublesome free trader and Métis agitator than it did with the proper conduct of innocents through the wilderness. Recognizing the main chance, Sinclair cooperated with the governor. Whether the colonists represented any threat to Red River tranquility is not apparent, but several of them were related to kinsmen who remained and were active in later disputes with the Company.[170]

As the party assembled, Sinclair checked off his final "List of Emigrants for the Columbia":[171]

?	No-1-1	Henry Buxton	1 wife & 1 child
2	2-2	James Birston	1 Do [ditto] & 3 do
	3-3	John Cunningham	1 Do & 1 do
	4-4	John Tait	-Do & -do
7	5-	Julien Bernier	1 Do & 2 Stout Boys
3	6-	Horatio Calder	1 Do & 7 Child 3 Some grown up
4	7-	William Flett	1 Mother 4 Children
	8-	John Spence	1 Wife 4 do
5{	9-	James Flett	1 do 4 do
{	10-	John Flett	1 do 4 do
{	11-	David Flett	1 do 2 d {one of the dec Jno Bird
+	12-	Joseph Klyne	1 do -do
8	13-	Toussaint Joyale	1 do 4 do query
	14-	Francois Gagnon	1 do 5 do
	15-	Bapte Rhelle	1 do 1 do
	16-	Pierre St.Germain	1 do 5 do
6	17-	Charles McKay	1 do 4 do

9	18-	Francois Jacques	1 do 4 do [Plourde *dit* Jacques]
10	19-	Alexr Birston	1 do 4 do
	20-	Gonracque Zastre	1 do 6 do trapper[?]
	21-	Pierre Larocque	1 do 3 do "
	22-	Louis Larocque	1 do 3 do "
11	23-	Archd Spence	1 do 7 do

Most of the males were relatively young fathers with large families or pregnant wives. They had grown up together in the communities of the old fur trade and shared a distaste for the limitations of the Red River community. In his study "Human Migration and the Marginal Man," Robert E. Park wrote that the movement of peoples was a positive step in the improvement of a stagnant society. As the grass on the northern plains greened, this corporate-contrived exodus from the Red River was going to test that thesis.

∽ 8 ∽

OVERLAND TO THE COLUMBIA

L ooking back after forty-four years, John Flett recalled the departure of the Puget Sound Agricultural Company colonists. "On the morning of the fifth of June we broke camp, and turning our backs on the rising sun, plunged into the wilderness."[172] It took a romantically inclined English gentleman to more fully describe a similar party:

> There was an infinite picturesqueness about them. Their long moving columns sparkled with life and gaiety. Cart tilts [covers] of every hue flashed brightly in the sun, hosts of wolfish dogs ran in and out among the vehicles, troops of loose horses pranced and galloped alongside. The smartly dressed men were riding their showiest steeds, their wives and daughters were traveling in the carts, enthroned on high heaps of baggage. Many of the women were clearly of unmingled Indian blood, tall and angular, long masses of straight black hair fell over their backs, blue and white cotton gowns, shapeless, stayless, uncrinolined, displayed the flatness of their unprojecting figures. Some wore a gaudy handkerchief on the head, the married, one also across the bosum.[173]

The colonists took fifty carts, sixty horses, seven oxen, and two English cows. Some families needed more than one vehicle to carry their outfits. Husbands handled several rigs by attaching the halter rope of an ox to the rear corner of the cart he was driving. As trailing animals walked in the wheel rut of the cart ahead, the train cut a wide swath through the tall grass. Prairie roses, hyacinths, and tiger lilies were blooming in prairie grass already as high as a horseman's knee.

After leaving the White Horse plains, the caravan traveled along the north bank of the Assiniboine River until they came to a swampy part of the trail called the "sloughs of despond." Five miles west of Portage La Prairie the track branched northwest.[174] At the third crossing of the Whitemud River on 9 June, they met two travelers who came from their destination. Chief Trader George Traill Allen carried the Columbia District express to meet Governor Simpson at the Red River. He was accompanied by Dr. William Fraser Tolmie, physician, fur trader, and latent agriculturalist, who was going home on furlough. Tolmie's itinerary included a meeting with the London committee of the HBC/PSAC to share his observations on the potential of western agriculture and to be appointed superintendent of the PSAC operations.

The migrants were most interested in Tolmie's views on the place called Nisqually, where they expected to settle. One of the families put the kettle on. "Breakfasted with . . . Charles McKay, a highland half-breed & were hospitably regaled with cold ham, veal steaks, bread, butter and tea with fresh milk from the cow." Allen was even more eloquent about the victuals and traveling style of the overlanders. "On proceeding to the tent of Mr. Alex [*sic*] McKay, for to him we stood indebted for the invitation to dejeurner, we found his wife, a nice tidy little woman, had laid the table in great style, consisting of bread, buffalo tongues and roast veal, flanked by a fine pork ham of stately proportions."[175]

Tolmie was disappointed that the party was taking only three English milch cows. Good breeding stock was needed to improve the wild California cattle. Letitia McKay's breakfast failed to dissipate the pessimism reflected in Tolmie's private journal. "Judging from what I saw, they will be quite an acquisition to the Walamet, for there they must inevitably go, altho their agreement or contract with the Coy. states the Cowlitz to be their destination." Although distressed by the bull dog flies and mosquitoes that rose out of the grass, the innocents were spared that first bite of disillusion.[176]

Swinging north to avoid yet another crossing of the Whitemud, the caravan came to a low drainage divide where the landmark Riding Mountain rose beyond a succession of sandy, rolling hills. At the crossing of the thirty-yard-wide Little Saskatchewan (Minnedosa), the steep banks had to be broken down before the brakeless carts could be lowered with ropes. Of no great depth, the ford was soon churned into mud by so many wheels.

A cart trip usually taking a week to cross the parklands between the Whitemud and Fort Ellice ate up thirteen days for this laden caravan. Conductor James Sinclair was not an aggressive traveler, and a later trail companion criticized his "mania for novels which led to early camping and other unnecessary procrastination."[177]

From the edge of the Assiniboine River valley they looked down on the Qu'Appelle River. A horse herd was grazing beneath Fort Ellice on the opposite height. Postmaster John Richards McKay rode out to greet his younger brother Charles and many old friends. As a surrogate father, John steered Charles away from a career in the disillusioning skin game. Now they had a lot to discuss about his future on the Columbia.

About the same time, far to the south on the Platte River, another party of overland travelers was dragging into Fort Laramie. They were a conglomeration of Missouri frontiersmen, two disenchanted schoolteachers, a former bank clerk absconding with funds, a widow looking for a husband, an English remittance man, a retired Iroquois bear fighter, and a party of Jesuit missionaries intent on converting the Flathead Indians. The first major overland party on the Oregon Trail, the Bidwell-Bartleson wagon train was appropriately guided by the greatest of the mountain men, Tom Fitzpatrick.

Unaware of each other, the two groups were in an undeclared race to occupy the Oregon country. Who got there first might very well decide the diplomatic division of the Pacific Northwest.[178]

Leaving Fort Ellice, the Red River carts climbed to the high plains, where herds of grazing buffalo had fouled the waterholes. Mirages were sometimes visible on the shimmering plains. Out of the vibrating heat waves rode a legendary northern plainsman. It was Jemmy Jock Bird, the Blackfoot man, coming to see his sisters and brother safely through the Indian country. Bird had left the world of his father years ago to live and hunt with the Piegan Blackfeet. He was accompanied by his favorite wife, and ponies dragging a travois.[179]

The saline plains southwest of Quill Lake had been scorched by prairie fires, and the travelers trudged through ashes until a hail storm flattened small trees, pummeled the animals, and drove the emigrants to cower under their carts. When they reached the mile-wide canyon of the south branch of the Saskatchewan River, discomfort gave way to real danger because the river was a third of a mile wide, running fast, and the Company ferry was too small.

> Putting their effects and carts on a huge raft [they] attempted to pole across. The current was very swift and they soon lost bottom, and drifted down at a fearful rate towards the rapids, a short distance below. As they passed by the island on which the first party had landed, they passed so near that a rope was

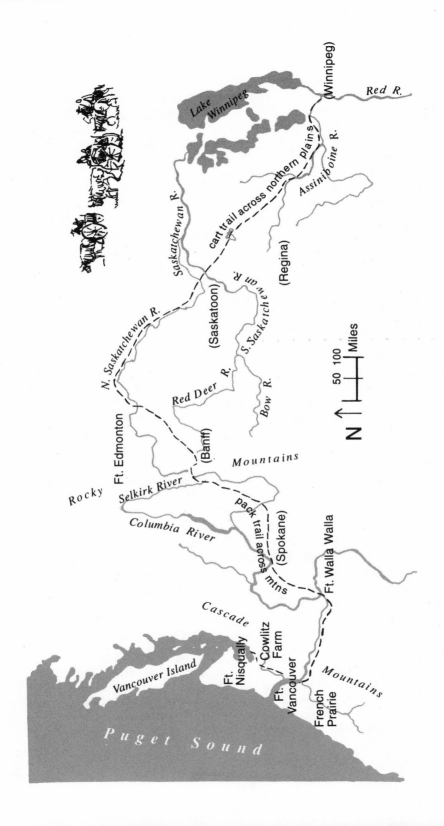

thrown to them, and after a long struggle, the raft was secured to the bank.[180]

After crossing the narrow neck of land between the two branches of the Saskatchewan, the caravan came to Fort Carlton, which was planted a quarter of a mile from the river to keep the wooden palisades and bastions above flood stage. About 300 Cree, Ojibwa, and Assiniboin Indians were more or less permanent residents near this provision post, which had been built by Chief Factor Bird and named for the Prince of Wales's residence in Pall Mall, London.[181]

It had been eighteen years since William Flett's seventy-five-year-old Indian mother, Saskatchewan, last saw the place of her birth. During the two resting days, she sat on the high banks of the river and recalled how she had given up her Indian family and community to become a trader's woman.[182] She had lived among aliens with strange habits and incomprehensible words. Old Flett took her thirteen-year-old son away to make him a boatman, and married off their daughters too soon. Now a grandmother, old Saskatchewan still missed her tribal sisters. She knew that she would never see this place again and that her bones would be buried in an alien land.[183]

After the Métis trader Patrick Small exchanged their tired stock for fresh animals, the party crossed the north branch on another ramshackle Company ferry. They were now traveling through the poplar parklands marking the southern edge of the northern forests. The woods were broken up by many small pools and lakes, and the travelers regretted leaving those shady places for the open, hilly country near Jackfish Lake.

There was an old sun dance site and buffalo pound left from the time before guns made hunting easy. Unable to resist a last opportunity to run buffalo, the Métis trotted out on their fastest ponies. Catching up with the stampeding shaggies, hunters bypassed the dangerous bulls and ranged alongside fat cows to fire, point blank, at the vulnerable spot just behind the shoulder. Without checking their racing horses, riders poured powder charges down the muzzles of their short-barreled fusels, spat saliva-patched bullets into barrels, and seated charges by banging stocks against saddle horns. In the excitement they killed more animals than they could use, and took only choice parts, or just tongues, leaving the carcasses to the wolves.[184]

The hunters returned to the carts, which had stopped for breakfast near the Turtlelake River. About noon, the corporate torpedo who had left Red River a month after they started overtook them.

Governor George Simpson was so pleased with this proof of his superior traveling ability that he "put the men in high spirits with a dram, while a donation of wine, tea and sugar rendered the women the merriest and happiest gossips in the world."[185]

While breakfast roasted over the coals, the governor and his traveling companion, Chief Factor John Rowand, spoke with "the elders of this little congregation." They encouraged the emigrants to push hard and avoid getting trapped in the mountains by an early snowfall, so they would arrive on Puget Sound in time to provide winter accommodations for themselves. "We therefore proposed that they should proceed by the Athabaska Portage to the Rocky Mountains to the Boat Encampment, and thence descend the Columbia to Vancouver. The people agreed to this change in their plan."

After enjoying a "complete specimen of a hunter's meal," the governor's party took to the trail again at three o'clock, leaving the colonists slogging behind in a cloud of corporate dust. But Simpson's concern suggests that there were some loose ends in the colonial scheme.

The bones of forty horses marked the site of a past battle between the Cree and the Blackfeet. The old enmity still prevailed, and excited war parties were skulking about to avenge the killing of a Cree chief and two of his followers. Nine offending Blackfeet had also fallen, and other warriors with ghastly wounds were lying around Fort Pitt.

The travelers made their most northern point by rounding the great bend of the Saskatchewan at 54 degrees north latitude. After another eight days of trying stream crossings, Edmonton came into view at the top of the steep, two-hundred-foot-high riverbank.

This was a homecoming for old John Tait, Horatio Calder, William Flett, and the Bird sisters. Letitia McKay was born here when her father was the trader in charge of the upper Saskatchewan District. During the sixteen years that the Bird family lived there, the Nor'westers went on to develop the Columbia, and the first American scalps came from the upper Missouri. Now John Rowand ruled from a three-story hewn-log mansion. The dining hall was painted in "a style of the most barbaric gaudiness, and the ceilings filled with center-pieces of fantastic gilt scrolls, making altogether a saloon which no white man could enter for the first time without a start, and which the Indians always looked upon with awe and wonder."[186]

Chief Trader John Harriot, who was in charge while Rowand accompanied the governor, relayed Simpson's latest instructions to Sinclair without comment.[187] The immigrants were expected to go north from Edmonton and cross the Athabaska River–Boat Encampment portage route. On the other side they could build boats for themselves and descend the upper Columbia River.

Joe Klyne, who grew up at Jasper's House, and Marcel Bernier, who was well acquainted with the Colvile District, warned that descending the awesome upper Columbia River in green wood boats was no casual undertaking. Three years ago fourteen travelers, some their friends, had met disaster. Going by boat also meant abandoning their precious cattle and most of their possessions. In a remarkable show of independence, the colonial tribe rejected the governor's instructions, forcing Sinclair to adhere to the original plan of crossing by a southerly pass.[188]

Although his former brother-in-law, Jemmy Jock Bird, was perfectly familiar with the country, Sinclair hired a Wetaskiwin Cree named Mackipictoon (Bras Croche or Broken Arm) as their guide. The widely traveled Mackipictoon assured Sinclair that the Blackfeet were off to the south hunting buffalo, so there was little danger. When most of the carts were left at Edmonton, Gonzarque Zarastre and his family of eight had second thoughts and dropped out.

The newly consolidated cart and pack train moved south between Whitemud and Blackmud Creeks to a string of narrow winding lakes that were marshy and overgrown with thickets. At the Battle River crossing, wasps upset the pack train, and at Gull Lake, mosquitos played hell. After fording the Little Red Deer, the trail plunged into a gorge so steep that horses had to scramble sideways.

Although the travelers slipped unnoticed by the big Cree camp on Gull Lake, there were still plenty of Indians around. Governor Simpson estimated that the region accommodated as many as 16,450 natives and 280 mixed bloods. Because living off the country required hunting in unfamiliar places, John Flett and his younger brother once found themselves in a thicket surrounded by hostile Indians. The two crouched in the brush with pounding hearts until the sun set and they could escape across the river. Slipping into the icy water, they clung to the tails of their swimming horses, only to have the animals come out on the wrong side of the river. John and his brother wandered for two days before finding the camp on the Bow River. Flett recalled, "Of all the dangers I have seen in a pioneer life of fifty years, the dangers of those two days were the worst."[189]

Forty river crossings were necessary as the migrants climbed the brush- and tree-tangled Little Red Deer valley. "As far as the eye can reach, mountain rose on mountain, while at our feet lay a valley surrounded by an amphitheater of cold, bare, rugged peaks. In these crags which were almost perpendicular, neither could tree plant its roots nor goat find a resting place: the Demon of the Mountains alone could fix his dwelling there."[190]

Passing beneath the Devil's Nose, the party entered a valley graced by four lakes about nine miles northeast of present Banff. After trailing along the long shore of Lake Minnewahkah, the group cut down the Carrot Creek gorge to the place where Bow Fort had been located several years before. All that remained of a vain attempt to hold the Piegan Blackfoot trade were the chimneys, and Jemmy Jock's campfire recital of those dangerous times:

> Prairie traveling ended here and packing begin in earnest. After a long debate about what should be taken and what should be left behind, we at last had our train in readiness and started on our way. The oxen, however, were unused to this mode of traveling and were frightened, and a stampede ensued. Then

Pack saddle brought to Nisqually by David Monroe in 1841 and returned there by John Flett in 1859. –Fort Nisqually Collection, Tacoma Parks Department, Author's photo.

what a sight, oxen bellowing, kicking, running; horses neigh-
ing, rearing, plunging; children squalling, women crying, men
swearing, shouting and laughing; while the air seemed full of
blankets, kettles, sacks of pots, pans and jerked buffalo. At last
the cattle were again secured, all our goods that could be found
were gathered up and the remnant repacked, and we again
started.[191]

By now the American overlanders had made the easy crossing
of the Continental Divide at South Pass and were at Soda Springs,
where they were deciding who was going to California and who
would continue on to Oregon. On 11 August three wagons and
the Catholic mission party headed for Fort Hall on the Snake
River to meet the Flathead Indians who were waiting to escort
the Jesuits. Only three families and some single men accompanied Frank Ermatinger and the Hudson's Bay Company pack
outfit toward the Columbia.

Climbing the valley between Mount Rundle and the Three Sisters, the Red River Métis found a wall of granite penetrated by
Goat Creek. Beyond the string of Spray Lakes they came to
Whiteman Pass, just above timberline at an elevation of 7,112
feet.

We reached the summit and found ourselves on a small plateau. Here we saw a huge snowdrift whose melted waters formed
three little rills; one running east through a deep canyon, and
finding its way through the Saskatchewan into Hudson's Bay;
another running southeast into the Missouri and at last the Gulf;
while the third sent its waters through those "continuous woods
where rolls the Oregon."[192]

Somewhere in the mountains, Jemmy Jock Bird bid farewell
to his relatives. His value as an insurance policy against Blackfoot
trouble ended, and he had raided into the Kutenai and Flathead
country too many times to risk going there alone. When Simpson
later branded Bird an undependable half-breed who deserted the
party, John Flett denounced the slur.[193]

The western waters were milky from glacial grindings. Although golden avalanche lilies bloomed in the miniature meadows, August mornings in these altitudes were frosty. Wading
across the roaring creeks was torture. The talus slopes and knife-
narrow ridges proved that this was no passage for vehicles. Perhaps the practical overland highway to the Pacific lay to the south.

Riding downhill on a sliding, checking horse is a jarring,
wrenching agony that turns knees to jelly and the spine into a
column of compressed bone. Several women were riding with

babes in arms, and at least one of them was expecting. Traveling into the tree line was no better because the animals had to pick through a jackstraw tangle of fallen trees and slippery, moss-camouflaged rocks. The travelers left a trail of horses with broken legs or blown-out hearts. Crossing the trough of the upper Kootenay River, they climbed up Swede Creek and came out

> on the steep and stoney edge of a glen down which rushed the sources of the Columbia. At one remarkable spot known as the Red Rock, our path climbed the dry part of the bed of a boiling torrent, while the narrow ravine was literally darkened by almost perpendicular walls of a thousand or fifteen hundred feet in height; and to render the chasm still more gloomy, the opposite crags threw forward each its own forest of somber pines into the intervening space.[194]

Flett recalled, "On the ninth day after we entered the Rocky Mountains we emerged on the western side at the Kootenay Plain." Sinclair made the date 27 August.[195]

The hard ride down the last canyon triggered labor in one of the women. There was nothing to do but wait until she recovered, but there were only enough provisions for another ten days, and the group had already eaten some of the cows. Sinclair sent young Joseph Klyne to Fort Colvile, where his brother-in-law was the trader. Archibald McDonald was asked to meet the party with food and fresh horses.

Klyne made the trip in nine days but found that McDonald was shorthanded because he had dispatched a river guide and four men to meet the colonists at the Boat Encampment, a wasted effort. The Colvile trader wrote a hasty response telling Sinclair to proceed down the trail and he would try to meet them near the Lake Pend Oreille crossing with whatever supplies he could scare up. McDonald packed sixteen horses with some moldy flour, bran, and dried peas—poor stuff but no worse than what the depot men were eating.

McDonald also started a letter to Fort Walla Walla, warning the officer there to expect the colonists and to anticipate their need for mounts. By coincidence, McDonald was also entertaining the visiting Presbyterian missionary Henry Spalding. Those compounded distractions were enough to make a saint short-tempered, and McDonald was so distracted that he blotted his letter book.[196]

Getting underway again, the immigrants moved up the Columbia past Thompson's first post and into the valley of the Kootenay River until they could cross over to the marshy and densely overgrown Moyie River. Flett recalled climbing the projecting point of a mountain to avoid some marshy ground:

> At our feet lay a valley of about thirty miles in length and six in width, bounded on the western side by lofty mountains, and on the eastern by a lower range of the same kind, while the verdant bottom, unbroken by a single mound or hillock, was threaded by a meandering stream, and studded on either side by lakes, diminishing in the distance to mere specks or stars.

Beyond, the trail opened southwest through grassy country to Pend Oreille Lake.

When Sinclair rode to Colvile to confer with McDonald, he learned that the Columbia District had been seeing quite a few Americans. Using Fort Nisqually as headquarters, Lieutenant Charles Wilkes of the United States Exploring Expedition sent parties inland to Fort Colvile and up the Columbia River. Two families of missionaries, the Walkers and the Eells, came to Tshimakain, north of old Spokane House, to establish an outpost of the Walla Walla Valley mission. Jesuits from St. Louis were in the Flathead country, and Frank Ermatinger was shepherding a party of settlers from Missouri.

A horse accident on the steep shore of Lake Pend Oreille almost claimed a life. "While traveling along a rocky cliff jutting towards the lake, a horse ridden by one of our women slipped, and horse and rider rolled into the lake, and were rescued with some difficulty." With winter closing in, the group could not afford another stall, so the suffering woman endured the ride along the Little Spokane River. All that remained of Spokane House, where Isidore Bernier had been born, were the chimneys and crumbling bastion.

Five-year-old Mary McKay remembered an incident with Spokane Indians who were fishing nearby. As Victorian ladies put it, the savages went about "stark-naked." When one of them became troublesome, one woman took a red-hot poker and chased the warrior away. "A woman with such an implement was more effective than a battalion of heavily armed men."[197]

Returning by way of Tshimakain, Sinclair caught the missionary Mary Walker at her washing. He told her that there were eighty children among the 125 travelers; several had been born along the way. Mary could understand their ordeal because she had been pregnant when the missionaries packed across the Rockies three years earlier. She closed her diary entry for 21 September with the laconic prophecy, "Thus we see Oregon filling up fast."[198]

The pack train strung out for the long, hot ride across the channeled scablands of northeastern Washington. After passing two lakes, the party picked up the broad valley where Cow Creek meanders between cliffs of columnar basalt, making a natural highway regularly used by Indians, fur traders, and missionaries.

The first waterfalls in the Palouse were unimpressive, but the second dropped off the plateau into a spectacular basin surrounded by perpendicular cliffs. Crossing the Snake River at Riparia, the travelers followed the old Indian trail up the Tucannon River and over to the Touchet, striking the Walla Walla Valley about midway between the Whitman mission station at Waiilatpu and old Fort Nez Perces at the mouth.

Archibald McKinlay had been in charge of Fort Walla Walla since the death of Pierre Pambrun the previous July. It had been twenty-three years since the location became the base for the Snake River trapping brigades and the remount depot for the Columbia District. The travelers must have found it curious that the running gear of an American wagon was parked just outside the gate.

On the night of 4 October, the colonists were camped about 300 yards from the fort when flames brightened the darkness. Although some of the missionary goods were lost, the Red River folk helped rescue the Company property and pile it in the open. There was worry that the temptation might prove irresistible to the troubled Cayuse Indians, making it dangerous to remain in the vicinity. The immigrants traveled across the arid Columbia River flats until midnight of the next day. Soon they were descending the ladder of rivulets that overlanders would soon call Fifteenmile, Eightmile, and Fivemile Creek in an expression of weary longing for the end of the trail.

William Overton, one of the American overland party, was resting at The Dalles. The American overlanders, who had started ten or thirteen days earlier, had beaten the Métis party by only four days. Henry Bridgman Brewer, the Methodist missionary, noticed the arrival of the Canadians in his diary:

> Oct 9, 1841. A large party of emigrants from the Red River country arrived. They are under the direction of the Hudson's Bay Company. Oct.12. A daughter of Mr. Archibald Spence came to us to live. She is 8 years old the 10th of last March. Also a daughter of Mr. McKay goes to Br.Lee and the daughter of Mr.[blank] goes to Br. Carters. May we have the wisdom to bring them up aright. The Company leaves us today for Ft. Vancouver.[199]

At Crates Point the remaining livestock were transported to the north side of the river, where some of the men and the boys would drive them on to Fort Vancouver. Entering Company boats at the Cascades, the rest of the party finished their odyssey in true voyageur style.

On 12 October 1841, 115 trail-worn Red River Métis stood on the beach before Fort Vancouver. They had completed the overland trip of 1,700 miles (2,000 according to Flett) in 130 days. Although the Oregon Trail from St. Louis was about 100 miles longer, and trail guide authors claimed that it was an easy passage, only twenty-four or twenty-five Americans managed to reach the disputed Oregon country in fall 1841.

∾ 9 ∾

BETRAYAL ON THE COLUMBIA

For seventeen years Fort Vancouver was the western depot and outfitting center of the Columbia Department of the Hudson's Bay Company. It regularly accommodated from 130 to 200 seasonal transients, including fur trade officers and laborers bringing out returns and picking up outfits. The arrival of nineteen families of overland colonists was not a great burden on that hospitality.

In 1841 the total labor force of the Columbia Department amounted to 616 Canadians, Europeans, mixed bloods, and Sandwich Islanders, recently augmented by new recruits from northern Scotland. Some were trip men and winterers from the interior posts. Others worked at the depot as blacksmiths, tinsmiths, carpenters, masons, tailors, shoemakers, farmers, or dairymen. Agriculturalists, as the gentlemen liked to describe them, were necessary to reduce provisioning expenses through the operation of Company farms and dairies at several posts. The 1,200 acres under cultivation at Fort Vancouver produced 4,000 bushels of wheat, 3,500 bushels of barley, oats, peas, and a large quantity of potatoes. Five hundred cattle and 1,500 sheep grazed on the pastures at Sauvies Island and the Scappoose plain, just across the Columbia. Another herd ranged at the Cowlitz River to the north.[200]

The clerk and six men at Nisqually were employees of the subsidiary Puget Sound Agricultural Company. There were the experienced herdsman Mr. Steel, two shepherds, five laborers, and occasional Indian laborers.[201] In a forecast of the Basque sheepherder wagons still being used in southeastern Oregon and Nevada, the Scots shepherd, Mr. Lewis, had a "moveable house on wheels." That winter, a Company steamer, the *Beaver*, was anchored offshore. While it was being overhauled, Captain William Henry McNeill kept his crew busy making a coal pit.[202]

But seeds of HBC deceit were rooted in that gravelly soil. From friends at Fort Vancouver, the colonists soon learned that Chief Factor Finlayson's description of the country and his promises of support were not entirely true. There were no houses or other buildings awaiting them at Nisqually. The virgin sod was unbroken, and skeptics believed that beneath the thin skin of soil hunched a base of round rocks. Food in the Columbia Department was going to be scarce that winter because most of the grain crop was reserved for shipment to the Russians. After winter rains turned the trails to mud, there would be little hope of hauling provisions from Fort Vancouver.

The western traders had never been enthusiastic about a colonial scheme that could only become an expensive burden on the Company and cut into their share of the profits. Chief Trader James Douglas had tried to warn the London directorate that "the soil about Nisqually and Puget Sound is unfit for tillage," and repeated that negative estimate to Governor Simpson in March 1838. Nevertheless, during the discussions relating to the renewal of the Exclusive License to Trade, the Company committed to the extension of cultivation and the establishment of an export trade in wool, hides, and tallow. In October, Douglas was reminded of the difficulties of agriculture in a country where a farmer not only had to be an all-around mechanic and artisan but also would lack extra labor to help him during harvest. Douglas might be dismissed as a timid naysayer, but as late as 20 November 1840 Chief Factor McLoughlin also warned, "Settlers will never settle on the Cowlitz till the Wallamette is settled." When he learned of Governor Simpson's colonial scheme, McLoughlin added, "I hope they will not be led to suppose they have any claims on us beyond our good will and the sale or loan of a few head of cattle or seed grain, if convenient." Although McLoughlin enjoyed broad authority in the Columbia Department and knew what was coming, he failed to press preparations for the colonists, or to ensure their support at Nisqually. Angus McDonald was sent north to juggle the hot potato with the following instructions:

> You will proceed to assume charge of the post of Nisqually which the HBC have transferred to the PS Assc. and where you are aware they are establishing a large sheep and cattle farm. . . . As I mentioned already Nisqually belongs to the PS Assc.—you will therefor charge all expense incurred for the HBC or anybody else—to the company or the person—you must in particular observe that you are not to feed passers by or others but let them have whatever you can and charge it—for instance Capt. McNeill

and his officers will be with you this winter and the best part of next summer—it would not be proper that they were supported or fed by the PS Assc. or that you were fed by the HBC.[203]

The disillusioned travelers simmered in growing apprehension for ten days, until Governor Simpson returned from his northern tour on the Company steamer, the *Beaver*. By then he understood the true situation at Nisqually and had to admit that the Company could not fulfill its obligations. Like a modern corporate executive, Simpson avoided the unpleasantness by letting an embarrassed James Douglas break the bad news.

Ironically, Douglas had been the voice of reality while contracts were being drawn. Those agreements specified that the PSAC would provide each head of family with a house ready for occupancy upon arrival, seed wheat sufficient to sow a certain number of acres, twenty milk cows, and a stated number of horses, as well as provisions when needed on the way out, and to provision the colony for the first year—"this to run for a term of [ten] years."[204]

John Flett later recalled the disappointing news he received, leaving his feelings to the imagination of the reader:

> Our agreement we cannot fulfill, we have neither horses [houses?] nor barns, nor fields for you, and you are at liberty to go where you please. You may go with the California trappers; we will give you an outfit as we give others. If you go over the river to the American side we will give none (very sickly). If you go to the Cowlitz we will help you some. To those who go to Nisqually we will fulfill our agreement.[205]

Letitia McKay recollected, "They promised us a farm and everything required to run it but when we arrived here they had no place to put us."[206] The disappointed colonists did not blame McLoughlin, or the mouthpiece Douglas, but "Sir George Simpson was regarded by us as a fraud."[207]

Beyond the minor embarrassment of renouncing a contract, the scheme was not much of a loss for the Company. The 121 bothersome half-breeds who had been siphoned away from the Red River settlement now had no alternative except to stay in the West as captive customers, debt-obligated settlers, and potential workmen.

Simpson wrote optimistically to the London committee on 25 November about the alternative he had proposed:

> ... of these, 14 heads of families, amounting in all to 77 souls principally English half-breeds, have located at Nisqually and are to hold their farms under the Puget Sound Company on

117

"halves," being provided with sheep, cattle, etc as per agreement entered into . . . [T]he remainder of the party, being 7 families containing 38 souls, are Canadians and half-breeds who being disinclined to crop the Cowlitz Portage to the seaboard, have been placed on the Cowlitz Farm where advances will be made to them by the Hudson's Bay Company in seed, agricultural implements, etc. instead of their being placed on farms under the Puget Sound Company, in like manner as the other people; as their previous habits of life, having devoted more of their time and attention to the chase than agricultural pursuits, it is more likely they could turn to good account any stock that might be placed in their hands.[208]

The governor was more specific in his letter to Sir John Henry Pelly and to Andrew Colvile, who were the London agents of the Puget Sound Agricultural Company:

The Nisqually settlers were to "get their farms on 'halves,' that is, they are to hold the land free of charge, the Puget Sound Company affording them the necessary means to assist in erecting buildings, with provisions until such can be raised from the produce of the farm, agricultural implements, and to each settler, two yoke of oxen, from 10 to 20 head of cattle, and from 50 to 100 sheep, as the farms may be in a condition to receive and take care of them, two pair of horses, with hogs, poultry, etc., all of which will be a charge upon the farm bearing interest, the Company and the farmer being equally interested in the marketable produce and increase of the stock; and from the cheap rate at which Indian labor may be provided, say from £8 to £10 per annum, besides provisions, there cannot be a doubt that this mode of farming will turn to profitable account, both to the settler and the Association."[209]

Despite the blatant misrepresentation and callous repudiation of legal contracts, three former HBC farmers decided to join the list of settlers. William Baldra, John Johnson, and Thomas Otchin had come to Rupert's Land in 1836 as part of a contingent of thirteen English agriculturalists to work on the Red River colony experimental farm. Two years later, they were reassigned to the Pacific posts: Otchin and his family at Fort Langley on the Fraser River, the Johnsons at the Cowlitz, and the Baldras to operate the Sauvies Island dairy. Because Company regulations required discharged employees to return to the place of their enlistment, getting these families to join the colonists saved the Company the expense of sending them east.[210]

Young Joe Klyne was the only colonist to throw up the arrangement entirely and join the California trapping brigade. He had no way of knowing that Simpson intended to go to California and close down that operation, which would put him out of a job within a year.

The two LaRocques, St. Germain, Bernier, Jacques, Gagnon, and Rhelle agreed to go to the Cowlitz to be near kinsmen and old friends who spoke French and worshipped at a Catholic mission church.

Young Buxton explained why eleven families of mixed English ancestry held to the original agreement.[211] "Here we were 2000 miles from our home that we had left and an wilderness intervening, winter approaching and entirely without resources, and in father's case, with a sick wife and only son looking to him as their protection."[212] Before the winter was out, his mother died from the injuries she received on the trip, after inadequate treatment at Nisqually.

Henry Buxton, Forest Grove, Oregon, immigrant of 1841. —Elwood Evans, *History of the Pacific Northwest: Oregon and Washington* (Portland: North Pacific Publishing, 1889).

The overland trail had reduced possessions to basics: clothes unsuitable for a wet climate, a few utensils, tools, and sentimental mementos. Charles McKay and William Flett received annuities from their fathers' estates, and those who sold possessions before leaving the Red River had a bit of ready cash. Perhaps old Chief Factor Bird gave his three departing daughters something to help them reestablish homes.[213] But for the most part, the settlers were totally dependent on the Company for their start-up capital.

Chief Factor Douglas and some of the leading settlers went ahead to scout for a more suitable location. Coasting along the east shore of Puget Sound on the steamer *Beaver*, they went as far north as Whidbey Island but felt that area was exposed to the northern Indians who coursed the inland waters in great war canoes. The main body of colonists followed on 8 November, driving their livestock along the trail that had been swamped out a year before.

Because Indians burned the meadows to keep them open for better hunting, the landscape alternated between open prairies and thick groves of fire-resistant giant fir trees. To the east, beautifully sculpted and snow-clad, Mount St. Helens smoldered with interior fires.

Along the banks of the Columbia River, rotting Indian canoes marked the burial grounds of those who had succumbed to smallpox, measles, and malaria. Nine-year-old Mary McKay recalled, "On the trip north we passed Indian burial grounds. Canoes and other sarcophagi hung from the tops of tall fir trees. I remember how my uncle Nicholas Bird climbed one of the trees and found a wooden image of the dead chief. It was about the size of a rag doll. My, how I appreciated that new addition to my toy world."[214]

At the Cowlitz farm, 3,000 acres of open prairie accommodated 206 cows, fifty horses, and some pigs in a ranching operation employing twenty-three Canadians and Kanakas. Twelve hundred additional acres were set aside for the use of the Catholic mission, with the expectation that the priests would convince the Willamette settlers to relocate. But only the families of Simon Plamondon, Francis Fraginent, Michel Cognoir, and Joseph Rochbrunne were there to welcome the seven French-speaking Red River immigrants who dropped out of the column.[215]

Earlier that year, the parklike beauty of the Nisqually plain strained the descriptive powers of the commander of the visiting American squadron. The sailor/explorer Lieutenant Charles Wilkes wrote, "One is lost on receiving everything upon the large scale that is presented of lawns, clumps, lakes, fine running brooks and coming upon lakes of some miles in extent with deer browsing quietly near them." Looming 14,411-feet above sea level, Mount Rainier made a dramatic backdrop.[216]

The Company storehouse, built near two Indian longhouses at the mouth of Sequalitchew Creek eight years earlier, had grown into a compound on the bluff above. Within a 200-yard square were crowded storehouses and a half-dozen bark-roofed houses. Fort Nisqually was already too small for the increased demands of the Puget Sound Agricultural Company, and now it had to accommodate seventy-seven additional people.[217]

The neighbors were "Clellams, Paaylaps, Scatchetts, the Checaylis and other tribes amounting in all, the Squallies included, to nearly a thousand souls," according to Simpson's estimate. The local Sequalitchew band of Nisqually were large men and stout, imposing women led by a headman named Lahalet, a friend to the traders.[218] However, they could become nuisances, as Captain McNeill of the Company ship *Cadboro* complained. "Indians are getting very daring. The herds[men] have detected them driving away cattle on two occasions. We shall be obliged to shoot in self-defense."[219]

The souls of the Nisqually were targeted by the Willamette Valley Methodist mission, which wanted to checkmate Catholic activities on the Cowlitz. After the arrival of the Great Reinforcement, the former whaling ship's carpenter, W. H. Wilson, built a Nisqually outpost, which was turned over to a greenhorn preacher. J. P. Richmond and his wife, America, claimed the distinction of being the first American family to live north of the Columbia, but after a year among the heathens, they were ready to pack up their supercilious opinions and go home.

Governor Simpson still believed that there would be many additional applications at the Red River to come to the Columbia. On 25 November he wrote to the agents of the PSAC that it was unnecessary to recruit emigrants from Europe. "We can from year to year have as many settlers from the Hudson's Bay Company's servants and from Red River Colony as can be advantageously employed, and these people are in every respect better adapted for our purpose."[220]

George Simpson finally attained the designation of governor-in-chief of HBC overseas operations in 1838. Earlier that year, he was knighted for his support of the arctic exploration of the experienced trader Peter Warren Dease and the governor's cousin Thomas Simpson. The latter two did the onerous legwork, but the accolade fell on the corporate manager, which said something about British priorities.

During his time at Fort Vancouver, Sir George hosted the officers of the United States Exploring Expedition. He used his considerable powers of dissimulation to pry the American view out of a junior officer and learned that Lieutenant Wilkes would recommend that the United States hold out for a boundary drawn at 54 degrees 40 minutes, the tip of Russian Alaska. That threatened the entire HBC western operation. Whether Simpson received an accurate piece of political intelligence or was taken in by a raw midshipman with real talent at dissimulation, the great man swallowed it whole. After holding out for twenty years for an international boundary down the middle of the Columbia River, Simpson abandoned his position almost overnight.[221]

It is preposterous to suggest that the failure of British claims to the Oregon country could have hung on the whim of a frustrated egocentric. The Oregon question had been a diplomatic stumbling block for half a century. Still, there is room for the human equation. If Napoleon was fatefully distracted by hemorrhoids at Waterloo, it is possible that another little man in a big position squirmed uncomfortably in his chair in the salon of a weather-bound Company ship.

When the *Cowlitz* sailed from Fort Vancouver, Simpson felt that he was finally embarking on the most exciting part of his round-the-world journey. Instead, he was stuck for three weeks in Bakers Bay at the mouth of the Columbia, with the shadow of John Jacob Astor's defeat looming over him.

Over the years the Company had lost several ships on the Columbia bar. On 10 March 1829, the supply brig *William & Ann* was wrecked crossing into the river. The HBC replaced that loss with the *Isabella,* which wrecked on the same bar on 2 May 1830. In 1841, the Wilkes expedition lost the *Peacock.* During his involuntary stay, Simpson brooded that the Columbia River was an impossible shipping point. The Company had to find a safer port, even if the cost were the Oregon country. The torpedo that sank the colonial scheme was already running as the immigrants trudged north.

Not until 21 December did the ship-greedy sands permit the *Cowlitz* to pass and sail for San Francisco Bay. After Simpson and McLoughlin made a joint inspection of the California operation, Simpson's abrupt and unilateral dismantling of the Vancouver operation led to a strained parting.

Simpson finally reached Honolulu, still steaming over the three-week delay on the Columbia bar.[222] On 1 March 1842, he outlined his sweeping changes in a long dispatch to London. The governor and committee were informed, "It is exceedingly desirable however for the British interest in this quarter, and for the national honor, that Her Majesties's Government should not submit to such degrading conditions [as a line along 49 degrees] but I think it is nevertheless well to be prepared for the worst."[223]

Serious consideration of a boundary down the middle of the Columbia River must have been abandoned sometime between November and March. That mooted plans for a PSAC colony at Nisqually. The only value of the colonists was as evidence for future claims settlement.

In June 1842, the London directorate sent a letter through Montreal to Finlayson at the Red River. That missive needed to arrive in time to prevent the enlistment of any more colonists, because management had decided that it was inadvisable to burden the fur trade with the expense of transporting settlers to the Columbia. The subsequent defection of the Nisqually and Cowlitz colonists had nothing to do with this change in attitude because the decision was made *before* they had the opportunity to demonstrate their feelings.[224]

When they arrived at Nisqually, the colonists found that they had to build their own homes. Flett drew an axe on 19 November, Calder obtained a pit saw on 25 January, and Buxton got a brace and bit on 27 March. Johnson and Otchin were billed for fifteen nails each, and the latter was also charged for one pane of glass. The mortise chisel that James Flett borrowed and neglected to return was charged against him in June.

Were the colonists supplied with livestock? The PSAC flock of 4,526 sheep included 3,200 that had been driven from California earlier in the year. The cattle herd counted 217 cows and heifers, 176 bulls, oxen, and steers, and 9 calves. Three hundred and forty cows, bulls, and oxen gathered from ranching operations at Walla Walla, Colvile, and Okanogan had been driven over the Cascade Indian trails in October, and 135 were still on the road. One hundred twenty-three calves brought the total to around 1,000 head.[225] The stock inventory taken on 31 December 1843 listed 43 bulls, 528 cows, 182 oxen, 4 bull calves, and 30 cow calves in the Fort Nisqually herd, for a total of 1,364 animals, a comfortable increase.

Only 100 to 120 of the cows were tamed for dairy purposes, and only a third were milked at any time. The herd was kept penned in rail-fenced yards, which were regularly moved to allow the even distribution of manure. John Flett recalled his unsuccessful attempt to get a cow, either by the agreement or by purchase: "Some got wild cows but no sheep." At the end of April,

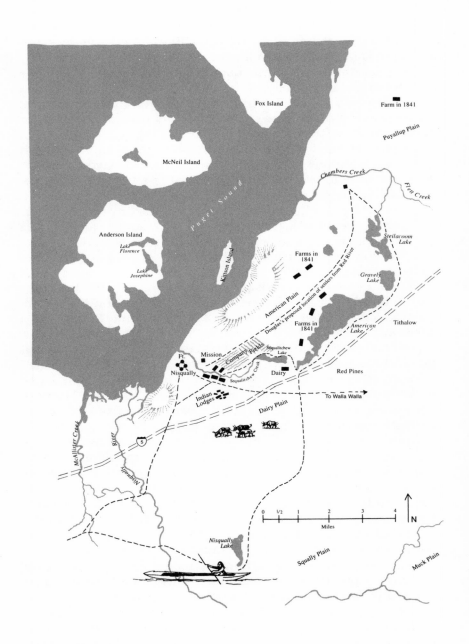

Fox Island

McNeil Island

Anderson Island

Lake
Florence

Lake
Josephine

Kittson Island

Puget Sound

Farm in 1841

Puyallup Plain

Chambers Creek

Flett Creek

Steilacoom
Lake

Farms in
1841

American Plain

Gravelly
Lake

Douglas's proposed location of settlers from Red River

Farms in
1841

American
Lake

Tithalow

Mission

Ft.
Nisqually

Company Fields

Squalitchew
Lake

Squalitchew Creek

Dairy

Red Pines

Indian
Lodges

To Walla Walla

Dairy Plain

McAllister Creek

Nisqually River

5

0   1/2   1   2   3   4
Miles

N

Nisqually
Lake

Squally Plain

Muck Plain

McLoughlin instructed McDonald to let Archibald Spence's eldest daughter, or any other girl who could milk, have the loan of a tame cow—for herself. Later, tin pans and cans were issued because whole milk was left standing in shallow pans and the cream that collected on top was skimmed off to make butter.

The colonists came to farm. After the first of the year, they were provided with two bushels of seed wheat, assorted tools, plow iron, a bullock, and a sow. The catch was that the heavy iron was forty miles away at the Cowlitz. Fortunately, Flett was a blacksmith and McKay was a harness maker. Before the Richmond family departed for more civilized pastures of the Lord, they sold their plow to Henry Buxton. John Tait also got tools by giving the Methodists a note on the Company, which caused the traders to complain that the emigrants "were a most extravagant set."[226]

The settlers received seventeen bullocks as draft animals. As the men worked desperately to get in crops, James Flett's ox died from bad treatment in January. Calder and Tate were also charged for two animals "killed in the yoke" as a consequence of trying to break up the rocky soil. In May, Otchin was held responsible for a mare and foal killed on the portage. But as harvest approached, only two or three Onsaburg bags were furnished to each family, because there was not going to be much grain to sack.

The question was, should the Columbia Department provide an adequate food supply until the colonists could become self-sufficient? By 14 December the colonists wanted someone to come from Fort Vancouver to regulate things, and McNeill noted that "they complain greatly about their food." Five days later, a call for grain was sent to Fort Colvile. But that was a disappointment because McDonald lacked men to thresh, and his mill was in constant use.[227]

Just before Christmas, McKay, Flett, and some other men went to Fort Vancouver. On 25 December one of the missionaries on the north Tualatin plains delivered twenty-four bushels of wheat, three bushels of peas, three bushels of oats, and nineteen bushels of potatoes to William Baldra, and nineteen bushels of potatoes to James Flett. But getting a pack train over the flooded rivers and muddy Cowlitz portage cost several horses, a loss that was later charged to the colonists. Captain McNeill was also obliged to hire thirty Indian horses at "an enormous price but in our present perdiculment it cannot be helped."[228]

From 9 November the Fort Nisqually account books recorded the items given to the settlers. The first advances were treated as sales debited to the settler. Early entries were for food: potatoes, turnips, peas, and salted salmon, usually in bushel and half-bushel lots. Some lucky individuals received "three ducks" or "one cod-fish." Small portions of molasses or California grease were allotted, and Buxton somehow obtained a bottle of rum. Between 9 November and 31 January, the McKays, a family of six, received seven pounds of beef, thirteen bushels of potatoes, fourteen bushels of peas, and eighty-two pounds of salted salmon. Around the first of March, after the coldest part of the winter, a few families also received two half-point blankets.[229] Cod lines, hooks, and barrels were requisitioned to take and put down spring salmon from the Nisqually River. In March, old John Tate was provided with a garden hoe, but what crop could have been tended so early?

Letitia McKay recalled that "we came near all starving and got disgusted and broke up." Young Henry Buxton was more explicit. "Would to God that I could forever draw a veil over my memory and never again recall the horrors of that winter. My mother, peace be to her ashes, died the following June."[230]

The Nisqually enterprise had been conceived as a ranching operation supplemented by subsistence farming. In reality, the Cowlitz was a better place for cropping, but the French-speaking Métis who were sent there were considered fit only for herding. At least two of the colonists were later successful as ranchers. With capital earned in the California gold rush, McKay entered the cattle business. John Flett later returned to the Steilacoom area and founded a dairy operation that is still in business.

The colonists were enterprising men. James Douglas identified a mill site on the Deschutes River about sixteen miles from Nisqually. There should have been a site in the wooded ravine where Sequalitchew Creek dropped 200 feet to the level of the Sound. On 28 February 1842, Captain McNeill wrote, "Charles McKay wishes me to say he will be obliged if you can forward the iron works for a mill he spoke to you about, he will pay for them in plank, or the interest on an annuity amounting to eight pounds per annum."[231] That was not the planning of a man who intended to desert the country.

Other colonists were not as determined. In June, McLoughlin noticed that Baldra, John Spence, and three of the Fletts had journeyed past Fort Vancouver. In a tardy attempt to stem any more leakage, McLoughlin went up to Nisqually:

> The remainder of the Nisqually settlers came to me when I was there in September and told me if I would promise to give them

half the increase of the Cattle they would remain till Spring 1843. I replied as to that they might do as they pleased, they knew that we had done every thing we could for them and would continue to do so, but that I could not think of altering the Agreements, well they said, we would have remained till next summer, if you would promise us we would be allowed to take with us half the increase of the Cattle, but since you will not, we will leave this season, I told them they might do as they pleased, I could not alter their Agreement, the fact is they wanted to go and if I had agreed to their proposal, it would have been burdening ourselves with the expense of feeding them during the Winter, for which we would have to give them half the increase of the Cattle in the Spring.[232]

On 10 October, when Johnson, McKay, Cunningham, Spence, Buxton, and Otchin headed for "the Fallatine Plains," Cunningham and Johnson were charged for horses "to be returned at the Cowlitz."

The families of James Birston, Alex Birston, H. M. Calder, William Flett, John Tait, and Toussaint Joyelle stayed at Nisqually for another year, but Dr. Tolmie, back from his furlough, found them "indolent and thriftless." McLoughlin wrote the finale on 15 November 1843:

A few days ago the remaining seven went. The fact is from the first moment I saw them after their arrival from the Red River, from their manner of speaking, I felt convinced they were desirous of going to the Willamette, and though the Willamette is a finer country for tillage than Nisqually, still beyond a doubt they might have made themselves comfortable and independent by stock raising at Nisqually *and their accounts show*, that every indulgence was allowed them that could be possibly made to induce them to remain.[233]

Doctor McLoughlin was consistent in his epitaph:

Though I have done everything I could to keep the settlers at Nisqually, still I am certain it is more advantageous to us, and to them, that they go to the Wallamette, as at Nisqually they would be a constant Bill of expense to us, and would never after all be satisfied, and by going to the Wallamette, they have no further claim on us and will exert themselves, as they have only that to look to for their support.[234]

In keeping with his weakness for close planning, Governor Simpson had designed a time schedule that the western officers were unable, or unwilling, to meet. After his decision to shift operations north, the colonists became redundant and were sacrificed for economy. Simpson's bookkeeper's mind could not grasp that pioneer development was an emotional process expressing the human need for freedom and self-determination, values that could not be entered in a ledger.

The persistence of Simpson's misunderstanding was revealed when he was called to London in 1844–45 to confer about the Oregon question, and to advise on defensive measures if the United States decided to force a military adventure. Simpson told the government that the defense of the West could be achieved by two British warships and two steamers filled with marines to seize the north side of the Columbia River at Cape Disappointment. They would find support from 2,000 western Métis and Indians who would rally to the call to serve under British officers.[235]

By then the Foreign Office had learned to doubt such optimistic assumptions and sent two undercover agents, Lieutenants Henry J. Warre and Mervin Vavasour, from Montreal in 1845. Their observations disclosed the actual support that Great Britain could expect from its former citizens. Within a year, the empire settled the Oregon boundary question.[236] To mask its failure, the overseas management of the Hudson's Bay Company made the colonists scapegoats.

✎ 10 ✎

STRANGERS IN PARADISE

The new peoples of French and Indian descent must be explained through British and American records. Even Marcel Giraud in his landmark study, *Le Métis canadien: son role dans l'histoire des provinces de l'ouest*, depended heavily on the records of the Hudson's Bay Company. The best sources of personal information about the French Prairie settlers are contained in the six volumes of *The Catholic Church Records of the Pacific Northwest*. This magnificent contribution of the late Harriet Duncan Munnick includes notices of baptisms, marriages, and burials, which made up the everyday history of the Oregon country Métis.

To fit Indian women into the Catholic structure, the church fathers used a combination of Christian and tribal names. The mothers of the Métis were known to the stranger's God as Marguerite Clacalam, Marie-Anne Chinook, or Catharine Cayuse. Others were called Marie Chehalis, Lisette Killimaux, and Marianne Walla Walla. Origins were widely spaced, as demonstrated by the names Marguerite Shasta, Catharine Shoshoni, and Louise Cowichan. Present maps still recall the geographical heritage of Charlotte Okanogan, Josephte Spokane, and Cecile Seattle. Although their husbands remembered a mother, a sister, or a sweetheart in the distant parish of Pointe-Claire, Bethier, l'Assumption, or Massconge, Catharine Marguerite Kalapuya, Genevieve Kalapuya, and Henrietta Rosalie Kalapuya were survivors of a lost people. Like the padre who bestowed names on them, we are puzzled by the ethnological mystery of Ceceile Tilehoska, Ester Tawalalit, and Camile Kwoithe. As a last resort, the priest put the bride, mother, or baby down as "of the country." These women kept a bottomless sorrow to themselves as they went about the household chores of a "Siwash kloochman."

But what memories flickered in the dancing firelight of those rude cabins where husbands and wives rocked and smoked in pensive silence.

Because the Pacific Fur Company recruited voyageurs from Montreal, Michilimackinac, and St. Louis and along the Missouri, the roll call of the Astorians was a sampling of Métis origins whose degree of Indianness is unclear. The lonely bachelors who took western wives became the fathers of the Northwest mixed bloods.

Lucier was a name well known in the British trade when Pacific Fur Company recruiters approached Etienne Lucier at Michilimackinac in July 1810. Lucier's brother Joseph and his Cree wife were engaged for the North West Company business on the Saskatchewan. Joining the Americans, the seventeen-year-old Etienne arrived in the West, where he soon formed a relationship with a woman of the country known as Josephte Nouite. Their daughter Felicite was born in 1814, and the last of their six children, Joseph, in 1838, six months before the mother's death. Taking Marie Marguerite Tchinook as his second wife, the French farmer fathered two more children before his death in 1853.[237]

Etienne's nephew Jean Baptiste Lucier *dit* Gardipee also crossed the mountains to earn a reputation as a scout and guide. His brother Paul Lucier *dit* Gardipee, also called July, lived in the Willamette settlement through the trying period of the Indian wars but spent his last years among the Flatheads at the St. Ignatius mission.

During the transition from hunting to farming, the former Astorian trappers were already familiar with the middle Willamette Valley. As early as 1828 Etienne Lucier had asked Chief Factor McLoughlin for assistance in starting a farm. But HBC regulations required men to be returned to the place of their enlistment, and all that the chief factor could do was offer the Lucier family passage to Canada. Realizing that his Indian wife and mixed-blood children would never fit into Canadian society, Etienne returned to trapping with the Southern Brigade.

Lucier and his trapping partner, Louis LaBonte, went to petition the chief factor again. Their persistence convinced McLoughlin that freemen could become responsible citizens, and he circumvented the regulation by keeping them on the Servants List without pay. The first settlers were advanced seed, flour, and four cows and were permitted to purchase necessary farm implements at fifty percent of cost.

Louis LaBonte's parents lived at La Prairie, across from Montreal, but he had worked in the western trade for several

Oregon's Oldest Woman
Passed to Her Reward, Friday at 2 p. m., June 6, 1919.

Adrian Lucier Lachepelle, daughter of Etienne Lucier. –Collection of Patricia Jo Kern-Bowers.

years before the Astorians recruited him.[238] The twenty-five-year-old trapper came west with the overland Hunt party but soon found himself working for the Nor'westers. Kilakotah, the daughter of the minor Clatsop Chief Coboway, became his country wife, and their first son, Louis Jr., was born in 1818. A suspect story holds that the rule requiring the return of discharged servants forced LaBonte to travel east of the mountains to receive his discharge. Only then could he return to take a farm just across the Willamette River from the French Prairie.

Julliene LaBonte, only recorded daughter of Louis LaBonte and Kilakotah Clatsop. She married Narcisse Vivet. –Helen Austin Collection.

Top: Louis LaBonte II, son of Astorian Louis LaBonte and Kilakotah, daughter of Clatsop Coboway. Left: The LaBonte brothers, four of whom died young of tuberculosis. Bottom: Kilakotah, daughter of Coboway and wife of Louis LaBonte. –Helen Austin Collection.

The Maskinonge habitant Joseph Gervais hunted buffalo on the Arkansas plains for ten years before joining the Pacific Fur Company at the age of thirty-four.[239] During his western trapping career Gervais had three Chinook wives: the first's name is unknown, the second was another daughter of Coboway, and the last was baptized Marie Angelique Chinook. Julie, a daughter of the first wife, was born in 1820, and the only known son, David, in 1823. Gervais took land at Grand Island on the Willamette about the same time that Lucier and LaBonte settled below.[240]

The name Gervais was also known to American trappers. Joseph's brother, Jean Baptiste Gervais, was one of the freemen who deserted Ogden in May 1825. That was a good career move because he rose to prominence among the American hunters and became one of the five partners of the Rocky Mountain Fur Company. As a leader of the French-speaking trappers, Gervais remained with that debt-burdened partnership from 1830 until 1834. After the dissolution of the Rocky Mountain Fur Company, he continued in the mountains as an independent trader/trapper and finally brought his family to live near his brother's location in 1850. Jean Baptiste Gervais declared U.S. citizenship to prove his donation land claim and was buried at St. Louis parish on 29 November 1870.

Another of the original French Prairie settlers, some say the first, was known as Jean Baptiste Desportes (Dupaty) *dit* McKay. Born about 1793, he was called an Algonquin from the Timishkaming region. He may have inherited his alternate name from the Berthierville family of McKays, who traded in the region toward James Bay. Dupaty was around Fort George in 1812 but was later listed as a freeman. When he "retired to pitch his tent permently" near Champoeg, his biographer was the sometime Fort Vancouver schoolteacher, John Ball. Dupaty had Kalapuya and Shasta wives, seven children, and a remarkable collection of cats and dogs. His two wives were, like a captain's paradise, from the opposite extremes of his travels with the southern hunting brigade. Agathe, born in 1825, and Francoise, born in 1828, were daughters by the Kalapuya wife, who died leaving Dupaty with a handful of motherless children. He sent some of them to the Methodist mission school, where Daniel Lee performed the marriage of Marie Lisette Dupaty to John Howard on 1 May 1837. But as soon as a Catholic priest was available, the couple was properly re-wed. Dupaty died in 1853, but the confusion between Desportes *dit* McKay and his neighbor Tom McKay continued after their descendants drifted south into the Umpqua country and resettled in the Roseburg area.[241]

The initial settlers were soon joined by other retiring trappers. In 1833, eight or nine farms could be counted in the Willamette Valley.[242] That planting continued as the mountain hunt declined, and the next year a dozen families were living on homesteads stretched for fifteen miles along the south bank of the Willamette River. The seventeen or eighteen families noted in 1836 had Indian or Métisse mothers, and fifty-nine children who were authentic sons and daughters of the country.[243]

The New England entrepreneur Nathaniel J. Wyeth also came to the French Prairie in 1834 to lay out what he envisioned as a farm to support his western operations. The iceman's expectations for the fur trade and salmon fishery contributed to the orderly development of the country by stranding twenty-two unattached men of doubtful character.[244] Then in October Ewing Young, a former trapper of the Southwest, arrived from California with sixteen men and a herd of around 200 probably stolen Spanish horses. Warned by Spanish authorities, McLoughlin gave the buckskin such a cold reception that Young went to the Chehalem Valley west of the French Prairie settlement to live in an independent sulk.[245]

Whatever their political origin, former trappers shared a unique experience, and there was little friction between the Americans and the nominally British. When the American agent Lieutenant William Slacum toured the French Prairie in early 1837, he found about nineteen families, totaling approximately 100 individuals, living in relative harmony but cultivating only about a section of land in total.[246]

Parallel to Willamette development, but less recognized, were the locations north of the Columbia River. The Company built Fort Langley in 1827 to receive and ship the trade of the Fraser River region. As the traffic between Fort Langley and Fort Vancouver increased, an intermediate depot was necessary on the lower lobe of Puget Sound, where cargos delivered by Company ships were received and stored.

Of the eleven men who began construction of the Nisqually depot in the summer of 1833, the most notable was Pierre Charles, an Abenaki mixed blood. He was reputed to be the best deer hunter west of the Rocky Mountains. Others in that cosmopolitan group were the Iroquois Louis Sagohanenchta, the Columbia Métis William Ouvre, and the handy Canadian Simon Plamondon, who had previously helped in the construction of Fort Langley.

When accommodations were ready, Chief Trader Francis Heron brought his country wife, Josephte, from Fort Colvile. When

Heron took furlough in 1834, the Irishman confirmed an already bad reputation by callously abandoning Josephte and their baby son, George. The experienced HBC man William Kittson, who was married to Helene McDonald, replaced Heron.

Simon Plamondon may have started farming on the Cowlitz plains about 1833 but moved his family to Fort Vancouver in October of the following year. It was three years before Plamondon and Francis Faignant returned to start farming in earnest.[247]

Plamondon left his St. Hyacinthe, Quebec, home at the age of fifteen and during years as a Mississippi River voyager traveled as far south as New Orleans. Entering the service of the HBC, he was on the Columbia as a middleman by 1827. His first country wife gave birth to children in 1830 and 1832. After her death, he married Emelie Finlay, the widow of Pierre Bercier, and came to the coast.[248]

Simon Plamondon. –Washington State Historical Society.

The two small farms were located on the open plain near the upper Cowlitz River (at present-day Toledo), where the HBC expanded farming operations in 1838. Two other servants, Michel Cognoir and Joseph Rochbrunne, were induced to join Plamondon and Faignant in laying the groundwork for the expected transfer of other Willamette settlers north of the Columbia. The first trip beyond Fort Vancouver by Fathers Blanchet and Demers attended the little group of Cowlitz Catholics, and invaluable clues about their lives and background went into the earliest church records. But the priests failed to induce the Willamette Valley settlers to join them.

When Governor Simpson visited the Cowlitz in 1841 he noticed that the six families and the Catholic mission occupied about 1,200 of the 3,000 open acres on the plain. The remaining 1,800 acres were reserved for the Puget Sound Agricultural Company. About 1,000 acres had been broken up and were planted with wheat, oats, barley, and peas. The Montreal man Charles Forest had charge of Company operations, which employed twenty-three servants, mostly Sandwich Islanders and Canadians.[249]

Access to religious instruction attracted seven families of Red River colonists later that year. Those who came to the Cowlitz community were not entirely strangers. Several of the men had previously served the HBC west of the mountains. The Métis who went to the Cowlitz were Julien Bernier, his wife, and two stout boys; Baptiste Rhelle, wife, and one child; Pierre St. Germain, wife, and five children; Francois Jacques, wife, and four children; Pierre Larocque with three children; and Louis Larocque, wife, and three children.[250] Toussaint Joyelle was the only French-speaking Catholic to accompany the English mixed bloods to Nisqually.

Within a year, Jacques, Gagnon, and the two Larocques moved south of the Columbia, where they were counted in the U.S. Indian subagent Elijah White's informal, and atrociously misspelled, late 1842 census. The families of Julien Bernier and his two stout boys, old St. Germain, and Jean Baptiste Rhelle, fourteen people in all, remained planted solidly on the Cowlitz plains. After the boundary settlement of 1846 they did not hesitate to declare United States citizenship in order to be eligible for the provisions of the donation land law. Nationality was not a big issue because they were Westerners by birth and habit. Being removed from the multiplying Oregon settlements insulated them from inevitable sneers about squaw wives and half-breed brats.

Julien Bernier maintained that he was born in Canada in 1794 or 1795, and at the age of nineteen was serving as a North West

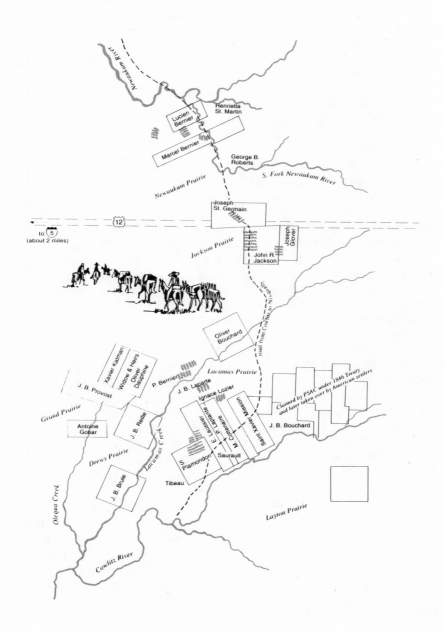

Newaukum River

Lucien Bernier

Henrietta St. Martin

Marcel Bernier

George B. Roberts

Newaukum Prairie

S. Fork Newaukum River

Joseph St. Germain

12

to 5
(about 2 miles)

Jackson Prairie

Joseph Glover

John R. Jackson

road from Cowlitz to Nisqually

Oliver Bouchard

Lacamas Prairie

Xavier Katman

Widow & Heirs Oliver Dauphine

P. Bernier

J. B. Provost

J. B. Laparte

Ignace Lozier

Claimed by PSAC under 1846 Treaty and later taken over by American settlers

Grand Prairie

Antoine Gobar

J. B. Reille

E. Laparte

P. Laparte

M. Cloutier

Saint Xavier Mission

J. B. Bouchard

Drews Prairie

S. Plamondon

Lacamas Creek

Saurault

Olequa Creek

J. B. Brule

Tibeau

Layton Prairie

Cowlitz River

Company *devant* (bowman) on Thompson's River. Marcel, his son by a western Indian mother, was born at Spokane House on 10 November 1819. The second boy, Isidore, came along in 1827.[251] Retiring from the fur trade around 1830, Bernier was obliged to return to the place of his enlistment for discharge. The family located in the Red River settlement, where Marcel attended the St. Boniface parish school. When the Berniers crossed the mountains in 1841, they were actually returning home.

Julien's family witnessed the baptism of Plamondon's stepdaughter, Cecile Bernier. Her father helped David Thompson cross the Rocky Mountains in 1808 and seventeen years later was one of the few Snake Brigade hunters to resist the subversion of American prices. Given the close relationship of the Cowlitz community, it was not surprising that Bernier married Cecile on 20 February 1844.[252] The union was another example of the overlapping bonds of affection and association that were the warp and woof of the Northwest Métis fabric.

Old Pierre St. Germain could claim a remarkable place in the catalog of exotic adventurers. Canadian born, he was one of six men bearing that name who were employed by the HBC between 1821 and 1824. St. Germain initially served the Nor'westers in the Athabaska country, and his son Joseph was born on the McKenzie River. In 1818 he transferred to the HBC and two years later was given permission to accompany the first Franklin exploring expedition probe toward the arctic coast. One of the British leaders described the interpreter, Pierre St. Germain, as a Chipawyan Bois Brule. The fateful expedition of 1820–22 ended in the deaths of half of the party, and tragic cannibalism.[253]

Pierre St. Germain retired to the Red River around 1835, where he had a lot of fifty acres, of which only two were under cultivation. Six years later St. Germain brought seven members of his family to Oregon. Although silent on the death of Madame St. Germain in 1844, church records do show the death of a four-year-old son. On 17 May 1847, Pierre St. Germain filed a preemption for 640 acres of land located on the west bank of Liquimah Creek, an indication that he had either remarried or misunderstood the rules. In the first tax list, he was a major taxpayer with assets of $200 worth of horses, $50 worth of cattle, and $50 worth of hogs.

By 1850 three more family members had disappeared, but Joseph St. Germain was married to one of the Plamondon girls and had a two-year-old daughter.[254] Joseph applied for a donation land claim on 8 November 1853.[255]

*Joseph St. Germain and Mariann Plamondon
St. Germain.* –Washington State Historical Society.

Jean Baptiste Reille was born in lower Canada about 1798 and entered the fur trade during its most competitive period. He failed to survive the personnel reductions following coalition, although three others of that name were retained. On the Lewis County

Left: Gravestone of Joseph and Mariann St. Germain. Right: Gravestone of Harriet Bouchard. Both sites are at St. Francis Xavier churchyard, Toledo, Washington. –Author's photos.

tax roll of 1847, the Reille household included one male over 18 and two females over 18. After the death of his overland wife, Reille remarried on 3 November 1848, qualifying the family to claim the maximum amount of land. In 1850 he was listed as a fifty-five-year-old farmer living with a twenty-year-old mixed-blood wife who had been born in Oregon Territory. When the donation land claim application was filed in 1854, the family resided on the claim. Donation Land Certificate Number 462 was finally issued on 30 June 1873.[256]

The Lewis County men who signed a petition against claim jumping in 1847 reveal the growth of the community north of the Columbia. They were John R. Jackson, William F. Tolmie, Charles Wren, Isidore Bernier, Peter Bernier, Lewis Bernier, Joseph St. Germain, Joseph Cunningham, Simon Plamondon, M. Bernier, P. St. Germain, and Julien Bernier, almost all former HBC men.[257]

Lacking the dedication of their neighbors for the Cowlitz, four Red River colonists soon left for the Willamette. After witnessing the marriage of Oliver Bouchard to Angelique Okanogan at the Cowlitz mission in June 1842, sixty-four-year-old Pierre Larocque

St. Paul Mission, Oregon Territory, 1847, from a wood-cut by Father Point. –St. Paul Mission Historical Society.

relocated in the fall to the French Prairie. He brought his Cree wife, Marguerite, and children: Louis born in 1823, Marianne in 1825, and Jean Baptiste in 1830. The children who later gave Oregon Territory as their place of birth were Moses, born in 1836, Francois in 1840, Agnes in 1842, and Marguerite in 1845. Their mother died in 1847.

After moving south, the families of Pierre and Louis Larocque were living in adjoining homes by 1844. But the next year, when Pierre signed Tom McKay's immigrant road petition, he seems to have been relocated between the homes of Francois Jacques and Luc Gagnon.

In August 1850 Louis Larocque and Marie Toussaint went to Fort Vancouver to have their daughter Sophie baptized. But they were missing from the census of that year, which may confirm John Flett's belief that they returned to the Red River. Twenty-six-year-old Sophie Larocque continued to live next door to Pierre, presiding over a flock of children who had been born in 1838, 1843, 1846, and 1848.

Another old trapper on the French Prairie was Joseph Sebastian Larocque, who married Elizabeth (Lizette) Walla Walla in 1824. Not long after they settled in the Willamette Valley, their son Joseph was baptized at the St. Paul mission. The father filed a Provisional Land Claim for 646 acres on the Pudding River in December 1846, but the young bachelor Joseph could ask for only 330 acres on Grand Prairie.[258]

The Walla Walla pioneer Nesmith Ankeny recalled that old Larocque, who had been in the country since 1823, brought his Indian wife and three children back to the Walla Walla Valley in 1854. They located about two miles west of the ruined Whitman mission, and within a year their raw new cabin became the high-water mark for the Oregon Mounted Volunteers' long charge against the Walla Walla Indians.

Francois Plourde *dit* Jacques brought his wife, Catharine Dubois, and four children to the Grand Prairie in 1841. By the time the Indian subagent White got around to counting them the next year, the family had increased to five. The children's names were Andre, Monique, Alexandre, Basile, and Joseph. Joseph Jacques, who married Elizabeth Bourjean on 23 July 1850, professed to be a native of Sorrel. His bride was a Métisse of the Oregon country.

Francois Gagnon was away from home when the enumeration was made in 1850, but his thirty-five-year-old wife, Angelique Marcellai, presided over a household that included Francois Jr., Ambroise, Louis, and Joseph, as well as Baptiste, Ursule, and Isidore, who were born after 1844. Gagnon did not hesitate to give up British citizenship and on 9 May 1849 filed his intention to become an American in order to obtain a land claim. He soon returned to California and died in the gold mines.

Edward Bellanger, a native of Montreal, was a forty-niner who arrived in the Oregon country in June 1852 and married the widow Gagnon. The wife relinquished the claim in favor of her new husband, but Bellanger could not resist going to the Colvile gold strike. He was paddling on the Pend Oreille River with Waken Umfreville in mid-September 1856 when their canoe upset. Wakan managed to save himself by clinging to a rock but Bellanger drowned.

An undiscouraged victim of compounding tragedies, Angelique took Charles Delorme as her third husband. By the time the land patent was finally issued, the claim had passed into the possession of an American settler named Benjamin Brown.[259]

Selling off their prime holdings was typical of many French Prairie families. As early as 1847 a recent American arrival, Hugh Cosgrove, noticed Métis disposing of their claims at ridiculously low prices. He paid $800 for a choice section near the Catholic mission, but others got claims for as little as $100.[260]

Top: Cyprien Beleque, youngest son of Pierre Beleque, his daughter Rose, and half-brother Narcisse Gardipee. Bottom right: Sophie, daughter of Pierre Beleque and Genevieve St. Martin, who married Narcisse Cornoyer. Bottom left: Pierre Beleque II, daughter Clementia, and son Gilbert. –Helen Austin Collection.

Edward LaFlemme house showing transition to community life. —Oregon State Library.

The old travelers on the brigade trail were natural horsemen and their children knew the rhythm of a cradleboard swinging from mother's saddle bow. But their carelessness with animals was the constant lament of their leaders. Even by broad frontier standards, they made poor farmers, a failing that only increased envy of their choice claims.

The desire for quick cash does not entirely explain why the French Prairie Métis disposed of those investments. Perhaps their former nomadic habits made them susceptible to the temptations of successive gold rushes. More likely, they felt the pinch of American encroachment and the dilution of the Francophone community. Some longed to return to communal tribal life.

The French Métis were dividing between those who drifted on and those who stayed, determined to integrate into the growing American community. It was the choice between seeking but never quite finding a place for themselves, or facing up to a world of racial and cultural absolutes.

Withdrawal was not limited to French-speaking Catholics. About the same time, two British mixed bloods, John Flett and Horatio Nelson Calder, left their Tualatin Valley claims to return to the Nisqually area. Another unattached man, Nicholas Garry Bird, went to end his days on the Umatilla Indian Reservation.

After the Cayuse war of 1847–48 several families called French-Canadian, but probably Métis, went to the Walla Walla Valley to found the little community called Frenchtown. In 1855, the community was disrupted by the Yakima/Walla Walla when some fled from hostile Indians at The Dalles and others from the volunteer army into Montana.

One of the French Métis, Toussaint Joyelle, cast his fortune with the English mixed bloods and went to Nisqually instead of the Cowlitz. Born in Canada about 1800, Joyelle was serving the HBC in 1821 and later worked as an occasional boatman with the freight brigades between the colony and York Factory. Those seasonal, temporary jobs, which paid cash, attracted mixed crews. Working together lessened the distinctions between Catholics and Protestants, Francophones and Anglophones, Métis and others of mixed descent, and Joyelle was comfortable with his English neighbors.

When Joyelle's wife died at Nisqually in 1842, he was left with the responsibility of four small children, and found a housekeeper among the nearby Nisqually Indians. Joyelle hung on until the last group of colonists left in 1843. By then his son, Etienne, was old enough to get a job with the Company at Fort Vancouver and four years later was working at the Cowlitz farm.

Toussaint followed his English-speaking friends to the Tualatin plains, where his name became an impossible burden upon the spelling of Sheriff Meek. The best that census taker Meek could manage in 1845 was Tuso Jugal, while the voters list for the next year put him down as Tow Saw Joiall. Three years later the name was listed as Joseph Yull and was eventually Americanized as Joe Yell.

When Tom McKay rode through the plains community with his road petition, Yell was living on the east plain between the houses of Thomas Otchin and Alason Pomeroy. Relatively well-to-do, Yell owned horses worth $125, cattle worth $200, and hogs worth $5, but as taxation was voluntary, he chose not to pay the levy of 78 cents.

Soon after the Whitman massacre, the Reverend J. S. Griffin began publishing an abstract of his religious views disguised as a sixteen-page, small-format newspaper. *The Oregon American and Evangelical Unionist* was really the sheet that Griffin and H. H. Spalding used to proclaim their rabid anti-Catholicism, but the tract occasionally allowed a rare news item to slip in. Under the headline "Give me justice against the arch scoundrel, or with the law in my own hands, my oath for it, the infernal rascal never disgraces another female" lay a tragedy.

Toussaint was working in Portland when a messenger brought bad news concerning the Nisqually Indian Chilos, who followed the colonists to the Tualatin plains six years earlier and lived with the Yell family. While Yell was away, Chilos came to the house demanding supper. Once inside, he bolted the door, trapping Joe's sixteen-year-old daughter. Neighbors living within hearing distance failed to respond to her screams.

Chilos was apprehended and tried by Twality County Judge Lenox on 16 June. Because there was no place to hold him, the accused was tied to a tree. The lack of a jail led the crowd to favor an immediate lynching, but the moralistic Reverend Griffin counseled that they should wait for ten days until a community meeting could *vote* on his disposal.

With justice taking a wrong turn, and fearful that Chilos would escape punishment, Yell called for a gun. A neighbor obliged but in his excitement Joe "choked the ball." While everyone was distracted by this uproar, Chilos slipped his bonds and ran for his life. With the mob in pursuit, the desperate man made an eighth of a mile before being overtaken and stabbed three times. While the mob was discussing whether to cut his throat and finish it, the rapist expired.[261]

Toussaint Joyelle revealed the short fuse that may have contributed to his death in December 1849 from apoplexy. The next year American neighbors were caring for his daughters, twenty-two-year-old Tusiah Yoycee and fourteen-year-old Mary A. Yell, both born at the Red River. Eight-year-old Joseph Joyelle, who was also born at the Red River, must have been one of the babies of the immigration. Because the community had no way of dealing with orphans, the family had been broken up and distributed among neighbors.[262] The fourth child may have been Antoine Yele or Yell, who was a twenty-four-year-old farm laborer in the Locust neighborhood of Umpqua County in 1860.

The north Tualatin plains were too confining for the grandiose visionary M. M. McCarver. His predilection for entrepreneurial ventures led him to conceive the future city of Tacoma, Washington, where the family moved in the fall of 1868. Mrs. McCarver recalled that "Joe Yell, whose father was French and his mother a Puyallup," drove the team that carried her family. Yell's wife, Katie, later served the family as a washerwoman.[263] At the Puyallup treaties, John Flett noticed that one of the chiefs was named Yell.

With their church as anchor, the French-speaking families of the Willamette Valley developed a parochialism that successfully resisted pressures from American culture and Protestant religion. Through that persistence they became the venerable French families of Marion County, Oregon. Others, who floated on the edge of the community, or displayed Indian characteristics, were up against a more difficult passage.

After the surviving Indians were shuffled out of sight to reservations, the latent prejudices of the pioneer community shifted to half-Indians settling on the best tracts. After 1849 the infusion of California gold provided capital for land investment and accelerated the process of Métis elimination. To poor subsistence farmers willing to relocate in more distant places, money in hand was irresistible. Some Willamette Valley French Catholics moved south into the hilly Umpqua country, or east to the dry plateau country. Others joined their tribal kinsmen on the reservations.

The ephemeral quality of Métis life in the Pacific Northwest is demonstrated in the dispersal of the Montour family. With a name that reflected a rich heritage of French, Algonquin, Oneida, Shawnee, and Cree ancestry and a long history in the western fur trade, the patriarch Nicholas Montour retired to the French Prairie in 1838. Montour and his son George took nice pieces of land near modern Gervais, Oregon, and made preemption declarations in accordance with the land rules of the provisional government. About the time of the gold rush, the father disappeared from the record, and his claim passed from a French immigrant to an ambitious Yankee landowner. When his wife died, George Montour lost interest in his claim and drifted into the territorial military and Indian service. At the end of his life, he was living near the Flatheads in western Montana. His brother Louis Robert (Louis Bob) also gave up trying to live in a predominantly white and Protestant community and moved to the Grande Ronde Indian Reservation with his Mollala wife. After Tom McKay's death in 1850, their sister, Isabelle, remarried and moved south into the Umpqua country, where her descendants vanished into the backcountry. Other daughters married into the French Prairie community, and within a generation the Montour name was forgotten on the French Prairie.[264]

Retreating to the reservation did not guarantee acceptance as an Indian. Thomas Pisk Kipling, a English-Cree Métis from the Albany River, came to the Columbia District as an HBC engagé and married a Chinook woman. Their daughter, known as Nancy Pisk, married a man of Iroquois descent named Sansregret, who became a leading figure on the Grande Ronde reservation. But when the Bureau of Indian Affairs compiled lists of those who

St. Paul, Oregon, cemetery.

were qualified for tribal enrollment, their daughter was obliged to collect a considerable body of evidence and supporting testimony to prove the degree of her Indian ancestry.[265] A similar sheaf of documents is preserved in the Federal Records Center, Seattle, showing the extent that the Flathead Métis were required to go to to prove their descent.

The French-speaking families of the 1841 immigration represented a new infusion into the Pacific Northwest mixed-blood community. Most were the children of the old fur trade, whose concentration at the Red River settlement over the past quarter of a century produced the distinct culture of the New Peoples. Some of the fathers had downstream French-Canadian origins, and others were the sons of such men, born in the country of Indian mothers. The mothers of the immigrant families were daughters of the country who had grown up in the floating communities of the fur trade. In the years since coalition they had joined the complex Red River society, contributing to and absorbing that conglomerate culture.

But a dozen families were not enough to transfer very much of the Métis culture to the Pacific Northwest. What they brought blended with the in-place habits of the former hunters. The common meeting point was in their Catholic faith, and their most obvious bond was the parish. The fusion occurred at the moment when the political organization of the Oregon country challenged that unity.

Daughters of 1812 memorial to early settlers, St. Paul, Oregon.

◦‿11‿◦

RAWHIDE KNOTS

The initial penetration into the old Oregon country was from the heights of the Columbia River drainage, with a definite British and French-Canadian flavor. There was the smoky taste of roasted haunch and broiled hump ribs in the mountain men who came through the valley of the Green. Although they were not as old hands as the Columbia freemen, the likes of Joseph Meek, Robert ("Doc") Newell, George Ebberts, Caleb Wilkins, John Larrison, and William Craig were far from Johnny-come-latelies. They had been smoke-cured around the campfires of the last bonanza beaver trapping.

Sons of the middle border and Ohio heartland, they lacked the taint of Indian blood when they were brought into the mountains on the conveyor belt of undercapitalized traders needing a resident trapping force comparable to the western freemen. Meek and Newell rode through the valley of the Green with the resupply column that Bill Sublette was bringing to meet his mountain resident partner, David E. Jackson. With any luck, the missing partner, Jedediah Smith, would also show up from his profitless adventuring in California with some pelts to put into the pot. Under the tutelage of Jackson, the greenhorns learned the survival rules of the skin game and played the tricks of young irresponsibles without losing their hair to the Blackfeet or their hides to a not entirely amused bourgeois.

One of the requirements of being a master mountain man was having a trustworthy partner to back you up when you had to wade in the icy water to retrieve last night's set. Meek and Newell, Craig and Larrison, Ebberts and Wilkins were the usual pairings. They were companions in the high country until the morning traps were no longer sprung.

Drawing of Joseph L. Meek, from Hillsboro Argus.
–Judith Gates Goldman Collection.

Along the trail, or more likely at the annual summer rendez-vous, the merry pranksters felt the sap rising and looked for brides. Just as the Chinook of the lower Columbia River birthed British and French-Canadian children of the new West, so the maidens of the Snake country and Clearwater contributed little mixed bloods to the buckskins. That required horse trappings, expensive trade goods, and lodges where papa could recline and dandle the young'un on a greasy knee.

Joe Meek inherited one of the Shoshone gems of the mountains, Umentucken Tukutey Undenwatsy, the Mountain Lamb, and had a glorious year before the Bannock rubbed her out. Next he tried a Nez Perce wife, who soon got homesick and abandoned Joe to return to her people, taking their daughter, young Helen Mar, with her. When the trappers visited the Nez Perce camp of Kowesota on the forks of the Salmon River, Joe replaced the fugitive with a young girl he promptly renamed Virginia. That union lasted, and Virginia gave her faithful husband a small tribe of mixed-blood children.[266]

Drawing of Virginia Meek, from Hillsboro Argus. –Judith Gates Goldman Collection.

Kowesota was a lesser chief of the Kamiah band of the Nez Perce. Doc Newell took Virginia's sister Kitty as his bride, and Caleb Wilkins married Catharine, so the former mountain pals were now brothers-in-law of a country kind.

Feeling like responsible family men took the edge off the fun and suffering. Like their Canadian associates, the trappers eventually began thinking about farms in Oregon. Missionaries had been passed along the caravan road from Missouri for the last six years, and in late summer 1840 a party of independent Congregationalists realized that they were not going to get their wagons beyond Fort Hall. Newell and Ebberts thought it would be a lark to take wheels all the way, and Meek was ready to drive Doc's team. The dried-out wheels didn't quite clear wormwood as high as the mules' backs, and after floating over sagebrush all that managed to roll into Walla Walla was the running gear. But that was enough to complete the trail to Oregon. Joe and Doc never got over arguing who was due the honor; Caleb never tried to shine so bright, although he was just as prime.

Craig and Larrison dropped off to stay among the Nez Perce, and Meek left his daughter Helen Mar, who had been retrieved from the absconding wife, with the Whitmans to be educated in the mission school.

After a cool welcome at Fort Vancouver, six sodden mountaineers decided to locate west of the Willamette Falls on the north Twality plains. William Dougherty, Joe Meek, Doc Newell, Caleb Wilkins, George Ebberts, Courtney Walker, and their families arrived on Christmas Day, while their companion on the trail, Jandeau, apparently went among the French-speaking settlers to the south.

The Nez Perce sisters, who were accustomed to living in the high country, endured a dismal first winter in sodden skin lodges. No wonder they felt lonesome for their own kind on the rain-pelted plains of Twality. The sniffing children came in soaked from dragging downed fir branches or mossy oak that did not take as kindly to the fire as dry pine. Rain dripping down the smoke hole hissed on the coals. Babies simmered in soggy cradleboards. At least the women could speak their own tongue to each other instead of the bastard Chinook jargon that most in the valley spoke. Their men were crazy to bring them to this drenched world. According to Virginia, it was Doc who helped them "face up to the new conditions under which they had to live. He even advised the women about the changes they would have to make in such matters as their housekeeping."[267] In addition to teaching the women how to make light bread, he cautioned his wife and her sister, "Be neat, lots of white women will soon come to settle."

In later years Virginia told her daughter-in-law:

> We did. We kept our houses clean and ourselves and our children and sure enough next summer they began to come, sometimes two or three wagons a day. They were the poorest, dirtiest, most ragged people you ever saw. Of course we knew they couldn't help it, traveling like that, but we wanted to laugh at Newell, and asked him if this was his nice white women.[268]

Joe found excuses to avoid finishing the cabin on the north plains, but Doc, ever the more responsible, completed his and then in a couple of years abandoned it to move over to old Champoeg on the French Prairie, where he was nearer the action as the missionary party made a play to dominate the new government. Meek didn't have to go far to seek his own salvation. The Reverend John C. Griffin was located just a mile or so to the south, piously explaining that the mountaineers asked him to come among them and save their somewhat tarnished souls. His ready sermons bit as sharply as the fleas in a buffalo robe, but Joe popped them with a joke. When Doc was driven to it, he had a talent for matching the pious, metaphor for metaphor. Squire Ebberts just took a jug over to Caleb's for a quiet evening in better company.

The Flett brothers were the first of the Red River half-bloods to come to the plains. They came with an old neighbor, Baldra, who had been the HBC dairyman on Sauvies Island when the mountaineers first arrived. They brought complaints about the Hudson's Bay Company. "Here Before Christ" might have been a good joke in the mountains but in the settlement, where the Company store loomed large and survival depended on what could be obtained there, it had a graver ring. The next spring, the Meeks entertained the McKay family until they could get properly located beside the creek that took Charley's name. He was as Scottish as wool but all beaver inside, and everyone got along "jest fine."

Everyone rode over the hills to attend the "wolf meetings" (see p. 173) and pull together for a provisional government. Most drew unpaying jobs in its service to keep the tight-assed missionaries from getting too firm a hold on the less enlightened. Back home, dealing their worn deck of greasy cards on the barrelhead, the mountaineers were coming to realize that they had to change with the times. Before long there would be no place left to spit except in your own boot top.

Virginia Meek, daughter of Nez Perce Kowesota and sister of the wives of Robert Newell and Caleb Wilkins. –Judith Gates Goldman Collection.

As sheriff, Joe also drew the challenging responsibility of collecting the voluntary tax contributions of the citizens. In his rounds during 1844 he got to know almost every citizen of the new republic. That included the former southwest trapper Joseph Gale, who lived over on the west side of the plains and bluntly stated, "Darn my sole if I pay." A greater problem for Joe was puzzling out some very imaginative spelling for the outlandish names of the French Canadians. "Jondra," his companion coming out of the mountains, who broke up McLoughlin with a demonstration of his prayer, was really Joseph Gendron.[269] John Larrison had apparently left Craig among the Nez Perce at Lapwai and come on to the valley by 1843.

Two of Kowesota's daughters didn't survive long in the pioneer community. Doc's wife, Kitty, became ill in late 1845, and he took a leave of absence from the provisional legislature to return home and nurse her until her death the next year. Later he married Rebecca Newman. Caleb Wilkins's wife, Catharine, died in childbirth in December 1848, leaving him with five children. He married an overland neighbor lady, the widow Enyart. Virginia Meek had a visit from her Nez Perce brother, which made her homesick, and she offered to return to her tribesmen so Joe could have a white wife. The husband was adamant in his refusal, and the growing family stayed on the north plains, having a total of twelve children, half of whom died before adulthood. As she aged, the daughter of Kowesota spent her last years recalling memories of her childhood and crooning the songs of her

160

Left: Clella and Lenora Meek, daughters of Courtney and Adele Meek. Below: Olive Meek Riley, daughter of Joseph L. and Virginia Meek, and her daughter Jennie Riley. —Judith Gates Goldman Collection.

native people. Taking sick on New Year's Day 1900, Virginia died quietly two months later.[270]

After the Cayuse killed Marcus and Narcissa Whitman, many of the old mountaineers took to the war trail with the volunteers. Never a proponent of militia, Doc rode ahead of the ragtag army with Joel Palmer and H. A. G. Lee to try for a peaceful solution. But blood was not so easily denied, and the McKays led in blowing the wind out of Cayuse sails at Sand Hollow.

Joe had left his half–Nez Perce daughter, Helen Mar, with the Whitmans. She had been named for a heroine in the book *The Scottish Chiefs*, which the trappers read to each other during the long winter camps. She was one of those who died of neglect after the killings, and Doc helped Joe put her into a decent grave. Then Meek and Ebberts headed east as what Joe liked to term "Envoys extraordinary and ministers plenipotentiary from the Republic of Oregon to the Court of the United States."[271]

Ebberts considered that duty fulfilled at the banks of the Missouri, but Joe went on to Washington to make sure that the delegate who was sent there by sea properly represented the situation. The politically flexible J. Quinn Thornton might sit among the senators without portfolio, but Meek had the ear of a newly discovered kinsman, President James Polk. The territorial bill hung up on the issue of slavery, and later in the discussions over statehood Thornton did some nefarious things concerning the rights of half-breeds and former British subjects, which even disinterested eastern congressmen could not swallow.

Meek fondly recalled the figure he cut in Washington society. At a senator's reception he spoke with a lady who inquired if he was married. "Yes, indeed, I have a wife and several children." His companion ventured that Joe's wife must be *so* afraid of Indians. "Afraid of Indians!" exclaimed Meek in his turn, "Why Madame, she is an Indian herself!"[272]

Now a United States marshall, Meek returned to Oregon Territory in 1848 with a new governor in tow. September was late in the season for crossing the plains with a party of fifty-five wagons, so they took the route to Santa Fe and crossed the southwest desert to San Francisco. The place was teeming with the first reaction to the gold discovery, and many of Meek's former comrades in arms were already there to skim the cream. Most of the governor's party evaporated to the mines, and only seven were aboard the *Jeanette* when it headed for the Columbia, top-heavy with the nouveau riche.

For a free spirit like Meek, federal service was a harder row to hoe than Virginia's potatoes. On 3 June 1850, his duty required him to hang the Cayuse who came and surrendered themselves for the Whitman murders. On the scaffold, one of them begged the marshall to kill him with a knife, but Joe cut the trip rope with his tomahawk instead. Three of the five martyrs died instantly, but Tamahas continued to struggle. "It was he who was cruel to my little girl at the time of the massacre; so I just put my foot on the knot to tighten it, and he got quiet."[273]

As a frontier lawman, Meek cut a wide swath and left sheaves of folk yarns. But his tenure was plagued by accounting deficiencies, and he was up against a new breed of sly politicians. When the Pierce administration came in, Joe returned to the north plains to become an admittedly indifferent farmer.

No one dared call Meek a "squaw man" to his face, but the hearsay smarted. It was his half-Indian children who stood to lose on the new social scale. Even the folk memory of how those husbands stood to defend the honor of their wives was a form of condescension. Among neighbors who knew them, it wasn't hard for the girls to find husbands, but Joe couldn't shield his boy Courtney from saloon bullies.

George W. Ebberts, American mountaineer.
—Elwood Evans, *History of the Pacific Northwest: Oregon and Washington* (Portland: North Pacific Publishing, 1889).

163

It is hard to think of Doc as Squire Newell, firmly planted in that house overlooking old Champoeg. He had a talent for public matters and a sympathetic inclination for the Indian service. In a time of few salaried jobs, the Indian superintendency was an attractive opportunity for men with an inroad to the tribes. Soon after Governor Joseph Lane arrived in 1849, he appointed Robert Newell one of three subagents of Indian affairs in the territory. His report for the "Sub-Agency, First District South of the Columbia River" was dated 10 August 1849. It was a first-hand summation of all the tribes as far east as the Shoshone, west of the Continental Divide to what remained of the Kalapuya of the Willamette, and an outline history of what had affected them since 1829. He reprised his role as intermediary during the Yakima/Walla Walla war by organizing a company of federal volunteers who might be held in reasonable check. Later, Doc became a champion of Kitty's Nez Perce tribesmen. But he did not return to the Clearwater in 1861 to accommodate her, because she died on 3 January 1845. A year and a half later, the thirty-nine-year-old Newell took a fourteen-year-old bride. Rebecca Newman had just two years on the oldest of the mixed-blood boys she was expected to stepmother.

Doc found the Indians on the reservation suffering from the opportunism of unscrupulous whiskey peddlers. A year later, he was recommended as someone "who would take a permanent interest in that faithful tribe."[274]

Bill Craig deserves better historical treatment than his thin record has received, although Merle Wells has done the best with that challenge. Craig had settled at Lapwai near his father-in-law, Hinmahtutekekaikt (Big Thunder), whom the intrusive missionary Henry Spalding insisted on rechristening James. Big Thunder had been a buffalo-hunting familiar of the mountaineers, and Craig's association with him put the mountaineer at odds with the missionary. Craig was determined to warn his adopted tribesmen of the danger of falling under an insidious influence and even filed on a land claim that encompassed the Lapwai mission site. But it was at his nearby house that the terrified Spaldings sheltered after the Cayuse killed the Whitmans.[275]

After speaking for the Nez Perce at the initial Walla Walla treaty in 1855, Craig was honored by being confirmed in his homestead among the tribesmen, which no other whites could do except by the express permission of the Nez Perce. During the abortive Yakima/Walla Walla war of 1855–56, Craig worked with the "law" faction of the Nez Perce to prevent the excited warriors from going over to the hostiles. As the plateau tribes fell before the military forces, his position was tenuous and risky. In 1858–59 Craig left his family at Lapwai and moved to the new town of Walla Walla as postmaster. During the Montana gold rush he operated a ferry across the Clearwater River but returned to Lapwai to die.

William Craig, by G. Sohon, June 1855. –Washington State Historical Society.

As the reservation slumped into mindless bureaucracy and sly petty graft, individual allotments became a big thing. In the 1855 treaty, the tribesmen asked that their trusted interpreter, Craig, be guaranteed land on the reservation. In the 1866 treaty in which the dupe Lawyer sold out the nontreaty bands, Newell also received special consideration and was granted a tract at Lewiston.[276] Individual ownership of reservation land once held in common opened opportunities for exploitation by outside opportunists. A half-century of homesteading had gobbled up the most desirable land, but whites were precluded from the reservations unless they could prove the necessary percentage of Indian blood. The comfortably established McKay family never quite got over the surprise visit of the former husband of their deceased daughter, who brought a suspect grandson in the hope of proving the boy was Indian enough to get some reservation land.

In time, Virginia Meek claimed parcels for herself and five children, and each of them applied for lots for grandchildren. As an example, Virginia's oldest son, Courtney, who had fled to those tribesmen after an unfortunate saloon incident, received an allotment of eighty acres for himself and as much for his only daughter, Lenora.[277]

The erosion of revised agreements drove a wedge between the treaty and nontreaty factions. Some diehards, like the old buffalo chief, Eagle from the Light, could not tolerate being nibbled to death and withdrew among the more insulated Flatheads. It was Bill Craig's father-in-law, Big Thunder, who questioned whether there would be any land left on which he could live. When Agent Newell confirmed that his lands lay within the boundaries of the new reservation, the consumptive old man accepted the treaty but refused to make his mark on it.[278]

In 1868 Lawyer received permission to come to Washington with three other chiefs. The delegation was accompanied by Robert Newell and Perin Whitman, the nephew of the murdered missionary and the more articulate interpreter. Sixty-one-year-old Doc had not been east since he visited St. Louis during the declining years of the mountain hunt. He was as astonished as the Indians by the state of the outside world. Although there were reservations about his drinking problem, Robert Newell was recommended as agent to the Nez Perce on 22 July. He took over at Lapwai at the end of the following September but was replaced by June 1869. On the 25th of that month he married Mrs. James M. Ward. The days were closing in around the old mountaineers.

Joseph L. Meek and Robert Newell. –Judith Gates Goldman Collection.

In August, Newell's old friend Craig suffered a stroke and died. Two months later, Doc Newell followed him to the grave.

There is a suggestion that one of the relatives of the obstinate nontreaty chief Eagle of the Light was the wife of another Métis in retreat, George Montour. After the Indian wars, Montour came to the Flathead country, where the Deer Lodge press disparaged him for selling liquor to disillusioned tribesmen. When the Nez Perce began their run for the Canadian line, the region was in an uproar, and Montour tried to mediate between terrorized settlers and apprehensive Indians. Resentful Kutenai and Pend d'Oreille Indians killed him shortly after the fugitive Nez Perce were run to ground just short of the border.

Joe Meek was buried in the nearby Scotch Presbyterian Church cemetery, where those who appreciated real pioneers put up a nice monument. Caleb Wilkins outlasted Joe, but before coming to the mountains he had worked in the hatters trade. It is possible that the St. Vitus Dance that marred his final years was actually the consequence of early mercury poisoning. After 4 October 1890, Caleb was carried to the Baptist church cemetery just north of his claim. His grave lies close to that of his old pal from the mountains, Squire Ebberts, partners to the end. Less was made of the Indian wives in a community more inclined to erect monuments to covered-wagon overlanders.

~12~

THE NEW REPUBLICANS

P eople didn't count. In the diplomatic poker game for the Oregon boundary the Columbia River was no longer in the pot because the stakes had been raised to 54 degrees 40 minutes north. When the ante came around again in 1845, the United States opened with nine families who were then living north of the Columbia, and the British countered with the thirteen Métis families at the Cowlitz. But the national affiliation of the Métis was uncertain, and British diplomats soon learned that they dare not risk a call on the basis of undependable half-breeds. As the Harvard historian Frederick Merk pointed out, settlement, by either faction, had little to do with the decision to locate the boundary at 49 degrees north latitude. But it had a good deal to do with what attitudes were going to prevail in the former Oregon country.

The men who crossed the mountains with the Nor'westers or who came up the Missouri River with entrepreneurial Americans tolerated their leaders because the success of the hunt depended on guided cooperative effort. If dictatorship became excessive, they voted with their feet. The tribal unity demonstrated by the defections from the Snake Brigade in 1825 was economically, not politically, motivated. The Hudson's Bay Company men's disparaging descriptions of the western freeman came from mercantile disappointment.

Economics rather than national interests forced the western trappers to give up the chase for a sedentary life. The communities that coalesced on the French Prairie and north Tualatin plains were casual, self-regulated, and without the incentive to change a near-perfect state of society. The shadows over their isolated Eden were cast by the selfish policies of a tightly administered British corporation, or the egocentric preaching of a rigidly centered missionary congregation. If the first served a greedy foreign mammon, the later considered themselves spokesmen of a stern New England God. Caught between abstractions, the children of the fur trade developed a certain xenophobia toward those professing to have their best interests at heart.

In 1842–43 the Hudson's Bay Company and Puget Sound Agricultural Company had 559 servants scattered at several posts in the Columbia Department, including the Fort Vancouver, Nisqually, and Cowlitz farming operations. While Governor George Simpson worried that American overlanders threatened, Chief Factor John McLoughlin could not restrain his sympathy for travel-blasted arrivals. That understanding was not reciprocal, because the frontiersmen he helped hated institutions, even their own government to some degree, and deeply resented a manipulative foreign corporation. Transplanted butternuts saw an imperially sanctioned monopoly standing in the way of their enterprise, and taking unfair advantage of its neighbors. Due to the Company's past overbearance, quite a few British subjects also shared that resentment.

John McLoughlin pragmatically cooperated with the fledgling provisional government, at the cost of admitting popular sovereignty and, finally, his forced retirement. But there was no denying that the corporation had lost its leverage and was in retreat before rampant democratic principles.

The original Oregon country freemen and the recently arrived Nisqually colonists were torn between their former corporate relationship and the readily expressed egalitarian views of their American neighbors. Many former trappers and Red River settlers owed debts to the Company, and others feared to risk offending the only store and sole market.

When the PSAC colonists abandoned Nisqually, the English-speaking Protestants went to the north Tualatin plains to join a fistful of American mountaineers who had found a pocket Eden. The French-speaking Catholics went to the Willamette, where the established Métis community was rapidly being surrounded by overland pioneers.

The rawhide knot of former mountain men taught the north plains settlers a broader version of participatory democracy. Soon Red River men who had been running buffalo during the Métis tribal hunt only a few years before were serving on juries, signing petitions, and making other expressions of political self-significance. The transition was slower for the French Prairie folk, whose language and religion isolated them from the town meeting. Those passive Catholics preferred to have their paternalistic Father Blanchet compose petitions and act as their spokesman.

Founded on the ideal of Christianizing the heathen, the Methodist mission had slipped too easily into subsidized colonization. In 1841, after the Protestants led the first attempt to organize a government, Governor Simpson could report with smug satisfaction:

> Last summer they made strong efforts to form a constitution for themselves, but the Company's influence over the Canadian settlers, in a great measure defeated that object, which however ridiculous it may at a distance appear, might nevertheless be here attended with much inconvenience, if these would-be authorities, had been able to carry their plans of self government into effect.[279]

In the first months of 1843 the mission party renewed its agitation with what was usually the first step in frontier organization, predator control. A meeting was called on 2 February 1843 to consider "the propriety of adopting measures for the protection of herds from beasts of prey." This led to a second, more inclusive meeting, which was held at the home of Joseph Gervais. Not entirely innocent of the implications, Gervais, Etienne Lucier, and Joseph Barnabe helped spread the word of the next "wolf meeting."

Although Nicholas Montour asked to be excused from the burden of being secretary, the French Prairie community was well represented on 6 March. Lucier, McKay, Montour, and Gervais were named to the committee to oversee the bounty system. McKay, Lucier, and Gervais were also nominated to another committee to consider the propriety of taking measures for the civil and military protection of the colony. But Métis were a constructive minority in councils dominated by the mission party bloc. Oddly, the leavening came from former American mountaineers like Doc Newell, who mistrusted anyone overly sanctimonious. A committee was scheduled to meet again at Oregon City to prepare presentations for a general meeting in May.

The mission party's real intention was expressed in another memorial to Congress, dated 25 March and heavy with anti-HBC sentiment and unseemly interest in McLoughlin's Willamette Falls waterpower site. Of the sixty-five signatures asking the United States to step in, only the names of Charles Compo and Charles Ray were associated with the Métis community.[280]

The development of government was not an overriding community obsession. In the scattered cabins and stump-cluttered

Who's for a divide? Theodore Gegoux painted this mural entitled "Inception of the Birth of Oregon, May 2, 1843." —Champoeg State Park Visitor Center.

fields of the pioneers, daily chores and the necessity of building for tomorrow were the real concerns. Families without cash, and with small credit, had to make most of the tools, equipment, and furnishings used on their raw farmsteads. Just getting an axe sharpened on a distant neighbor's grindstone could be an all-day chore. Exhausted men and women did not stay up discussing politics.

Many of those who assembled at Champoeg in May, and those who pointedly stayed away, meant to guard against the intrusion of authority. They needed to protect themselves from the meddling Methodists, misguided Catholics, the greedy Company, and political opportunists. Morally and ethically self-sufficient, most felt little compulsion for law. Presented with the potential authority of a governor, the frontiersmen diluted that power by devising a committee of three executives, and *voluntary* taxation.

Oregon mythology holds that the voice vote on the question of organization was too close for certainty. The former mountaineer Joe Meek called for a divide, the frontier method used to select wagon train captains, or school-yard teams. When those favoring an organization made a "tail" behind him, the final count may have been fifty-two to fifty, with two French Canadians as the swing votes.[281]

The three old Oregon hands from the French Prairie who joined the organization were Lucier, the former Astorian turned early settler; Mathieu, a French Canadian who came west after the 1837–38 Canadian rebellion; and Charles Compo, a former mountain trapper. Compo had a lot to answer for because he had nursed the missionary intrusion by wasting a summer's trapping to guide the religious explorer Samuel Parker on a tour of the Northwest. The man of God quibbled over the payment, but Compo was a slow learner. In 1839 the Compo family was helping out around the Whitman mission. When Mary Walker experienced difficulty nursing her new baby boy, Madame Compo suckled the little white child beside her mixed-blood babe. To

Pioneer Catholic missionaries.
—Elwood Evans, *History of the Pacific Northwest: Oregon and Washington* (Portland: North Pacific Publishing, 1889).

BISHOP BLANCHET.

FATHER DE SMET.

ARCHBISHOP BLANCHET.

FATHER BROUILLET

BISHOP DEMERS.

PIONEER CATHOLIC MISSIONARIES

avoid offending the delicate sympathies of the Protestants, the Compos agreed to a Protestant wedding but later came back to the true church in St. Louis parish.[282]

Most of the French Prairie folk preferred to sit back against the cabin wall and observe the development of early Oregon politics. Their feelings are difficult to recover because the historical record was appropriated by the activists. Lacking the democratic habits that American frontiersmen had been perfecting through several generations, and overwhelmed by stump politicians, the Métis lost their political voice by default rather than defeat. The French Canadians and Métis came to the May meeting with a seventeen-article declaration that was so hastily devised by Father Blanchet that it lacked the names of its adherents. What this made clear was that the French Prairie settlers also wanted law and order, but not too much.[283]

The Métis were reluctant to ask the United States to assume control until a boundary decision confirmed their status. They occupied choice claims, and it was not unimaginable that a biased interim local government might put their holdings in legal jeopardy. The integrity of their organization-minded American neighbors was suspect, and they were reluctant to create legislatures, or other bodies, that would pass judgment on them, or laws that could become an opportunity for roguery. As cashless subsistence farmers and struggling ranchers, they feared being "loaded" with taxes, and saw the danger of causing "bad suspicion to the Indians" by the creation of a militia.

Blanchet's letter expressed the Métis desire for peace, prosperity, and harmony, with the due protection of individual rights. Although the document was shadowed by some corporate manipulation, some religious sectarianism, and only a vague appreciation of the international situation, it also displayed the Oregonian distrust of authority. After stating a position that came close to being a half-breed bill of rights, the French Prairie folk withdrew.

Two Hudson's Bay Company observers, George Roberts and Joseph William McKay, sniffed at the nomination of old hunters, trappers, and illiterate French Canadians.[284] Although the sanctimonious missionaries despised "squaw men" with half-breed families, the former mountaineer Joseph L. Meek was chosen sheriff, and his trapper cronies Robert Newell and William Doughtery were seated on the legislative committee. George Ebberts became a constable. Another representative from the Tualatin plains community was Charles McKay, a Red River colonist, who was appointed to the committee to look into the propriety of taking measures for the civil and military protection of the community.[285]

It was commendable that the land claims of the aging Columbia freemen were protected by a preemption policy that anticipated the territorial donation land law. By registering their claims, the Métis could guard their holdings as the country filled up with more overland Americans.

Four years later, the republic of Oregon was gifted with a unifying national disaster comparable to the Alamo in Texas. In late 1847 the Cayuse Indians destroyed the Whitman mission in the Walla Walla Valley, and the provisional government was obliged to respond. In contrast to the heroic posturing of their American neighbors, the Métis took action; their talent as scouts, interpreters, and experienced Indian fighters made them particularly effective during the Cayuse War.[286]

Mixed bloods slipped easily into the roles of interpreter and intermediary. The former trader Tom McKay used his command

Group gathered around the Champoeg monument includes Louis LaBonte II, F. X. Mathieu, and his sons Charles and Lester. —Helen Austin Collection.

of Chinook trade jargon to introduce the first Cayuse Laws imposed by Subagent White in 1842, and five years later he rallied the half-breed company in the same tongue to enforce them. His sons William, Alexander, and Donal continued that tradition during later Indian affairs. Charles McKay Jr. and George Montour took large risks as intermediaries during the Yakima and Spokane Indian wars. In another trying time when good men attempted to find reasonable compromises to the impossible problem of Indian dispossession, John Flett served the Oregon Territorial Indian Superintendency and helped Superintendent Joel Palmer negotiate most of the Oregon Indian treaties. He continued that service for the Washington superintendency around Nisqually.

Anglophobia focused on the Hudson's Bay Company. The Company's betrayal of the Red River colonists drew the sympathy of their American neighbors, which was demonstrated in 1854, when the three English agriculturalists, Baldra, Johnson, and Otchin, brought lawsuits over their broken contracts. But the sympathetic jury was frustrated in October when the tobacco-juice justice of Columbia country ran into changes of venue and legalistic stalling. The supreme court of the territory finally disqualified the award through the statute of limitations.[287] But the suits demonstrated that bonds had developed between the American community and the children of the fur trade. Now, people did count.

⌒13⌒

CHARLES MCKAY: A PUBLIC MAN

Métis trying to adapt to the rapidly changing situation through obscurity, passivity, or retreat had yet another alternative. They could embrace the new order and become part of it. In the formation of the provisional government, Charles McKay was the only representative of the disappointed Red River colonists. His American associates were conditioned to frontier democracy, but he was the product of an autocratic world, in which one learned by doing.

McKay was born at Brandon House on the Assiniboine River in 1808, about the same time that other mixed bloods were going into the mountains. The place had been founded by his notorious uncle, "Mad Donald" McKay, and his father, John, spent most of his career there as master. His mother, Mary Favel, was the daughter of an Albany River English trader and a Swampy Cree country wife; she died when he was just two years old.[288] After the grieving father soon followed her into an unmarked prairie grave, the responsibility for the family of eight fell upon the eldest, eighteen-year-old John Richards McKay, who had recently returned home with a Scottish education.[289]

Charley was eight years old in 1816 when the area roiled in the Pemmican War between rival Hudson's Bay Company and North West Company interests. Young Nor'wester clerks were sent in to promote a new sense of Métis identity. Early on a June morning, Métis nationalists painted like Indian warriors charged through the gate to capture Brandon House. Charles would remember the tall, limping stranger who carried the same name, Thomas McKay.[290] The war party rode on to confront the Selkirk colonists and kill the HBC governor and twenty-one settlers. It was an unforgettable lesson in the abuse of power.

Charles may have attended the Red River school or been educated at home by his brother. He was sixteen when John Richards

McKay was released by the HBC and saw few options for useful employment in the isolated community. Supercilious officers of the reformed Company snickered over McKay's advertisement of a school for gentlemen with a curriculum that included instruction in swordsmanship and dancing. Those smiles faded when McKay crossed the Mandan Connection to join American traders on the upper Missouri River and make inroads into the Assiniboin Indian business. Within a year, the HBC was forced to rehire him.[291]

John Richards returned to his trading station on the Assiniboine River, and Charley was apprenticed to a colony harness maker. He must have shown promise because his acquaintance with the favorite daughter of retired Chief Factor James Bird led to their marriage in 1827. Marrying Letitia Bird brought him the opportunity to live on her father's large land grant. The small acreage provided subsistence while the harness business grew to the point that McKay required the assistance of two male servants.[292]

In the close community of former traders, Letitia's brother John married Charles's sister Mary. Both clans were shocked by the news when Thomas Simpson, the governor's cousin, murdered John on the overland trail to St. Paul. The Company hierarchy preferred to gloss over the scandal, but the example of social privilege hung over the mixed bloods.

The Puget Sound Agricultural Company colonial proposals offered an alternative to life in a dead-end world. The husbands of three of Bird's daughters joined the party, which was conducted by another brother-in-law and accompanied by an unmarried brother. Mary McKay's orphan son was taken west by his aunt and uncle, the David Fletts.

During the overland journey and in the trying year at Nisqually, Charles McKay showed leadership and the incentive to better himself. On arriving at the Twality plains in October 1842, the McKay family enjoyed the hospitality of Joe and Virginia Meek. They were soon introduced to the little community of retired mountain men, and when Joel Walker, an overland pioneer of 1840, moved to the Champoeg area, the McKays took over his cabin. The claim was along the banks of a meandering creek that took their name.[293] Its central location made the McKay house a convenient place for pioneer gatherings.

Cooperating with his neighbors during the busy winter of 1842–43, Charles McKay helped lay out a road to the Willamette River and build a bridge across Dairy Creek.[294] The introduction of predator controls interested him, so he rode to the wolf meetings with his neighbors, Meek, Newell, Gale, and Dougherty. In the resulting expression of frontier democracy, McKay found himself appointed to the standing committee of eight to receive proofs of bounty claims, and to the committee of twelve to consider "the civil and military protection of the colony." At a later conference in Oregon City, the committee of twelve decided to call a May general meeting in Champoeg.

Most of the men who came to Champoeg felt quite capable of running local affairs and were there to protect their interests from the meddling of Methodists, Catholics, and Company men. Rightfully suspicious of the patriotic pronouncements of politicized New Englanders, the Twality men made another ride across the Chehalem Hills on 2 May to address the question of forming a government.

When matters came to a vote, Charley McKay stepped behind Joe Meek and became one of the fifty-two favoring organization. By pushing the Pacific Northwest toward affiliation with the United States, McKay was deliberately deciding to abandon British citizenship. Of the British subjects who sided with the Americans, two were Canadians, five English, two Scots, and one Irish; all were already Americans in practice.[295] Only four of the fifty-two voting for organization were Catholic.[296]

The vote at Champoeg was a distant sidebar to the international problem of the Oregon boundary. Diplomatic representatives from the United States and Great Britain were also considering several other complex matters. But the vote had local importance because it committed the informal community to an organization that meant to unify the factions.

After the French Prairie folk lost their appeal for a cautious approach and withdrew, the remaining parties proceeded with the appointment of officers. Of the old mountaineers, Meek was chosen sheriff, Newell and Dougherty were seated on the legislative committee, and Ebberts was made a constable. McKay was appointed to the committee charged with looking into the propriety of taking measures for the civil and military protection of the community.[297]

At the next public meeting, on the fifth of July, the legislative committee presented the regulations of the new government. Joe McLoughlin, the neglected Métis son of the former HBC chief factor, moved for the adoption of the first article. Another Company outcast, Charles McKay, stood in support of the third article, which stated, "Religion, morality and knowledge being necessary to good government and the happiness of mankind, schools and the means of education shall forever be encouraged." It continued in a less abstract vein:

> The utmost good faith shall always be observed [towards deleted] the Indians; their lands and property shall never be taken from them without their consent, and in their property, rights and liberty, they shall never be invaded or disturbed, unless in just and lawful wars authorized by the representatives of the people, but laws, founded in justice and humanity, shall from time to time, be made, for preventing [injustice] being done to them, and for the preserving of peace and friendship with them.[298]

On 10 October 1843, McKay took an oath of office as one of the three captains of militia, taking command of one of three planned companies of mounted riflemen. A major commanded the battalion, but any commissioned officer could call it out in case of insurrection or invasion. This militia was to be drawn from men between the ages of sixteen and sixty.[299]

Charles McKay.
—Oregon Historical
Society, 19919.

Doc Newell restated the Canadians' concern that a show of force would be "a danger of bad suspicion to the Indians," pointing out that there were only sixty-three Americans qualified for military duty. That puny force could very well find itself facing as many as 400 British subjects or 15,000 Indians. Newell's biographer believes that the companies were never formed because wiser counsel prevailed.[300] Perhaps Captain McKay's first service was in failing to carry out his sworn duty. His brief military career peaked in the election of 1847, when he was an unsuccessful candidate for the office of major of the territorial militia.

The Twality founders of the republic of Oregon returned to the mundane duty of building the Dairy Creek bridge, which was still unfinished when McKay and his neighbors petitioned the provisional government to be excused from working on the road to Yamhill. They argued that it would be of no use to them, and the legislative committee generously gave them the alternative of building a road from their neighborhood to the Linn Town river shipping point. After Flett and McKay laid out the trace, everyone brought axes, picks, and shovels to complete a rough road by December 1844.[301]

Soon after his arrival at Fort Vancouver in 1845, the young HBC clerk Thomas Lowe toured the northern plains. He found

Grand Ball at Fort Victoria, 6 October 1845. —Pencil sketch by H. J. Warre, National Archives of Canada, C-058113.

that "McKay's was a central place on the plains," and a vote had been held to consider whether it should become the seat of Twality County. However, the question was decided in favor of Columbia, on the northwest corner of David Hill's claim.[302]

The Hudson's Bay Company and the Methodist mission party found common ground in the control of liquor. Dick McCary, who came to Oregon with Wyeth, and James Conner, a former mountaineer, set up a still along the lower Willamette River. Their fires soon attracted the attention of the officious Indian subagent White, who overturned the malt tubs and put them out of business. The disgruntled McCary moved over the hill and began living with one of the daughters of McKay's neighbor, Birston.

The availability of liquor on the north plains attracted the crew of the British warship, which was laying on station in the Columbia River. Offended bluenoses described the "Bacchanalian carousals (one was a most disgraceful drunken row kept up for several days by the officers of the *Modeste*, in honor of the Queen's birthday) which came off in the Tualatin Plains, on Vancouver rum, last winter and spring, at the expense of the good morals of our farming community."[303] Charley McKay, who once told a friend that he would give a horse for a gallon of whiskey, voted for an amendment of the organic laws to allow the sale of liquor.[304]

At the last auction of the Ewing Young estate, McKay bought a herd of wild mares and a cowhide. By 1844 he had a tanning operation that turned out inferior but badly needed leather. The rapidly tanned hides had a raw streak in the center. Shoes made from the leather had to be soaked in water overnight to keep them soft enough to wear during the day. The sale of some leather on 10 December 1844 suggests that McKay had his operation going before the pioneer Lownsdale Portland tannery was established.[305]

McKay used the modest annuity from his father's estate for a pioneer development that came up for sale in October 1846. This was a sawmill located just off the trail to Sauvies Island (Logie Trail), about six miles from Linnton. In 1843 the former mountaineer Joseph Gale had a flour mill in operation on the west side of the plains, so the sawmill in progress must have been McKay's. Charley recognized that the waterfall on an upper branch of McKay Creek was the best head of waterpower in the north end of the Twality plains, and began reassembling the ironwork originally obtained for a mill at Nisqually. Three years later, just when the sawmill was ready to go into operation, the provisional government announced a land policy that denied the re-

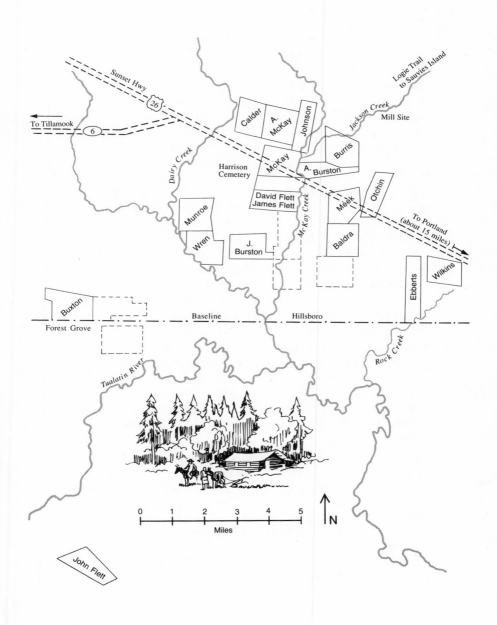

Sunset Hwy

26

To Tillamook

6

Dairy Creek

Calder

A. McKay

Johnson

Jackson Creek

Logie Trail to Sauvies Island

Mill Site

Harrison Cemetery

McKay

Burris

A. Burston

David Flett
James Flett

McKay Creek

Otchin

Meek

To Portland (about 15 miles)

Munroe

Wren

J. Burston

Baldra

Wilkins

Ebberts

Buxton

Baseline

Hillsboro

Forest Grove

Rock Creek

Tualatin River

0   1   2   3   4   5

Miles

N

John Flett

sional government announced a land policy that denied the retention of more than one land claim. Like Tom McKay and his Scappoose horse ranch, Charley had to divest himself of improvements he didn't quite own. The operation passed into the hands of an experienced Virginian miller, John B. Jackson, who improved the facility and operated it until the flood of 1857.[306]

On Monday, 6 November 1847, a diarist at Fort Vancouver recorded appalling news. "In the evening Beauchemin [a company employee] arrived from Walla Walla with the startling intelligence that Dr. Whitman and his lady, beside nine other Americans have been massacred by the Cayuse Indians at Wailatpu." The former Snake Brigade leader Peter Skene Ogden immediately started for Walla Walla to ransom the survivors with Company goods. As the returning boats rowed up the Willamette River with the surviving women and children, they were saluted by the volunteer army marching to punish the Cayuse Indians.

Perhaps McKay's recent defeat in the election for major of militia kept him from marching with his neighbors. Instead, he joined the French Canadians and Métis being organized by the experienced Indian fighter Tom McKay.[307] The Tualatin mixed bloods who joined those thirty-four experienced Indian fighters included Charles McKay, his brother-in-law Nicholas Garry Bird, John Cunningham, John Spence, Tom's son Alex McKay, and the Kanaka (Hawaiian fur trade employee) Charles Cawanaia.[308]

The Canadian volunteers elected Tom captain and Charley first lieutenant. The final roster of Company D listed thirty-three experienced Oregonians and three recently arrived immigrants who were too late to join any other outfit. Their departure was noted by the Oregon City newspaper the *Oregon Spectator* on 10 February 1848:

> The last of the French Company under Thomas McKay left the city on the 3rd inst. for the field of action. The number of the company passing through this place was about 40, which number we understand was expected to increase to about 50. The company left this place in high spirits—they will render efficient service on the battlefield. A flag emblematic of the present situation in the country—lone star with several stripes—made by some citizens for the company was presented to the company by their captain accompanied by the following short but appropriate address: "This is the flag which you are expected to defend and you must defend it too."[309]

Charley McKay was riding with the limping half-breed warrior who had helped capture Brandon House so many years earlier. Tom thought so highly of their association that he later named a team of his horses Tom and Charley.[310]

The mixed bloods caught up with the self-righteous avengers, who had rushed upriver to The Dalles and been milling about for three months. When the campaign finally got into gear, three peace commissioners accompanied the army in the faint hope of negotiating a solution. When other Columbia River Indians refused to support the Cayuse, the apprehensive tribesmen sent messages and emissaries. The ragged column of unforgiving volunteers grimly rode past Wells Springs on the immigrant road to sandy flats eight miles beyond.

A cold wind scoured the bluffs where nervous Indian horsemen hovered and Indian women and children watched. The army halted in a loose semicircle around the supply wagons while the peace commissioners rode forward to speak with Cayuse heralds. Holding his company in a tight formation on the right, Captain Tom McKay called to some nearby Indians to withdraw before it was too late.[311]

Indians were led by persuasion and example. The night before, around the campfires, a medicine chief named Tom-tice-tom-let (Grey Eagle) boasted that he could swallow the bullets of the Bostons. Not to be outdone, the Umatilla leader, Five Crows, also claimed to be invulnerable. Now they saw their tribesmen beginning to lose nerve. In an attempt to precipitate a charge, they killed a stray dog.[312]

Charley McKay penned a description of what followed for his Oregon City friends, Brooks, Smith, McLoughlin, and Wilson, who had it published in the *Spectator*.

> Dear Friends — This is the first opportunity I have had to send any intelligence of our proceeding since we left the Dalles, which I embrace; but as time is pressing I write but one to all of you.
>
> The first circumstance of importance which has occurred since we joined the army was the making of a treaty with those of the DeChutes Indians with whom Col. Gillam fought before our arrival. On the 2nd day after the making of this treaty, we met a combined force of Cayuse, Walla Walla and Indians of other tribes, amounting in all to 418 armed men, and about 100 more without guns who remained spectator to the conflict. Is impossible at present to give a perfect description of the engagement, but it is enough to say, that the enemy had every advantage of position, added to a through knowledge of the hills and ravines which marked the face of the country. Our lines were extended and nearly formed a circle with the horses, cattle and wagons in the center. The enemy commenced the action by

charging toward us, and firing, which was briskly returned by our party.

Some of the Indians more venturesome than the rest came so near to us that they were shot. Two of them were men of influence, one of whom was Great Eagle, a Cayuse medicine man who was killed by Thomas McKay. "Five Crows" the fellow who took one of the girls [after the Whitman massacre] was shot in two places, smashing his left arm into splinters, by myself— he dropped his gun which I obtained and if my horse had been good he would not have escaped me.

After this the Indians kept up their firing, but at a great distance off. Their fuzees throw balls further than our rifles in which they had the advantage. The firing continued until within an hour of sunset, when the Indians cleared out and left us masters of the field. The canon was discharged twice, but without much effect. Five of our men were wounded, one severely, being shot in the right breast—there is well grounded hopes for his recovery. On the next day a truce was agreed upon, when some false reports were explained to the Walla Walla, Nez Perce and other tribes; that is to say; That the Americans were intending to kill them all, and take their lands—upon hearing which, they refused further interfering in the matter and immediately departed for home. We understand (but it is impossible to arrive at the exact truth) that three of the enemy were killed and several of the enemy and a great many horses wounded.

It is indeed a handsome sight to see fighting men galloping on their horses and the spectators on the hills (even women were there) to witness the conquest of the Americans. The enemy had threatened that "the Americans should never drink the waters of the Umatilla." They had further threatened that they would beat the Yankees to death with clubs, and then proceed to the Willamette and take women and everything; but in this the Indians were egregiously mistaken. By the Indians account their loss was sustained from that portion of the field where our party was stationed; but I imagine that they sustained loss from other portions of the army. March 1st. We have had a talk with the Indians, and proposed a treaty with those *only* who are friendly. but we have since heard that they are all combined with the exception of Yellow Snake [Peo-Peo-Mox-Mox of the Walla Walla]. We expect to be at Whitmans today. Some of our party were foolish enough to tell the Indians that Thomas McKay and myself shot the two Indians above mentioned—so we have to look out. Excuse abruptness as the courier is departing. Yours truly C. McKay.[313]

With their war medicine discredited, the Cayuse bravado evaporated. When the provisional government army reached

Waiilatpu to rebury the slain missionaries, Charley helped his old friend Joe Meek cover the body of his daughter, Helen Mar. After shaking hands, Joe and Squire Ebberts rode on east to ask for assistance from the United States government.

The hostiles declined another direct confrontation. Confining their resistance to skirmishes, the Cayuse retreated beyond reach and managed to remain undefeated in the field. But they lost confidence in exile and eventually surrendered their ringleaders for trial and hanging.

Lieutenant McKay returned downriver with the peace commissioners. A charming, and perhaps even true, McKay family yarn held that Charley and Five Crows became friends after the war and that the Cayuse leader visited the McKay home when he brought horses down to trade. The story is not unbelievable—the family was sympathetic to Indians. Local tribesmen came to the McKays when they were sick or in trouble. Letitia's grandchildren remembered Indian camps along the creek below the McKay home.[314] Adventurers exploring the Claskanine River in early fall 1848 were guided by information obtained from Charley McKay through "his Indians."[315]

The glittering promise of the California gold discovery reached the Willamette Valley, and in a twinkling two-thirds of the male population started south with pack trains or wagon parties. Two of McKay's neighbors, Otchin and Burris, filled pokes in the mines, and Charley did well enough to afford ship passage home, sharing the lee rail of Captain John H. Couch's brig *Madonna* with Ben Stark and W. H. Bennett. The latter was pleased to step ashore in style, to a town where three years before he barely made a living by splitting shakes.

McKay realized the opportunities in supplying the miners. "With the money he had brought back from California he began buying cattle throughout the valley, driving them to Portland where he sold them to the butchers."[316] Traveling around the country as a cattle buyer helped enlarge Charley's reputation as a local character. One yarn recalled that he was hiking along the Columbia River with his cash and lunch wrapped in his bedroll when he came to a house offering the enticing prospect of a hot dinner. But when he returned to recover the hidden bedroll, his cache was missing. With the latchstring hospitality of the community at stake, everyone turned out to search for the thief. They soon found a trail of gold pieces scattered along the road; at the end lay a semiwild hog enjoying the last of the lunch.[317]

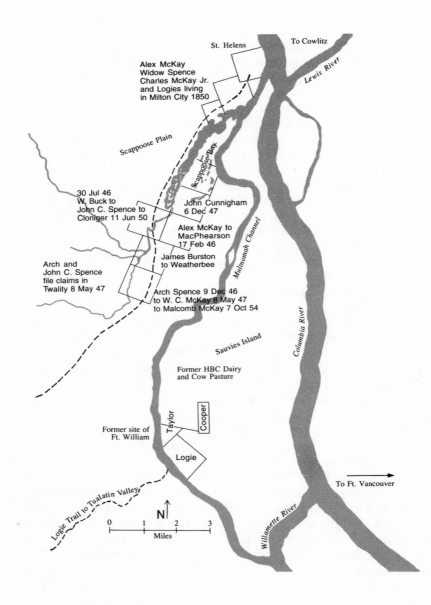

To Cowlitz

St. Helens

Lewis River

Alex McKay
Widow Spence
Charles McKay Jr.
and Logies living
in Milton City 1850

Scappoose Plain

Scappoose Bay

30 Jul 46
W. Buck to
John C. Spence to
Cloniger 11 Jun 50

John Cunnigham
6 Dec 47

Alex McKay to
MacPhearson
17 Feb 46

Multnomah Channel

James Burston
to Weatherbee

Arch and
John C. Spence
file claims in
Twality 8 May 47

Arch Spence 9 Dec 46
to W. C. McKay 8 May 47
to Malcomb McKay 7 Oct 54

Sauvies Island

Columbia River

Former HBC Dairy
and Cow Pasture

Taylor

Cooper

Former site of
Ft. William

Logie

To Ft. Vancouver

Logie Trail to Tualatin Valley

N

Willamette River

0   1   2   3
Miles

near friends who shared in the division of Tom McKay's horse ranch. Both of the Spence brothers died in the gold rush, and Charley was obliged to assume the administration of the estate of his sister Mary's second husband. Needing investment capital, McKay advertised his Twality land claim for sale, as well as property and town lots in the town of St. Helens.[318] Later, the McKays moved to fast-growing Portland, where Charley drove in cattle and operated a butcher shop. By now eastern shippers were getting cargoes to California and undercutting the price of Oregon products. When the brief boom evaporated, the McKays moved back to the north plains. But Charley was unable to give up traveling, and continued going up the Columbia River to trade horses from Five Crows and other former enemies.

The verification of his land claim made Charles McKay an American citizen in 1851.[319] That Halloween, the pioneer Episcopalian minister the Reverend William Richmond came from Oregon City to hold services for about twenty people in the McKay house. Of the seven children baptized by Richmond, he identified five as Indians.[320]

McKay's former brother-in-law James Sinclair was another wanderer drawn to the gold rush, accompanied by Letitia's brother Levi. Traveling between California and the Red River, Sinclair stopped at the McKays' with relatively recent news and with letters from friends and family. During one of his visits, Sinclair bought the annuity that McKay was still receiving from his father's estate. Charley needed to convert a modest guaranteed income into ready cash.[321]

In late 1854 Sinclair returned with a second party of Red River immigrants and news of Governor Simpson's appointment as the HBC trader at old Fort Walla Walla. Through mutual inexperience and hysteria, Sinclair and the U.S. Indian subagent, Nathan Olney, managed to project the innocent Walla Walla Indians into the Yakima Indian War of 1855.[322]

Once again the citizens of Oregon rallied for a war east of the mountains. But now they were younger men, which left old campaigners like Charley McKay and Joe Meek feeling overlooked. In a clumsy attempt to relive past glories, they wrangled an unofficial presence with the First Regiment of Oregon Mounted Volunteers. Sinclair, who met Charley in the volunteer camp, wrote home that he was "sober when he cannot procure whiskey." But it was Sinclair who was killed in a surprise attack on the Cascade portage, and all that McKay had to show for his service was a claim for a horse that he lost, or ate, during that hard winter.[323]

The defeat of the plateau tribes opened the interior for settlement. Soon cattlemen were moving into the Yakima country. In 1860 a pioneer rancher, A. J. Splawn, stopped at the McKay home to hear large yarns. "We spent the night with Charles McKay, brother of the celebrated Thomas McKay. . . . I listened to tales of Indian warfare from one who had taken part in it for a lifetime."[324]

Bypassed frontiersmen, like genies, disappeared back into the bottle, and later references to McKay show his drift into alcoholism. In later years, most of Charley's business transactions were land sales, until Letitia was forced to prevent the wastage of the entire estate through legal action.

The Portland *Oregonian* of 28 May 1873 carried a notice:

> We are informed that Charles McKay, well known in Portland, in fact all over Oregon and in many other places died at his residence at Glencoe, Washington County, last Tuesday night. He was an old pioneer coming to Oregon about 40 years ago as a trapper in the employ of the Hudson's Bay Company. He was a Scotsman by birth and possessed all the national traits of that people, many of which are found in the composition of every good man. His death was sudden and many will miss Old Charley McKay as he was familiarly known from the walks of man. May he rest in peace.

During thirty-two years in the Pacific Northwest, Charles McKay demonstrated that a half-blood from a different culture, environment, and political philosophy could successfully adapt to the American frontier. He showed leadership on the overland trail and during the struggle to establish farms at Nisqually. Those attributes carried through in Oregon, where American associates nominated him for responsible positions in the provisional government. McKay's successes in business, politics, and pioneer development were remarkable in a man formed in an insular, authoritarian corporate world. They go far in disproving the negative stereotype of the disreputable half-breed. By refusing to be impeded by his racial or social peculiarity, Charles McKay shouldered a place in the new community without losing connection to the Indian side of his heritage.

∽14∾

A TRANSPLANTED SISTERHOOD

I n the records of the fur trade, daughters of the country were usually invisible due to the genteel oversight of the wives and children in bark canoes, York boats, or with trapping brigades. Although ill-informed accountants thought them a burden on the business, women living in the camps and cramped posts performed a multitude of services for which they were not, or were inadequately, compensated. Against the movie image of a wild-spirited, sexually promiscuous half-breed girl must be balanced the reality of a quiet helpmate seeing to camp chores and packing the horses.

Métisse were preferred because, in the perception of prospective husbands, they were less brown than their tribal sisters but dark enough to get along in a country where a pale European woman would falter and faint. The trappers liked to get them young—virgins if possible, who were certifiably free of disease.

One of the first Métisse born in the Pacific Northwest was Helene McDonald, the country daughter of the red-haired Nor'wester Finan McDonald and the Pend d'Oreille girl named Marguerite.[325] After Finan's imprudence in the Blackfoot country forced North West Company operations to fall back to Spokane House, the marriage was arranged. Helene was born there on 19 June 1811.

Not all the amenities of famed Spokane were taken from the admirable kitchen garden. "There was a ball room, and no females in the land so fair to look upon as the nymphs of Spokane. No damsels could dance so gracefully as they; none were so attractive."[326]

Having grown up around the depot and its outposts, Helene was eleven in spring 1822, when her father and mother joined the hunting brigade that coursed the eastern Snake plain and

"My partner at a Grand Ball given at Fort Victoria."
—Pencil sketch by H. J. Warre, National Archives of Canada, C-058104.

the Salmon River country. The young girl probably saw the scorched bodies of the slain Blackfeet and the Métis scalp dance. Five years later, when her father left the country, she was considered old enough to be settled with a promising clerk, William Kittson. Their son, Pierre Charles, was born on 6 April 1832, and daughter, Eloise Jemima, on 25 July 1836. Three years later, a Catholic priest legitimized the marriage and children at Fort Nisqually.

Brave, dapper, little Kittson succumbed to illness and drink. The widow fell on the indulgence of Fort Vancouver officers until Richard Grant married her on 29 March 1845. Grant's post was Fort Hall, along the Oregon trail, and Helene was the first daughter of the country that most overlanders saw. Several of them described her admiringly in their journals.

When the census of 1860 was taken, Helene was living with her notable family in the lower Bitterroot Valley. When she died three years later, a life ended that had spanned the initial development of the Oregon country. Helene was representative of those anonymous mixed-blood wives and mothers who shared the brigade trails, the dangerous river journeys, and the long, lonely winters at some remote post.

The freeman trappers usually found wives among the local Indian women, who were then taken far afield by the hunt. Chinook brides from the lower Columbia River fishing people had to learn nomadic skills that were far outside their experience and training. Other hunters preferred brides from interior tribes, because they already understood the arts of packing and camping. Mixing women from many tribal origins in the brigades created homely collisions of habit, custom, and taboo and surely generated personal crises of confidence. Somehow those wives were able to meld different customs into acceptable behavior patterns to be passed on to their children, the true sons and daughters of the country.

During the years of the bonanza hunt, trappers' wives were living demonstrations of their husbands' prowess with their displays of heavily beaded and decorated costumes or elaborate horse gear. Two famous mountaineers had the privilege of knowing the Shoshone beauty Umentucken Tukutsey Undewatsey, the Mountain Lamb. Joe Meek never forgot.

> She was the most beautiful Indian woman I ever saw and when she was mounted on her dapple gray horse, which cost me three hundred dollars, she made a fine show. She wore a skirt of beautiful blue broadcloth, and a bodice and leggins of scarlet cloth,

of the very finest make. Her hair was braided and fell over her shoulders, a scarlet silk handkerchief, tied on hood fashion, covered her head; and the finest embroidered moccasins her feet. She rode like all the Indian women, astride, and carried on one side of the saddle the tomahawk of war, and on the other the pipe of peace.[327]

Helene Lattie, daughter of Columbia bar pilot Alexander Lattie and wife of Antoine Cloutier, who operated Summer House at Seaside, Oregon, for many years. —Oregon State Library.

Decorative styles reflected the patterns and symbols of coastal and plateau heritages, with broad borrowing from the radiant plains culture. Travelers probably brought examples of the developing eastern Métis decorative arts, but as Juliet Pollard points out, the nomadic hunting life of the Pacific Northwest Métis was their real culture. When that was lost with the decline of the hunt, displaced trapping families living on reduced incomes were no longer in a position to make elaborate displays. The women of the 1841 party probably brought examples of Métis handiwork but those mementoes made little impression on a culture already in retreat before the rapidly expanding American community.

The preference for disease-free brides led to very young mothers, while the combination of genes from large-boned Europeans and smaller Indian women produced big babies that were difficult to birth. At the time of delivery, those young mothers were often far away from experienced matrons or supportive tribal sisters, facing uncertainty and fear alone. One of the first mixed-blood babies, young Baptist Charbonneau, was assisted into the world by unlikely midwives named Lewis and Clark.

Bemused observers liked to draw the comparison between the hardy woman who stepped down along the trail for a casual delivery, and the delicate flower of society who birthed her baby in bed. Was that a backhanded way of showing the difference between insensitive savages, or half-savages, and truly refined ladies of quality? By implication, did a half-breed mother feel only half the pain?

At least three of the overland colonist mothers had babies during the 1841 trip. With the exception of William Flett's seventy-five-year-old Indian mother, Saskatchewan, they were daughters of daughters of the country, several steps removed from tribal experience and full confidence in Indian birth practices. Governor Simpson tossed off their experience lightly.

> The band contained several very young travelers, who had, in fact, made their appearance in this world since the commencement of the journey. Beyond the inevitable detention which seldom exceeded a few hours, those interesting events had never interfered with the progress of the brigade; and both mother and child used to jog on, as if jogging on were the condition of human existence.[328]

Compare that supercilious opinion to the trail birth observed by a gold miner in 1850:

> We found a company of Oregon men also on the "Gold Lake" hunt—The men here were Fox, Battis [Bercier?]—the French half-breed Oregonian—he is called Battateaux generally, and is brother of Captain Warner's guide, murdered with poor Warner. He has a Digger squaw, whom he alternately caresses and whips—and is a poor drunken devil. . . . July 29, 1850—On the ride out, at a deep hollow—some 20 miles distant from the settlements, the Frenchman's squaw had to dismount and cause a slight detention, while she gave birth to a child. It was enveloped in a rag, and its mother mounted her pony astraddle, in half an hour after, with the infant mountaineer, and rode about 35 miles, without serious inconvenience. The child did not survive the ride, and was buried. This shows the difference between artificial and natural folks.[329]

The colonial party was stalled on the west side of the mountains by a birth that was probably induced by a long downhill ride. Jane Bruce née Work, the daughter of Alexander Work and a native woman named Isabelle, had been born at the Red River in 1824, and married a son of the country named John Cunningham. She was seventeen when their daughter was born on the trail. James, the son of Grizzel Birston, claimed to have been born in the Rocky Mountains, and Letitia McKay rode into the Oregon country with a new babe in arms.

Her accidental horse fall at Lake Pend Oreille made Frances Buxton a casualty who never fully recovered; she died at Puget Sound during the first winter. Her widower went to the north Tualatin plains, where he married one of the independent missionary women. The widow Munger also knew tragedy. Her husband, Ashael, in a fit of monomania, nailed his hand to the fireplace and roasted himself to death.

The tangled relationships of the Flett, Tait, and Birston families stretched back to the floating community of the North Saskatchewan. William and Elizabeth Flett were the children of the Hudson's Bay Company postmaster William Flett, Senior, and the Indian woman Saskatchewan. Elizabeth's marriage to Robert Rowland produced a daughter, Grizzel, who married James Birston at the Red River. James's brother, Alexander Birston, was married to Janette Tait, the only daughter of old John Tait, who, like Saskatchewan, accompanied the families west.

Janette Birston was quick to grasp the advantages for women of the donation land law, which allowed single men to claim 320 acres of free land but doubled the acreage for couples. More than romance was involved in some precipitous unions, and to ensure against fraud, the woman's half belonged to her. When Janette exercised her legal prerogative, the land-accumulating Virginian Ulysses Jackson got a convincing lesson in woman's rights.

After selling portions of their claim in 1851, 1858, and 1860, the Birstons disposed of the last 280 acres and moved across the Columbia River to the Fort Vancouver plains, where Alex died in 1867. Two years later, Jackson, who obtained most of the former Alex Birston land claim from a third party, was surprised to find that he was being sued by Janette Birston. She contended that she had not been consulted about the sale of her half of the land. Embarrassed by the lack of a valid deed, Jackson appealed the judgment to the state supreme court. The case mounted the ladder of Oregon jurisprudence until Jackson's title was confirmed, with the provision that he make an additional settlement with the widow.[330]

Just across the creek, 200 acres of the claim of Charley and Letitia McKay were already disposed of by 1865. Charley was of-

Letitia Bird McKay. —Oregon Historical Society, 91510.

fering another 200 acres for $1,000, but Letitia, who cared for a large number of foundlings and orphans, was concerned about losing her only base of support. She petitioned the court to have the remaining half of the claim set aside for her, since it was her responsibility to raise and support the large family.

A well-known local figure, Letitia McKay earned the respect of her community through good works and charity, a result of the sense of public responsibility inherited from her patriarchal father. Born at Edmonton House on 10 February 1810, Letitia spent her childhood playing with the other children of the Saskatchewan River community. She was about thirteen or fourteen when her parents settled on Bird's large Selkirk land grant. Her education at the Red River Academy included imported English graces and social attitudes. At the age of seventeen she married Charles McKay, and the couple had four children, aged twelve to two, when they decided to move to Oregon.

With the self-confidence of the daughter of a major fur trade figure, Letitia McKay was more than equal in character to her American sisters. Through her mother she could trace a remarkable lineage that included roots in the Cree, Shawnee, Oneida Iroquois, and Algonquin tribes. But pioneer Oregon was no place to emphasize that heritage.

As a consequence of her practice as a midwife and nurse, Letitia became the foster mother of as many as twenty-two orphans and foundlings. A grandson, James McKay, recalled her habits:

> My grandmother traveled all over that part of the country to help the wives of the settlers when the babies arrived. She was a famous midwife but she would never charge for her services. She used to say that she enjoyed being neighborly. She used to come out and say to me, "Jimmie, get my mare, I'll probably be gone for a day or two." Once in awhile babies arrived when they weren't ordered, so the mother of the baby didn't have a husband. My grandmother would advise her to get a job working for someone in a neighborhood where she wasn't known, and grandmother would adopt the baby.[331]

Letitia helped ease the differences between the Red River and Tualatin Valley communities. Among the Métis, morality, ethics, and custom owed as much to tribal values as to Christian ethics, and carnal sin was no big deal. In comparison, Americans tended to be easy with truth and manners but made an issue of sexual morality. The loudest voice of God on the north Tualatin plains was the Reverend J. W. Griffin, who felt it his duty to intervene and correct the mistaken. His ingenuous explanation that the retired mountaineers invited him to settle among them to look after their benighted souls would have drawn snorts, and he went too far when those beliefs took a prohibitionist turn.

The old friends William Johnson, Dick McCary, and James Conner had their Willamette still overturned by the sanctimonious Indian subagent White. When the indignant Conner challenged White to a duel, he was excommunicated for life, and McCary wisely withdrew to the north plains. There he married sixteen-year-old Catharine Birston and kept her fifteen-year-old sister in the household as company. Until thirsty Oregonians could express themselves at the polls, temperance prevailed.[332]

Letitia McKay was a mother with nubile daughters to guard, especially when Charley's hospitality included inviting sailors to the 1844 Christmas festivities. Captain Avery Sylvester of the brig *Cheminus* wrote:

> On our arrival at Mr. McCoys we were presented to some *shining fairies* and a good supper. You may censure me for mentioning "shining fairies," being married, but though I never forget my plurality in that respect, yet I don't think it my duty to deprive myself altogether of the pleasures derived from the company of handsome, chatty young ladies. We continued our cruise for 8 days during which time I have seldom enjoyed myself better.

Avery returned to his ship convinced that it was unfortunate that many of the impoverished settlers had native wives who were not acquainted with the business of a farmer's wife, but "if you wish a bit of a spree, there is no people more ready. In fact they are 'a right smart chance' of people."[333] The church element countered the decline in morality by holding a camp meeting at Alexander McKay's place on 12 April 1846.

The plains also attracted the officers and sailors of the British ship *Modeste,* which was anchored in the Columbia River from 30 November 1845 until May 1847.[334] Lowe, the Fort Vancouver clerk, noted in his 20 April 1846 diary entry:

> Mr. Hobbs [another HBC man] returned in the evening from the plains where he had been at balls given in the honor of the marriage of Miss Christy Munro to Michael Calder [Wren], and Miss Margarette Flett with Charles Kawiniha. Captain Baille, Mr. Rodney and some more of the Modeste's officers were also present.

The Reverend Harvey Clark performed the ceremonies.

Eligible brides did not hang very long on the vine. The Kanaka (Hawaiian engagé) Charles Cawanaia came to the north plains to marry fourteen-year-old Margarette Flett in 1846. In spite of her youth, she had produced a son and a daughter by 1850. On her death, Cawanaia remarried another daughter of the country, Amelia Johnson, whose father had been Cahanaiah's trapping companion on the Umpqua and in California.[335]

In May, the appreciative British tars reciprocated the hospitality they had been shown by inviting the plains folk to theatricals followed by a picnic on the dairy plains below Fort Vancouver. According to the social page of the *Oregon Spectator*, the fine weather brought out the butterflies and a list of guests that included:

> A. L. Lewis from Lewis Lake, Mr. & Mrs. Birnie of Fort George, Mr. McPhearson, Mr. Roe and Mr. Buck from Scappoose, Mr. & Mrs T. Smith from Tuality Plains, Mr. & Mrs. Raines [Wren], Mr. & Mrs. C. McKay and family, Mr. Burston, Mrs. A. McKay, Miss Mary Spence, Captain H. M. Knighton and Mr. Phineas Hunt of Oregon City, Captain Newell of Champoeg, Captain Cook of the Callepooiah, Miss Buck and Miss Anny Raines from Tuality Co, Mr. & Mrs. William McKay of the falls, Mrs. Solomon Smith from Clatsop, Mr. & Mrs. Burris, Mr. William Flett, Mr. & Mrs. Roumia, all of Tuality Plains and Mrs. Logie of Sauvies Island.[336]

Indignant moralists condemned "the bacchanalian carousals," and Mary Beck Otchin soon found that she was accused of lewdness (the charge discreetly says rudeness) with someone identified only as Bob. Convicted by a Twality grand jury of twelve prim neighbors, she appealed to the supreme court, was exonerated, and was authorized to recover the cost of defending her character.

Less resistant to disease than their American neighbors, the Red River folk lost six men and six women and an unknown number of their children during their first decade in Oregon. Unprepared to face a sodden climate, they learned hard lessons during the first winter at Puget Sound. Even more appalling was the condition of the Kalapuya Indians, most of whom had been destroyed by previous epidemics, who shared with the mixed bloods that antique oddity—consumption. Mary McKay remembered the sick Indians lying in her father's tan house and believed that they suffered from winter fever, which they tried to cure, over the objections of her parents, by the usually fatal combination of steaming and cold dips.[337]

Everyone in the Willamette Valley seemed at risk from cholera, scurvy, and diphtheria. Measles arrived with the wagons of 1848, typhoid in 1849, and camp fever or ague (malaria?) in 1850. The overlanders of 1844 who thought they had camp fever prob-

Mary McKay Elliot,
age 87. —Marg Caire
Collection.

Maria Brooks
Jackson, grand-
daughter of Charles
and Letitia McKay
and one of the
twenty-two orphans
raised by Letitia.
—Author's collection.

Mollie Brooks, daughter of Isabelle McKay and John Privity Brooks. —Author's collection.

ably suffered from anthrax, acquired from eating their infected livestock. Some of those animals survived the trip and entered into the Willamette breeding pool. With increased population, communities also lost the shield of distance between sources of infection.

As an untrained visiting nurse, Letitia McKay provided warm broths, hot or cold packs, and encouragement. Most patent medicines were of doubtful value, and guesswork prescription could be fatal. Even the healthy aspects of vigorous outdoor life were offset by the perpetually damp climate. Fine wool blanket capots soaked up water and didn't dry completely until spring. Homesick women, with few cherished mementos, found their bright kerchiefs molding and their precious books rotting. Marriage certificates and letters dissolved.

Loneliness, when combined with the dreary Oregon weather, could be a fatal disease. The tragedy of one family was a horrible example. The Englishman William Burris came by ship to Fort Vancouver, where he served as steward until he left the Company in 1844. Burris took his English wife and children to the north Tualatin plains settlement, where they purchased a claim near the Birston family. By August 1845 Burris was elected a district judge.

One young Métisse thought that Burris was even more religious than the stern Reverend Griffin. Something cracked in the man, causing him to kill his wife and three children "while they were still good, so they would be sure to go to heaven." By then Tualatin had managed to build a jail, but it had no facilities for the criminally insane. Burris was lodged behind bars for eighteen months until, mercifully, he expired.[338]

In addition to sudden wealth, and a crop of new clocks, the gold rush produced a lode of Oregon widows. F. X. Mathieu, who went to California with one of the Larocques, reported that 80 out of a company of 120 miners from Oregon died of scurvy or diarrhea.[339]

In June 1850, John Spence was camped on the Deer Creek tributary of the upper Sacramento River, just south of the Red Bluffs, and near the camp of a forty-niner named J. Goldsborough Bruff. The Easterner liked to keep a diary.

> Today a lad, the son of Jno. Spence, an Oregonian French man, from their camp a short distance above, called and asked me for an emetic for this father, who was ill-supposed to be bilious. He had been drinking hard and caught a severe cold. Dr. Bowman was absent and I had no other emetic than Lobelia. Saw 2

bottles of lobelia & composition powder with full directions on them, measured out the doses, gave them to the lad and told him very particularly how to administer them. He returned to camp, gave his father the lobelia first and the composition tea afterwards. Excessive vomiting ensued, and I gave laudanum to relieve him.

Lobelia was an accepted herbal purgative of the day. It had been invented by a New Englander who was eventually prosecuted because too many of his patients died. The composition salts intended to raise a fever were concocted from cayenne pepper. Laudanum, the aspirin of another day, was opium based. For John Spence, the prescription was fatal.

The boy this morning reported him dead—died about 2 O'clock this morning. About 9 A.M. the lad called again requesting me to go to camp and prepare his father for burial. I went there and found some superstitious ideas prevented the Frenchmen from laying out their dead comrade.[340]

Bruff, who had contributed perhaps too much already, decently helped plant his unlucky patient in a corner of Peter Lassen's wheat field.

Spence's brother Archibald, William Flett, Francois Gagnon, and Charles McKay's brother-in-law John Calder also died in the gold rush. Their widows were quick to remarry. Arabella Spence, who held a claim at Sauvies Island, attracted the interest of her next-door neighbor's boarder, James Taylor. David Monroe's daughter, Ellen, who lost her husband in 1855, married the widower John Flett within three years.

Red River Métis continued coming to the Pacific Northwest as individuals until 1854, when James Sinclair brought a second party of Métis families. Several of the new arrivals were relatives of Letitia McKay, and they also located on the north plains. Despite their father's pessimism, Letitia's two younger brothers, Philip and Arthur, came, as did the daughter of Bird's second wife, with her husband, Roderick Sutherland.

Only three of Letitia McKay's ten children survived her, but there was a large crop of orphan grandchildren and other relations. In 1869 the McKays posted a $1,200 performance bond so they could assume the guardianship of three granddaughters orphaned by the death of Isabelle Brooks. Looking to probate courts for assistance was so unrewarding that near the end of her life Letitia was reduced to trading in what has been called "horse futures." In 1873 she petitioned the government to obtain payment for the horse that Charley lost during the Yakima

Nicholas Garry Bird, Red River immigrant of 1841.
—Buchtel & Stolze photo, Portland. Author's collection.

Indian War eighteen years earlier. In 1883 she petitioned for the estate of Lawrence Birston, who had been in her care for ten years before he died. That estate also consisted of two horses lost during the Yakima campaign by Birston's mother's first husband.

Finances were so tight that Letitia was unable to furnish her brother, Nicholas Garry Bird, with a little tobacco when he visited from the Umatilla Indian Reservation. In 1896 Nick wrote to the lawyer T. A. Wood, "I tried to borrow a dollar and could not even get a ten cent piece. I do without medicine and tobacco, and this is pretty rough you can bet after using it since I was 18 year old. I am in a worce fix now than I ever was."[341]

John T. Caples presented Letitia to the twenty-fourth annual meeting of the Oregon Pioneer Association. "I want you all to join me in giving three cheers for this grand old woman, who in her early days encountered hardships and privations that would put to blush the Spartan mothers of legendary lore."

When the pioneer mother died on 16 February 1897, she was the last survivor of the overland colonists of 1841. Her death was reported in the local papers and picked up in an April edition of the Winnipeg *Nor'wester*, a final proof of the lasting relationship between those distant places.

The experience of the daughters of the fur trade who settled in the Pacific Northwest was not that much different from that of other pioneer women. White and Métisse faced the same drudgery of household chores and farmstead duties and shared the same concerns for their children. If the Métisse are overlooked in the historical documents, it is because they left no written records; generally, only urbanized, educated women had the leisure time to write diaries and letters.

The daughters of the country who survived the trail, childbirth, and hard work often outlived their men, and passed from widowhood into the state of lonely grandmothers. The erosion of the years altered their appearance and time obscured their peculiar heritage. When children playing in the forest of aprons and cotton stockings beneath the quilting frame overheard puzzling tidbits, they found it difficult to connect Indianness to the venerable old woman who peeled apples for them and baked bannock to feed the dogs.

~ 15 ~

HALF-INDIAN TROUBLES

We call them savage—O be just,
their outraged feelings scan:
A voice calls forth, "tis from the dust—
the Savage was a man."

—Ruth Rover

I n her poetry, the Methodist missionary Margaret Jewett Baily
was more understanding of the Indians than she was of her
estranged husband, Dr. William Baily, whom she dissected
in a thinly disguised roman à clef that was the first Northwest
novel.[342] Margaret skipped over the practice (rather than profession) of the Methodist mission, which was less interested in re-
deeming the benighted heathens than in perpetuating itself. Like
Ruth Rover's Indian, the stereotyped half-breed passed through
the history of the Pacific Northwest in a fog of misinterpretation
and under a shadow of domestic and imported prejudice.

Corporate prejudice against mixed bloods within the Hudson's
Bay Company was to some degree attributable to the Oregon
country freemen who early on offended Governor George
Simpson with their sense of independence. The influential man
returned from his 1824–25 visit to the Columbia fuming over
several instances of servant and hunter ingratitude. Those attitudes took root in his mind and continued to be expressed
through discriminatory practices toward Métis. Perhaps it
stretches a point to suggest that the social discrimination that
upset the tranquility of the Red River settlement was totally in-
stigated by one small man, but in Rupert's Land the governor's
views carried considerable weight. He encouraged negative attitudes toward country marriages, and limited the prospects for
mixed-blood children.

215

*Toostum, father of
Chechalis and last of
the Clatsop chiefs.*
—Oregon State Library.

Corporate attitudes also infected western operations, where exploited freeman hunters dealt Company and imperial expectations several telling blows. The children of the fur trade learned to tolerate business injustices much better than their American neighbors, who arrived at the end of the overland trail with a large measure of Anglophobia.

Frontier prejudice expressed the accumulation of 200 years of injustice and unrelieved guilt. Those attitudes originated in colonial fears of the brooding wilderness, in the grim repetition of border wars, and from the guilty images of a defeated culture in

Indian Lize, last of the Kalapuya tribe. —Oregon State Library.

retreat. Disrespect for Indians in general also rubbed off on their partial kinsmen, whose very existence affronted concepts of racial purity and fears of miscegenation.

That is not to say that all frontiersmen hated Indians. Most Rocky Mountaineers learned to respect the tribesmen they lived with, fought, and sometimes married. They were often partners on the brigade trail and in the winter lodge, together for mutual protection against other enemies. But in pioneer Oregon, old trappers were only slightly less disgraceful than Indians and were soon submerged under the flooding tide.

The missionaries who came intending to recreate the New England church on the hill were closely shadowed by other skewed idealists and visionary entrepreneurs. The one-issue reformer, the "Wanabee" Indian, and the Apple (red outside, white within) are nothing new. Reason could not overcome the bitterness of people capable of projecting fear, envy, and the responsibility for personal failure upon others. The more pragmatic pioneers built from whatever raw materials were ready at hand, including the marginal men and women whose experience was invaluable in many ways. But utility was not enough to spare the Métis of the Pacific Northwest the impact of social intolerance. That blow fell on them a quarter of a century before the incoming Canadians drove their Red River Métis cousins against the wall.

Interracial union and the specter of miscegenation was a problem as soon as the first Europeans planted their late Renaissance boot heels on North America's Atlantic shore. In New France or Virginia there were not enough women to go around. After centuries of interbreeding within the close confines of shire, canton, and department, Europeans were surprised to find that that stagnant pool could be stirred by a new current. The tolerant culture of the American Indians accommodated extratribal relationships, so it was the intruders who wrestled with guilty consciences.

Three hundred years later, when the overland pioneers staggered into Oregon, they were greeted by children of the fur trade who were second-, third-, or in at least one instance, sixth-generation Métis. The conglomerate Americans recoiled from the mongrelization of their species.

However, it was unwise to slur a man cradling a trade fusee that he knew how to use. The children of the fur trade who settled near the Cowlitz, the Nisqually, the Twality, or the French Prairie were, after the Indians of course, the first inhabitants. They were proud of themselves and confident of the place they had earned in the new country. Why were their American neighbors so sensitive about biological distinctions?

Most early overlanders came from communities that feared and firmly repudiated racial intermarriage, believing it a threat to frontier survival. In the Northwest, it was difficult to maintain that attitude when mixed bloods were a result of interdependence. When squaw men like the former mountaineer Doc Newell tried to offset the pushy puritanism of the New England missionaries, he risked being identified as one of the French-speaking, hopelessly Catholic mixed bloods.

The early Methodist missionary Jason Lee abandoned his original goal of proselytizing the Flatheads and inflicted himself upon the last survivors of the Willamette Valley tribes. The mission he founded just above the Champoeg settlement was heavy with self-interest. When the Oregon Institute was established in March 1842, its constitution called for the education of the children of white men, but no person would be excluded on account of color, "if he has good moral character and can read, write and speak the English language intelligibly." Those requirements effectively excluded Indians and a good portion of the neighboring Métis.[343] However, Lee was willing to educate a few native Elishas if they would wander among their brethren and exhort them to become Christians.

Margaret Jewett's shipmate on the *Lausanne* in 1840 was Dr. John P. Richmond, said to be the best educated and most intellectual member of the Great Reinforcement. Richmond immediately concluded that the savages were doomed to extinction but thought it might be possible to educate their children "to estimate themselves properly as human beings." After a year at Nisqually, Richmond gave up that idea and returned home, leaving a bias that lingered as late as May 1854, when the wife of a later Puget Sound missionary expressed her disgust that Washington Territory had passed a law permitting the mixed bloods to vote. "It will be no difficult matter to get any number of Indians to pass as half-breeds. . . . You talk about the stupidity and awkwardness of the Irish. You ought to have to put up with our Indians."[344]

Lee's associate, David Leslie, was concerned that associating with the heathens would lead to the moral and physical contamination of Methodist children. Nevertheless, the school brought in Indian youngsters from the lodges, who were "already infected by the most revolting vices." Given the Protestant attitudes, it is not surprising that the Indian Manual Labor School at Chemeketa had only thirty pupils in 1844.

The high-minded Lee suggested that the amalgamation of the races was really a policy of conquest, with the object of producing mixed bloods. He prophesied, "There will be more Indian blood running in the veins of white men a hundred years hence than would have been running in the veins of Indians, if they had been left to themselves." He admitted that the missionaries had performed many such marriages themselves. Breeding the Indians out of existence was a novel humanitarian concept in a society that was generally willing to kill them.

The proximity of the Methodist mission to the French Prairie settlement threatened the dedicated Catholics. Before long the Willamette community was sending plaintive letters to the nearest see. The arrival of priests in 1838 transplanted the Christian schism and helped accentuate the differences between Catholic children of the country and predominantly Protestant overlanders. The children of the fur trade became involuntary pawns of colliding doctrines. In several instances, priests encouraged their parishioners to repeat Protestant marriages in the true church. That became a concern when settlers had to legalize their country marriages in order to qualify for land. Until the United States extended jurisdiction, the pioneer development of Oregon was essentially an unauthorized taking, and possession was a gentleman's agreement enforced by good marksmanship. Accurate surveys were not initiated until after 1852 and took several years to complete. There was plenty of opportunity for private argument, local disagreement, and general disharmony.

Sectarian differences were not as evident on the Tualatin plains because the English-speaking Métis were Anglican, but they were not spared the word of the enthusiastic preacher John S. Griffin. Although 125 American overlanders arrived in the fall of 1842, the balance of political power remained split more or less evenly between American and British subjects. The 1843 Champoeg decision to organize revealed the narrow margin, but by autumn there was no question where power lay after 1,000 Americans trailed in.

The historian Frederick Merk suggests that a majority of the incoming Americans "were Missouri people from border communities notorious for turbulence and a readiness for self help, who had already driven fifteen thousand Mormons from their homes."[345] That blanket indictment does not ring true, because neither the composition of the Great Migration nor its politics were quite that clear-cut.

The newcomers first saw people of mixed ancestry hanging around Fort Laramie. There were more examples of degenerate compromise scattered along the trail at Black's Fork of the Green, where Bridger and Vasquez had some houses and a blacksmith shop. At Fort Hall pioneers had their first significant experience with western fur trade culture. Because that place was operated by the HBC, many overlanders perceived it through the lens of Anglophobia. From there, the pilgrims straggled across the Snake plains to Fort Boise, another outpost of John Bull. Even the Whitman mission, the first bastion of American interest, lay in the shadow of Fort Walla Walla. When necessities passed over the counter in the trade shop at steep prices, the Oregon question became quite real.

Whitman collected Indians and part Indians for conversion into something more acceptable. More mixed bloods loitered around Fort Walla Walla and at The Dalles. By then, the pilgrims were so trail weary and experience blasted that they really didn't care who ferried them over the next troublesome creek or ran them down the roaring cascades. But it must have seemed that the end of the long trail was a thinly populated Métis corridor, channeling them to the promised land and then blocking their efforts to realize their dreams. People of Indian descent were already in possession of the choice locations. George Wilkes, who came in the immigration of 1843, wrote a glowing description of the country tempered by a disturbing account of some of the residents.

> There is another and pretty numerous branch of the population growing up here which cannot be passed without notice. This is the class of half-breeds, the issue of Indian women who are either married to or fall otherwise into the hand of the careless trapper, or indifferent woodsman. As there is a great scarcity of white women in the territory, this state of things naturally results, and the consequences will be that the half-breeds during the next five or six years, will form by far the most numerous native born population. Some of these are fine specimens of the two races and if the cross turns out many such men as [Tom] McKay there will be no reason to regret this perversion of family or rather this push of necessity on the part of their male progenitors.[346]

When Wilkes's book was published in 1845, Easterners were astonished to read that the Oregon country was filled with mongrels. Young Riley Cave was sent to the first school on the north Tualatin plains. His time in that log cabin, with its dirt floor and split benches, was memorable because he had to sit beside Indians and mixed bloods.

Other immigrants were denied choice claims already held by French-speaking Catholics with snotty-nosed little half-breeds hanging around cabin stoops. J. M. Bacon, who arrived in 1844, toured the Chehallem Valley looking over the prospects.

> I shall always remember the first night I was there, because it was an old mountaineer that owned the place where I stopped. He was standing at the gate when I got there. I told him I was hunting for work and asked if he had work making rails. After

making a bargain he says, "Come, let us go into the house." I started in and who in the world should I see there but a squaw? Says I to myself, will I have to eat after the squaw? I watched her slyly to see whether she was clean or not. I could not see anything out of the way: everything appeared as neat as a white woman. She was real jovial afterwards. She shamed me about it. "What did you watch me for when you came here first?" she asked. I said she was the first Indian woman I had ever eaten after and I wanted to see if you were clean. She was a sensible and real nice woman I found out afterwards.[347]

Concerned for the choice holdings of the HBC and its retired servants, Chief Factor John McLoughlin wrote in/March 1845:

It is reported that some of the immigrants last come have said that every man who has an Indian wife ought to be driven out of the country, and that the half-breeds should not be allowed to hold lands. This report was communicated to the Canadians by one of the American trappers who has an Indian wife, and excited great sensation among the Americans and Canadians who have half-breed families. But the persons accused of suggesting this measure deny it, but others say still it is true, and one of the American trappers believes it so firmly, that he bought powder and ball to prepare himself to resist.[348]

McLoughlin's informant was the Tualatin plains visionary M. M. McCarver, who came to the Oregon City Company store to buy ammunition against the unlikely threat of an uprising by the Fallatine Indians. McCarver caught the attention of McLoughlin, who asked him to inquire about the threats to the half-breeds.

On his way home conversing on the way, on these reports and expressing his astonishment at them, to his surprise one of his companions told him that such a design had been entertained, and the narrator confessed he was one of the thirty or forty, who entered into a written agreement to carry it into execution, but finding so few would join them they dropped it, and I am happy to be able to say the American emigrants, except the few conspirators who are not known, are quite indignant at so atrocious a plot, and on account of the immorality alone they would of themselves most certainly put it down, but besides, if this was not sufficient they are to much interested in the peace and prosperity of the country to give the least encouragement to any idea of the kind, as they must be aware if such was attempted, it would destroy all their prospects in this quarter.[349]

During the winter of 1845–46, two undercover British observers reconnoitered the Oregon country in case the boundary matter came to war. In mid-June 1846 they crossed Sauvies Island to "Shapoose," where they found a half dozen American and Canadian families located on the low ground between the river and the hills. About 150 Canadian, mixed-blood, and American families lived on the Tualatin plains, where their cattle ran wild. Between the north plains and Oregon City, patches of open ground were also occupied by Canadian and American families. A village yet to be named Portland had commenced since summer. Lieutenants Warre and Vavasour reported:

> To show the feeling of the American population against the British subjects, it may be well to inform your lordship of two measures which were proposed as laws, but rejected. 1st, For the prevention of the half-breed population from holding land or property in the country under the Organic laws which would be equivalent to a separation between the two parties, the half-breeds, children of the gentlemen and servants of the Company and of the Red River settlers forming the principle and most numerous portion of Her Majesties's subjects in the country. 2nd. For the taxation of the Sandwich Islanders, employed almost exclusively as servants and laborers by the H.B.Company, and intended mainly to annoy and embarrass the gentlemen in charge of said company.[350]

When article four of the Organic Law passed by the provisional government limited citizenship to "every free male descendent of a white man," which seemed to exclude a sizable portion of the pioneer community, Doc Newell rose to the touchy point. The former mountaineer, who had a Nez Perce wife and mixed-blood children, employed whimsy to point out the thin line between the factions.

> Wall now Mr. Speaker, I think we have got quite high enough among the dark clouds. I do not believe we ought to go any higher. It is well enough to admit the English, the French, the Spanish and the half-breeds, but the Indian and the negro is a little too dark for me. I think we had better stop at the half-breeds.[351]

The decline of Métis and mountaineer political influence can be seen in Twality County. Men like Joseph Meek, Charles McKay, Doc Newell, and William M. Dougherty initially represented mixed-blood interests in the first provisional government, but by 1844 they had been replaced by Peter Burnett and M. M. McCarver. Those overlanders and businessmen continued to voice support for the minority, but the large immigration of 1845 brought in a voting bloc that seized control of the legislature and made laws for its own benefit.

Until Indian title was extinguished there could be no land grants. The Organic Law in 1843 set up a system for recording preemptions in square or oblong blocks of 640 acres. By mid-decade many thought that too many of those sometimes vague, poorly surveyed, and occasionally overlapping claims were held by the wrong kind of people. When Samuel R. Thurston went to Congress as Oregon's first territorial delegate, he got a debate on land policy going by May 1850. The resolution he introduced inquired into the justification of donating land to American citizens then in the territory, and to all foreigners who were willing to become citizens. "On May 28 Thurston offered an amendment providing that a grant of land be made to 'every white male settler or occupant of the public lands, American half-breeds included' but not to include 'members and servants of the Hudson's Bay and Pugets Sound Agricultural Company.'"

In an objection to the amendment,

> James Bowlin of Missouri pointed out that there should not be two different sets of requirements, one for settlers already there, and another for those who came later. Bowlin also believed that land should not be reclaimed, merely because the settler was a former HBC employee. Thurston replied that only two of the territorial committee members had been in favor of giving land to HBC employees, and that such a practice would be the same as forgetting that England was an enemy of the United States. Furthermore Thurston had been instructed by his legislature to request land donations for American citizens only. He would therefore oppose any amendment that would give land to anyone connected with the HBC.[352]

Fortunately for the interests of the Oregon Métis the terms of the 1846 boundary agreement with Great Britain precluded blatant denial of the rights of the British settlers south of the Columbia River. In a fine twist of irony, the Red River colonists, who helped disappoint imperial pretensions, fell under the protection of that provision. In working out the donation land act, exclusion of the half-breeds was dropped because proponents realized that liberal-minded eastern legislators would see through and block the whole process. The donation land act was finally passed on 1 December 1850.

In the next five years the donation land act was the means of distributing 2.5 million acres of public land to more than 7,000 claimants. While there were fringe locations along the coast, around The Dalles of the Columbia, or in the middle Umpqua Valley, the most densely settled areas were the long Willamette Valley and the enclave of the Tualatin Valley.

The records of the provisional government and donation land act claims show the decline of the Métis community. Although they enjoyed no legality beyond common agreement, the early claims were sold or traded as settlers jockeyed to improve their holdings. Susceptible to easy money and convinced by prior wandering that the West was infinite, the old trappers sold out to the pilgrims. The infusion of gold rush capital accelerated the process.

The following provisional and territorial papers refer to Métis problems: 7726, a bill to enable certain half-breeds to acquire citizenship; 10863, report of a committee to let half-breeds vote; 11639, a bill to remove the incompetency of half-breeds as witnesses in courts of justice, section two repeals provisions passed 7 January 1854; 11672, a bill to submit to the people the question of permitting half-breeds to vote and testify.

The real tests were in the Willamette Valley, where newcomers envied the fine holdings of the French-speaking, Catholic Métis. Those who came west with inflated expectations were disappointed to find the undeserving squatting on choice acres and wasting the rich soil on horse pasturage. With half-Indians hogging the promised land, the arguments that exploded under the witness tree were too often projected in racist terms.

Callously applied social pressure encouraged the Métis to move on. It was hard to ignore the whispers, the malicious laughs behind a hand, or dark glances in the store. The mixed-blood son of Joe Meek was goaded into a fight by a notorious saloon bully. When the desperate boy drew a penknife to defend himself against the larger man, the ridiculous weapon found an artery. After hiding out for some time among his Nez Perce kinsmen, Courtney Meek returned to face an understanding jury. Doc Newell's children also retreated from the French Prairie to live with their Nez Perce relatives

After the Cayuse War, there was some kind of scheme to relocate Métis in the conquered Walla Walla or Grande Ronde valleys. James Taylor and Philip Thompson were granted concessions to colonize under the protection of a company of guards left at Fort Waters. Taylor recruited twenty-five interested mixed-blood families, but the desertion of the guards to the gold rush caused the enterprise to be abandoned.[353]

One of the demagogues who exploited unrest was William Henry Gray, the same despicable character who abandoned his Iroquois companions to the mercies of the Sioux. Attacking the HBC as a "Squawtocracy of British skin traders," Gray cited In-

Courtney W. Meek, son of Joseph L. and Virginia Meek. —Judith Gates Goldman Collection.

dian troubles at Oregon City in 1844 as proof that Company servants and Frenchmen would not turn out for a militia call.[354] As late as 1874 the former territorial delegate and later supreme court justice J. Quinn Thorton delivered the Gray line to the annual meeting of the Oregon Pioneer Association. He repeated the shopworn slander that any attempt to remove the British would have led to the arming of the 800 mixed bloods who were under HBC control.[355]

The U.S. census of 1850, which asked detailed questions about race, place of origin, family, and occupation, showed that Oregon now contained 13,294 people living in ten counties. Twality, renamed Washington, had 2,652. Marion, which included the French Prairie, had 2,749 and was the most densely populated. Of the total population, only 1,144 people admitted foreign birth, and many of those had lived in other parts of the United States before coming west. Indian parentage was noted only if the individual was willing to share that fact, and a check of the Red River people reveals that they were not forward about a potential social embarrassment.

An understanding census enumerator put down England as the place of birth for James Birston, and Hudson Bay as the home of his wife. He identified mixed bloods in the Calder, Cunningham, James and Alexander Birston, Wren, and Monroe families. Ten years later, the families of James Birston, Alex Birston, Horatio Nelson Calder, and Michel Wren were still recognized as half-breeds.

The question of James Birston's Indian ancestry arose when he filed his land claim application. Stating that his father was an Orkneyman, he described himself as a half-breed. John Flett gave an affidavit that he was acquainted with James's sister and believed that she was partly of white blood, although the mother had died ten or twelve years before he knew the family.

The Indian ancestry of Janette Birston followed her until the 1870 census, when she was living in the Falls Precinct of Hood River, near a knot of Red River half-breeds that included her sons, Magnus and William, and the related William Gibson, Henry Humphrey, and Thomas Thossell families. By then, the U.S. census had refined the definition into the terms of half- or quarter-breed. Twelve persons who called themselves half-breeds were still living in Washington County.

Scientific interest in miscegenation and racial hybridization became a late nineteenth-century concern. In 1878, Doctor V. Havard, the assistant surgeon general, described the Métis population of the United States. Havard believed there were about 300 half-breed offspring to be found on the French Prairie and in the valleys of the Willamette and "Kaoulis Rivers." The total living in Washington Territory was thought to number 250. His study, one of the earliest dealing with the social phenomenon of the Métis, expressed views that seem quaint today but were common at that time.

> The blood of the inter-marrying races becomes mixed in various proportions. A white man marrying a squaw begets half-breeds; those by successive marriages with either white or red blood will procreate quarter-breeds or quadroons in the second, and eighth-breeds or octoroons in the third generation. Marriages between the first and second generations are common, producing three-eighth breeds, either white or red. Of course, marriage between the offspring of the same generation, or between half–breeds, would not alter the relative proportion of either blood.
>
> From these possible combinations it is seen that the caste of Indian mixed bloods is neither fixed nor well defined. Like all hybrid races, it is liable to many changes, and generally tends to approximate one or the other of the types of its progenitors. If a district, inhabited by half-breeds or quarter-breeds, becomes settled by white people, and correspondingly abandoned by the Indians, the reversion, naturally, will be toward the white race,

and the red blood may become so diluted as to scarcely give traces of its presence either in the complexion or intellectual acquirements. . . . Again, if half-breeds live exclusively among Indians, the reversion will be towards the red type, so that a point is reached when it is impossible to discriminate between a mixed-blood and a pure-blood native. We find such individuals among the Northwestern tribes, of which they are a component part. Between these extremes is a large middle ground occupied by intermarried mixed-bloods, ranging from quarter white to quarter red, and including many half-breeds. These true representatives of the race are most numerous on the Red River of the North and the Winnipeg Basin.[356]

Some Oregon Métis kept ahead of intensified social pressure by moving on, but James Birston, Michael Wren, David Monroe, and Charles McKay persisted on the north Tualatin plains. Those Red River Métis passed into the bucolic Victorianism of the Tualatin plains because of their physical, social, religious, and cultural similarity with the dominant American community. They simply stepped into the background, and within a generation or so, their descendants forgot the Red River and the fur trade. Although Letitia McKay was honored as a pioneer mother, the history card that she filled out falsely indicated that her deceased husband had been "born at sea," a way of disguising his country origin. She gave her mother's name as Montour, which sounded a great deal more French Canadian than it actually was. But the bannock biscuits that her granddaughter learned to bake were an old Métis recipe, and Christmas packages of dried fruit and nuts were regularly sent to relatives on the American Blackfoot reservation. Her great-granddaughters believed that their mother and grandmother were so sensitive about the Indian heritage that they never spoke of it.

John Flett, the spokesman of the 1841 immigrants, took exception to implications that his friends of the crossing were tainted by Indian blood. A Nisqually friend, Henry Sicade, expressed the reasons for Flett's anger when he recalled in 1917 how it was to be recognized as an Indian:

> When the French came from Canada, explorers and teachers of religion, most of the men took native wives and settled down, their settlements being up the Willamette Valley and from the Columbia River to and including Puget Sound. There are many descendants of these early French settlers, and the women are noted for their prettiness, vivaciousness and general hospitality. There were never any wars or troubles with the French. I might add it is a common saying among us, that among whites

whose blood has Indian origin, some feature show. There children are apt to head to the aboriginal features; the most common give-away is a sudden stare when you meet a real Indian. My family and I have found ourselves put to much embarrassment when we travel bout, when people are much given to staring at us, noting everything we do or say; but that's another kind of story.[357]

A core of French-speaking, Catholic Métis of the Willamette Valley, now known as French Canadians, also held on. Their antiquity, determined respectability, and acculturation were finally accepted as a part of the prevailing culture. With solidly established Catholic churches as their foundations, they successfully resisted the social inundation and made the names of Gervais, LaBonte, and others respected.

Other children of the children of the trade gave up the struggle to adapt to new social, racial, or religious attitudes, and retreated to new homes on less critical frontiers. During the last quarter of the century, many refugees found niches in the marginal hill country of southern Oregon or on the sagebrush uplands of middle Oregon. Some went to the Grande Ronde Indian Reservation, others to the Umatilla or Nez Perce reserves. A little knot of Canadians retreated up the Walla Walla Valley, eventually ending up in Flathead country.

The mindless bureaucracy of the United States Indian service demanded a mathematical definition of the extent of Indian blood to determine who was entitled to inclusion on reservation rolls. This complex quartering of that exotic heraldry, and the compilation of elaborate lineages, entitled the successful to become perpetual wards of the state. Those who found a plausible trail through the forest of past relationships became official Indians, and Métis names can be found on most tribal rolls or in the sad little cemeteries. Those who wear them would find it difficult to explain the details of their heritage, because, in coming full circle, the Pacific Northwest Métis had to forget themselves.

Assimilation is a hard nut of concession and surrender. Accepting the dominant culture, or running away from it, was a dilemma that split the Métis soul. In an unrelenting world of racial absolutes, taking one path meant turning your back on the other side of your being. If the veil that they drew across their dark faces was white, it carried the risk of the resurfacing of an embarrassing memory, exclusion from the lodge hall, a snide remark in the pool room. There could be an eloquent silence in the store where neighbor ladies came to trade their eggs. Buried secrets could follow like an inescapable shadow.

If the mask was beaded, acceptance was burdened by the distinctions between pure bloods and mixed bloods. Those were economic as well as social differences, because the Bureau of Indian Affairs relied on its crude percentage tables to determine the distribution of government handouts. The competition for tribal council office could become an excuse for wounding insinuations. Marginality was as disfiguring as a blatant birthmark, a sensitivity that had to be lived with because amputation of part of one's being meant the perpetual burden of buried consciousness and pretense. Métis men like Ranald McDonald or David McLoughlin who ran away from themselves often became wanderers, lonely recluses, and sterile bachelors. As self-outcasts they cut themselves off from the weed of their being and all too often wasted their genetic brilliance in alcoholic rivers of no return.

Jette Farm Sign, Champoeg, Oregon.

∽ 16 ∽

JOHN FLETT:
A MAN BETWEEN

Marginal men often serve as intermediaries between cultures in collision. Half-bloods warned against the loss of Indian culture, mixed bloods led and participated in the surge of the takeover, and Métis helped negotiate the dispossession. Beginning as children of ambiguity, some matured into partners in the hustling settlements while others withered on the reservations they helped define. North American history is replete with examples of the half-breed guide, the mixed-blood interpreter, the Métis courier, but such stereotypes fail to show how those men reconciled the conflicts of their own duality.

The first Métis sent across the Rocky Mountains by the Nor'westers went to prepare the western tribes to receive traders. Popular fixation on the captive Shoshone girl Sacagawea ignores the fact that it was her Métis husband whom Lewis and Clark hired. Charbonneau and the other Mandan resident, LePage, knew more about the upper Missouri than anyone else available to the explorers. The Astorians, the Nor'westers, and men of the Hudson's Bay Company used sons or daughters of the country to find their way and advance their business. The success of the American trapping/trading partnerships owed a good deal to their happy connection with western freemen. Iroquois mixed bloods going to St. Louis stimulated missionary interest in the Pacific Northwest.

On the other side of the equation, there were mixed bloods and squaw men who had firsthand experience with the realities of eastern dispossession and warned western tribesmen of the danger. When their activities conflicted with the interests of the new order, the myth of the untrustworthy half-breed was confirmed. As early as 1841 Baptiste Dorion circulated a rumor to the Cayuse that "the Americans were coming to make war upon them and take their country." His joke referred to the straggling Bidwell-Bartleson party, but the tribesmen took it to heart. At Tiloukait's fishing camp on the Grande Ronde River, another mixed blood, the Iroquois Joe Gray, told the Cayuse that the missionaries were making them miserable and ought to pay for the lands they appropriated. At Henry Spalding's Lapwai Mission, the transplanted Delaware Tom Hill echoed that warning. In western Montana, Jemmy Jock Bird tried to discourage Jesuit intrusions by encouraging Protestant competitors. Those forecasts went beyond misanthropy because the prophets knew what had been lost when the eastern tribes were driven across the Mississippi River. It is doubtful that the western folk could fully comprehend the implications, but the pioneers did, and they damned the half-breeds as troublemakers.[358]

Mixed bloods participating in the treaties of cession also helped salvage something for a world in retreat. Leadership on the newly created reservations often devolved on relatively sophisticated mixed bloods who were better equipped to deal with government men.

Métis participation in Pacific Northwest Indian affairs was a complex blend of honor and dishonor, of good intention gone wrong, and unavoidable tragedy. Ironically, Dorion, the mixed blood who warned the Cayuse to beware of intruding missionaries, returned in a few years to stomp down the fallen Cayuse who had taken his advice. Tom McKay helped interpret the Cayuse Laws and later returned as a soldier to enforce them. His son, William C. McKay, served as secretary for the Yakima treaty and later fought Indians resisting containment.

John Flett, who served the Indian superintendencies of Oregon and Washington, left a record of painful disillusionment. He was the son of George Flett of Firth, Mainland, Orkney, who came to the Saskatchewan River for the Hudson's Bay Company in 1796 and took the Métisse daughter of James Peter Whitford as his country wife. After twenty-five years of faithful service, George was declared excess to the needs of the combined organization, and at the age of forty-seven he gave up the only career he had ever known to start over in the Red River settlement.[359]

By 1835 the limitations of a dead-end community led Flett to load his wife, six sons, and one daughter into carts that they drove to the St. Peter's River (Minnesota). They sought more promising prospects in the United States. Finding only one person at the unpromising place called Pig's Eye (St. Paul), the family drifted

John Flett, settler in Pierce County, W.T. —Elwood
Evans, *History of the Pacific Northwest: Oregon and
Washington* (Portland: North Pacific Publishing, 1889).

on to the lead-mining region around Dubuque and Galena. But that roughneck mining community was too much to endure, and they doubled back to the Chicago portage, and on to Sault Ste. Marie.[360]

By winter 1835–36, Black Hawk and his band had been defeated, and most eastern tribes were being relocated west of the Mississippi River. A few remnant Ojibwa still worked the old Soo rapids fishery, and in the smoke of their drying fires Baptist, Methodist, Episcopalian, and Catholic missionaries trolled for souls.[361] Nineteen-year-old John Flett was sympathetic toward Indians beset by jealous, conflicting dogmas whose only point of agreement was that Indian beliefs had to go.[362]

Failing to find an alternative home during their circle tour, the Fletts returned to the Red River settlement, where a Company officer gloated over the defeated dream. "Old Flett . . . with a bag of 800 dollars on his back set out to find 'el dorado' below St. Louis [but] now intends planting his tent permanently on the upper part of our late Experimental farm—[he] brings news of Yankee roguery in the back states."[363]

No surprise then that three of George Flett's sons signed Duncan Finlayson's colonial contract in spring 1841. David Flett was married to Letitia, the daughter of William Hemmings Cook, a retired chief factor. James Flett was the husband of Chloe Bird, whose sister Charlotte was his brother John's wife.

The Flett brothers became the first colonists to abandon Nisqually and follow William Baldra to the Tualatin plains. David and James found choice locations on the north plains, but John Flett was attracted to the highly prized beaver-dam soil on the west side of Wapato Lake.[364] The marshes of this seasonal lake supported camas beds that drew the last survivors of the Twality band of Kalapuya Indians each root-digging season.

The U.S. naval observer W. A. Slacum estimated that there were about 1,200 Kalapuya Indians in 1836–37. Four years later, Lieutenant Charles Wilkes of the United States Exploring Expedition thought that the number had dropped to 600. By 1846 the Twality band could count only sixty souls, half of them men.[365]

Dr. Elijah White, who was previously attached to the Methodist mission, returned to Oregon in fall 1842 with the appointment of U.S. Indian subagent for the Oregon country.[366] Two years later he was approached by the deeply concerned leader of the northern Kalapuya.

> The chief of the Twality Plains, whose orderly conduct and that of his clan did honor to the Nez Perce Laws, and the engage-

ment we had mutually entered into . . . invited me to come and
see him and his people; he said all was not right in his lodge; his
tribe divided, and all was not right; his influence was waning
and some of his people were becoming very bitter toward the
Americans.

The camas, their principal dependence for food was cut off
last season by reason of drought; and the deer are hunted so
much by the late hungry western immigrant riflemen that they
have become wild, poor, and few in number.

The old man's gun was broken and he could not even hunt in
competition with the newcomers. White learned later that in
desperation the Kalapuya killed and ate a settler's cow. On the
owner's complaint, the executive committee of the provisional
government called out the militia. This reluctant constabulary
stopped six miles short of the Indians, made a few heroic ges-
tures, and went home. But that was enough to bring in the fright-
ened Twality chief, who confessed to killing the ox because his
people were starving.

He told the agent:

I am a true man and carry an honest heart. . . . I am ashamed to
see a white man's face; they look cold at me and shake the head.
I can not bear it. . . . I can not live so; I come to you to help me, I
do not want such feeling to exist, nor do I want to be hunted as
a bear or wild beast for slaughter. I stand here a wisher for peace,
willing to have you dictate the terms but wish to have it remembered that we were distressed with hunger.

White gave the old man a letter and sent him to make amends
with the owner, who magnanimously took the Indian's broken
gun and eight horses as reparations.[367]

In 1846 the experienced mountaineer Doc Newell, whose wife
was Nez Perce, wrote:

[The Indians] are with us and among us and anxiously awaiting
the time when the government will come to treat with them for
their lands as they have been told will be done. Their long pa-
tience and kind treatment to the settlers when they had the
power deserves credit. But few depredations have been committed by them considering all the circumstances. They are generally poor and quiet, have little inclination to work the land, in
fact do nothing in that way for themselves but rove from fishing to mountains in search of something to eat.[368]

When writing about a meeting between the Twality Indians
and neighboring settlers on 24 May 1847, A. T. Smith gave no
indication of what was discussed, or if his neighbor, John Flett,
participated.[369] After the murder of the Whitman missionaries,

resentment of the Indians hardened, stray natives were murdered at the Cascades, and the Indian town at the Willamette Falls eel fishery was burned. The volunteers returned even more intolerant of local tribesmen.[370] In October 1849 the recently appointed territorial governor, Joseph Lane, showed that he was no fan of Indians by calling the sixty Twality Indians "a degraded, mischievous and thievish set," luckily lacking arms, whose land title needed to be "extinguished."[371]

Congress authorized the appointment of commissioners to meet with the Indians west of the Cascade mountains. In the first treaty, concluded at Champoeg in April 1850, the Twality band ceded the country between the Yamhill and Tualatin rivers, an area embracing the present sites of Lafayette, Dayton, Newburg, McMinnville, Yamhill, and the ironically named Amity.

Land north of the Tualatin River was excluded because it had fallen under the domination of other tribesmen. The Klickitat Indians, who lived north of the Columbia River, often traveled down the west side of the Willamette Valley and contemptuously threw down the rail fences that got in their way. Due to prior claims, the treaty failed to be ratified by Congress and the Indians were left in their deplorable condition.

In 1850, one of the three Oregonians who served as peace commissioners during the Cayuse War was appointed United States Indian Superintendent for Oregon and Washington. Joel Palmer recognized that "settlers have taken and now occupy within this reserve all the lands susceptible of cultivation without regard for the occupancy of the Indians who in several instances have been driven from their huts, their fences thrown down, and property destroyed."[372]

The hogs rooting out the wapato and camas may have belonged to John Flett or his neighbor, William Dougherty, who taught the Chinook trade jargon to Flett. When Palmer met the tribesmen at Wapato Lake in March 1854, John Flett acted as his interpreter because the Indians trusted him to accurately transmit their feelings.

The Indians agreed to cede their lands to the United States in exchange for forty acres on a yet to be determined reservation, where they would be provided with schools, hospitals, and vocational guidance. But the distant Congress found even this modest agreement too expensive.[373]

In August, Palmer, Flett, and six other men rode over the Barlow Road and south along the east side of the Cascades to Klamath

Lake. After confronting the notorious Modoc Indians who had been attacking wagon parties, the superintendent's party was home by the end of the month. They took the trail again to the Umpqua Valley treaty, where Chris Taylor acted as Palmer's interpreter. On 4 January 1855, when the superintendent met the upper Willamette Valley Kalapuyas and Mollalas at his Dayton home, Flett helped bring the costs down to a figure acceptable to Congress. The treaty was finally proclaimed on 10 April, but before the Indians could be moved, the Yakima Indian War erupted in the plateau country. That was not a good time to announce that the Grande Ronde Indian Reservation was located so close to the settlements.

Flett, who joined the Palmer superintendency out of need for a paying job, discovered that he could not blind his conscience to what was happening to the native peoples. His letters and reminiscences go beyond experience and reveal deeper feelings. He was disturbed by the callous treatment that the Indians were receiving and worked beside Palmer to mitigate the impact.

Pacific Northwest Indian matters could be divided geographically into coastal, valley, and plateau situations. In recently created Washington Territory, the Puget Sound and shore tribes were tied to, and jealous of, accustomed fishing places, which their treaties generally recognized. Those agreements were accomplished by Governor Isaac Stevens, who failed to foresee how fisheries would become the object of later dispute. The coastal tribes of Oregon were relocated on the Siletz reservation near the familiar shore.

Already thinned by epidemics, the western valley peoples moved around in localized seasonal harvesting cycles. Palmer meant to concentrate them on the Grande Ronde reservation in the foothills of the Coast Range.

Bringing Coyote's people to heel was quite something else. The plateau nations of the Klickitat, Yakima, Cayuse, Walla Walla, Palouse, and Spokane were accustomed to ranging widely. Insulated from degrading intimacy with the pioneer population, they were in a less accepting frame of mind. The Nez Perce, who straddled the Washington and Oregon jurisdictions, had old ties to the Flathead country. Because his wards rode across the border, the Oregon superintendent was obliged to attend the meeting that Governor Isaac Stevens of Washington called in the Walla Walla Valley.

The Klickitat flatly refused to attend, and those tribes that did come were sullen and belligerent. Flett recalled electric tension

Arrival of the Nez Perce at the Walla Walla Council, 1855. —Washington State Historical Society.

Chiefs at dinner during the Walla Walla Council, 1855. —Washington State Historical Society.

when a famous Blackfoot war chief rode around the camp displaying a bunch of fresh scalps on a pole and assuring the plateau delegates that his people were prepared to help their brothers resist the whites. Flett feared that frustrated warriors would kill the small treaty party.[374]

Governor Stevens began by explaining the United States' rights of discovery and international agreement, but assured the mystified Indians that his country had no desire for a war to prove them. Astute Indian leaders, who saw through the pretentious government man, had to recognize that he spoke for the great tribe of the Americans, but they were not convinced to sell the mother earth.

When he saw the issue hanging in dangerous balance, Palmer resorted to the thinly veiled threat of inevitability. Repeating those bitter words, John Flett told the Indians that the white men held the country by right of conquest and numerical superiority. The Indians' only option was to cede most of their ranges and agree to live on designated reservations. Biting their lips until they bled, the treaty chiefs came to the table and made their marks.

It wasn't the loss of land that cut so deep. Most reservations would still encompass more space than Indians could fully utilize. What galled was the idea of containment, of being fenced and harnessed in a way they never chose.

Flett's Red River cousin John Whitford was also present at the treaty, as Stevens's agent to invite the fierce Yakima. Billy McKay, the educated son of the deceased Tom McKay, was the secretary of the treaty council. Another local Métis, Narcisse Raymond, represented the French-Canadian and Métis settlers living in the middle Walla Walla Valley, whose duality made them suspect as Indian sympathizers.

When the negotiations were finished, Stevens proceeded eastward to deal with the Blackfeet, and the Oregon delegation returned by way of The Dalles. There, in June, they brought the Wasco Indians into legal relationship with the United States.[375]

The Indian treaties in which John Flett participated included the Rogue River treaty, 15 November 1854; the Shasta treaty at the mouth of Applegate Creek, 18 November 1854; the Umpqua and Kalapuya treaty at Calapooya Creek, 29 November 1854; the Kalapuya treaty at Dayton, 4 January 1855; the Mollala treaty at Dayton, 9 January 1855; the Willamette bands treaty at Linn City, 19 January 1855; the Santiam bands treaty at Dayton, 23 January 1855; the Walla Walla treaty, 9 June 1855; the Yakima treaty, 9 June 1855; the Nez Perce treaty, 11 June 1855; and the middle Oregon tribes at Wasco, near The Dalles, 25 June 1855.[376]

Their tribal constituents felt that the returning delegates had betrayed them by giving away the mother earth. By October, the Yakimas had murdered their Indian agent, nearly overpowered a punitive army column, and were committed to war. The puny federal military force was inadequate to deal with the situation, and the volunteer militia was called out. Settlers throughout the region grew increasingly fearful.

Klickitat Indians living just across the Columbia River seemed to threaten the settlers on the Tualatin plains. Reports that a large band of those malcontents lurked near the mouth of the Lewis River led apprehensive settlers to erect a stockade around the Hillsboro courthouse, "for the protection of their females." Another palisade sprouted around the Forest Grove Academy, and a third defensive stronghold guarded John Flett's house at Wapato Lake. Tension ran high until someone had the common sense to cross the river, where he found thirty equally terrified Indians who readily agreed to disarm and live under supervision.[377]

In the hysterical public reaction to the call for volunteers, Flett saw the wild threats and sanguine vows thrown at the conciliatory Oregon Indian superintendency.

> In the eventful winter of 1855-6 and immediately preceding the time . . . I was in the Oregon Indian service employed as an interpreter by General Joel Palmer, Superintendent of Indian Affairs for the Territory. Two encampments were under my charge besides the one at my home, which was composed of Klickitats who had refused to go either to Fort Vancouver or the encampment at Milton, Oregon. Chief McKay with six young men and their women had been living in a remote part of Sauvies Island. He became very saucy and it was generally believed that his presence there was to enable him to communicate information to the hostile on their war path, and to the Indian spies visiting the white settlements in the Upper Willamette. The Vancouver and Milton agents had failed to control him and his discontented band, or to effect their coming to either of those encampments. I received orders from General Palmer to move them if possible to the encampment at my place. This had been accomplished and they had been disarmed. They however continued restless and required the closest watching.[378]

As the war east of the mountains became general, another conflict developed between the Rogue River Valley Indians and obnoxious miners. Palmer and his staff faced the difficult task of limiting the damage by drawing as many tribesmen as possible to a neutral place, where they would be removed from the temptation of war and protected from rampaging whites.

Turning his camp over to Fred Florey on 5 January 1856, Flett rode south with Palmer to defuse the Rogue River War. Rain driven by a cold wind cut their faces as they came to Ford's Crossing on the swollen Rickreall River. The ferryman not only refused to cross them but also threatened to have 500 men waiting if the superintendent tried to bring any damn Indians into the middle valley. Palmer and Flett swam their horses across the river.

At the Umpqua River, Flett rode ahead to meet the Indian leaders: Chief Joe, head Chief Jackson, and two others whom he convinced to bring their people under the superintendent's protection.

> So great was the anger and opposition of the white people of the Willamette in having these savages brought to their door, so loud their threats against both Indians and agents, that it was deemed prudent to ask General Wool [the U.S. Army commandant] for an escort and guard [to move the Rogue Indians north].

Leaving Agent Metcalf to conduct the removal to the Grande Ronde Indian Reservation, the superintendent's party rode ahead but found that enraged valley settlers refused shelter at four

Fort Yamhill blockhouse from Grande Rhonde reservation, 1856. —Author's photo.

243

houses. Flett never forgot that 400-mile round-trip through the saturated country where "the ice . . . would not bear our horses, [and] the snow in places was four inches deep."

During Flett's absence, the renegade Klickitat Chief McKay murdered one of his own men just behind Flett's house and broke into the stores. The ammunition carried off by the murderers was believed sold to the hostiles.

A thaw and warm weather allowed Metcalf to herd 400–500 Indians north. Supplied with beef but no flour, the tribesmen developed diarrhea, and many died along the way. To help supervise them, Flett moved to the Grande Ronde Agency. He found that there was little he could do to alleviate the suffering.

Burdened by his part in bringing them to this terrible place, Flett watched the pitiful survivors of Chief Jackson's band die. The chief's sister was a shaman who danced, sang, and made magic in efforts to cure her people. When her desperate ministrations failed, sorrow-crazed tribesmen hacked her to pieces behind the agency building. When some of the Indians were relocated to the Siletz reservation, Flett saw an old woman carried into the brush and left to die.

The 1856 census of the Grande Ronde Indian Reservation recorded a total of 1,925 Indians, including 909 southern Umpqua and 600 surviving Kalapuya. A year later, the total had dropped to 1,495. No more than 3,000 Indians remained of all the tribes that had once occupied western Oregon. Saving those few cost Palmer his superintendency, and John Flett his home. His neighbors wanted no truck with an Indian sympathizer.

An alternative to community hostility arose through Cushing Eells, one of the Presbyterian missionaries driven out of eastern Washington by the Whitman massacre and the recent Indian war. Eells was concerned that opportunists were moving in on the abandoned Waiilatpu property. On 3 October 1857 he wrote to the secretary of the American Board of Commissioners for Foreign Missions proposing a solution:

> A thought I will take the liberty to suggest is that all efforts for the moral improvement of the Indian will doubtless be effected by the character and habits of the Indian Superintendent and agents. In this respect a loss has been sustained by the removal of Gen. Palmer. There is a half-caste man residing in this country by the name of John Flett. He received his early training at the Red River settlement—has been for some ten years a worthy and esteemed character with remarkable correctness and facility. Under General Palmer he had been a most successful assis-

Ellen Monroe Flett, immigrant of 1841. —Ellen Fleckleton Collection.

tant in Indian negotiations and removals. He understands to a considerable extent the Nez Perce language.

In receipt of your favor of July 1st it occurred to me that I knew no person from whom I should be likely to obtain more reliable information than Mr. Flett. I early sought an opportunity to see him. The interest which he manifested in the subject of your letter was gratifying. A few days later he made this proposition, viz, that if Mr. Walker and myself thought best, he would go as soon as practible and occupy the Waiilatpu mission station—thus protect it against the intrusion of unworthy and troublesome persons."[379]

The Board was prepared to engage Flett; however, there was a possibility that he might be called upon to conduct some of the chiefs to Washington. As it turned out, Flett's association with Palmer had ruined his expectations in the Oregon superintendency. Doc Newell shepherded the chiefs in their visit to the Great White Father, and Cushing Eells was sent to hold the Whitman mission as a farm until 1872.[380]

On 18 July 1857, John Flett sold some of the Wapato Lake land to his neighbor, Samuel Slott, and deeded the rest to his namesake son.[381] After sixteen years, he intended to return to the Nisqually area, where, like other fugitive Métis, he might find sanctuary on a neglected frontier.

John and his third wife, Ellen Monroe, relocated to South Prairie in Pierce County, Washington Territory, and later moved to Lakeview, only a few miles from the old Fort Nisqually farm. From 1862 until 1878 Flett was employed on the Puyallup Indian Reservation as a farmer and interpreter.

Not far to the north, the Puyallup reserve at the head of Commencement Bay had been established by Governor Stevens's ill-advised treaty of Medicine Creek in 1856. More enlightened than most, this treaty was one of a dozen, out of about 400 agreements between the United States and Indians, that mandated health services. In this case, that provision set up a fatal collision of science and belief. In 1863 Dr. Spinning worked with the tribesmen, blending medicine and ethnocentricity to discredit the native shamans. By 1871 he had finally succeeded in having native doctors banned from practicing.

It was mystifying why so many young Indians died. Indian Agent Edwin Eells knew of twenty out of fifty-two Indian families with no surviving children. Perhaps it could be explained because the tribesmen were rotten with syphilis and other obnoxious diseases, but why did the young people wither at maturity?

In 1872 the Clark County Medical Society heard that "all careful observers are fully satisfied that the mixture of races results in unhealthy and short-lived offspring." Perhaps they nodded in sage agreement, never realizing that it was one of their colleagues who may have been contributing to the problem. The agency doctor used a combination of mercury-iodide and arsenic to treat syphilis. He was unintentionally poisoning his patents.[382]

On 23 November 1876, the chiefs and headmen of the Puyallup Indian tribe and reservation entered into an agreement with the Northern Pacific Railroad allowing the right of way for a branch line from Tacoma to the Puyallup coal fields. John Flett witnessed the signature of a subchief named Joseph Yall. The following year, another Puyallup known as Pago-wilish gave his English name as Richard Yell. It appears Joseph and Richard were related to Flett's trail companion, the Red River immigrant Toussaint Joyelle.[383]

During his career in the Indian service, John Flett watched the dispossession of the Northwest Indians and helped shuffle the last of them to reservations, where their poverty and cultural disintegration were kept out of sight. He found the Puget Sound reservations discouraging and worked in a modest way to improve conditions. Saddened by what he had seen, Flett neared the end of his life without forgetting the changes that had adversely affected the native people.

Acknowledging his participation in significant events of Pacific Northwest history, John Flett became one of the founders of the Washington State Historical Society. Among the several reminiscences that Flett contributed to the Tacoma papers was an old injustice that he refused to allow to go unchallenged.

Cashing in on an undeserved reputation as pioneer missionaries in the Pacific Northwest, the J. P. Richmond family published a version of their experiences in the *Pacific Christian Advocate,* which included slighting remarks about the racial inferiority of the Red River half-breeds. Flett indignantly responded. "There were 17 families and but one Indian woman among them. Three of the women of the party are still living. I cannot account for the desire of the reverend gentleman to see an Indian in every family but his own, unless he has Indian on the brain."[384]

John Flett died at his Lakeview home on 12 December 1892, but the family name is still conspicuous around Tacoma through the family dairy operation.

Flett's career was not a complete model of the marginal man tortured by the opposing forces of a dual origin. As the son of a transplanted Orkney laborer and a Métisse daughter of the country, he grew up insulated from close association with his Indian heritage. His writings do not suggest that he ever thought of himself as anything except a white man. His sympathies grew from the accident of his location near the Wapato root diggers, his facility in Indian language, and the chance of a job. But what he saw in the painful process of Indian dispossession compelled John Flett to try to mitigate that terrible impact.

∽17∽

A Dispersed Community

After the Indian wars of 1855–56 and 1858–59 stifled the resentment of the plateau tribes, the old Flathead country began attracting the jetsam of the fur trade and the flotsam of the gold rush. By 1 August 1860, the mountain interior between Fort Benton on the upper Missouri and Fort Walla Walla on the middle Columbia was linked by the Mullan Road. Children of the country returned to the places of their birth and youth, and newcomers filtered north from the Oregon Trail, which had become almost a year-round highway. That thin line of contact stretched from Fort Laramie to The Dalles, tying together entrepreneurial way stations like Fort Bridger and the several river crossings where ferrymen lived with their native wives. The last British stores still trading were Fort Colvile; Fort Shepherd, on the border; and Fort Connah, just below Flathead Lake.

Ranching developed when traders along the immigrant road salvaged worn-out livestock, restored them on free grass, and traded the fresh animals to the next batch of overlanders. Before long, those road traders were driving their herds into the lush valleys of western Montana.

Richard Grant, the former Hudson's Bay Company man at Fort Hall, and his wife, Helene McDonald, brought their boys, Johnny and James, to the Beaverhead country. In spring 1858 they dropped over the divide into the Deer Lodge Valley.[385] The "tail" of followers of Laird Grant included Antoine Pourrier, the budding entrepreneur Louis R. Maillet, and Thomas Pambrun and his Snake wife, Margaret. Others in that area whose names suggest mixed ancestry were Antoine Courtei (Courtin?) and two big transplanted Delawares, Jim and Ben Simons. They traded with the Snakes who dared to come north after treaties emasculated the terrible Blackfeet. The Shoshone marksman Pushigan, who cleaned out the competitive shooters at Grantville in 1861, was a brother of the Lemhi chief Tendoy and of Johnny's wife, Catharine. Ten lodges of displaced Nez Perce also wintered nearby.[386]

Moving to the place where the Little Blackfoot River enters the Clark Fork, the Grants built cabins by 1859 and trailed a herd all the way to Sacramento, California, the next year. When his herds grew to 1,400 head, John Francis Grant was locked into ranching.[387] Johnny stayed in the Deer Lodge Valley, where the Grant-Kohrs Ranch is now a National Park Service site.[388]

Two itinerant Virginians, Granville and James Stuart, trailed cattle from the immigrant road in fall 1860. Two other entrepreneurs packed a trading outfit from Walla Walla on seventy-five Cayuse ponies and opened a store at Hell Gate, which put them in competition with Major John Owens's ten-year-old business at the former St. Mary's Catholic mission. Unfortunately, Fort Owens was thirty-five miles south of the new Mullan Road, and the winter of 1859–60 was the last good year of business there.

Over the next couple of years, the Stuarts recorded the names of Bercier, Oliver LeClair, young Michel LeClair, Le Gris, Joe Piou, Decoteau, Dave Contois, Louis Descheneau, and Baptiste Quesnell. Americans with Indian wives were Tollman (Frank Tallman from the Walla Walla Valley settlement), Frank (Francis) Newell, and the trail trader Bob Dempsey, who had a Snake wife. Pierre Ish Tabbobo was also married to a Snake woman, while Thomas Adams had a brief relationship with Louise, the Flathead stepdaughter of Lone Penny. As marriage became epidemic in the Deer Lodge Valley, James Stuart could not resist the wife of a Snake who had been killed by two Flatheads. Her fair complexion, red cheeks, and brown hair suggested that she was at least half white. Three days after Stuart ransomed her from the usual indignities visited upon Flathead captives, he decided to "marry" her. His brother Granville held out as a bachelor until the sap began to rise about the first of May 1862.[389]

When elections were held in July 1862, the three polling places in Missoula County, Washington Territory, were Fort Owens, Hell Gate, and Gold Creek. Another settlement had started about twenty miles west of Hell Gate, where Louis Broun and his wife, "a fairly civilized Indian woman," had settled their family in 1858. Frenchtown began to take shape when the Brouns were joined by Baptiste DuCharme and Mose Reeves, who built a cabin.[390] Reeves had a contract to carry mail between Walla Walla and Fort

Benton, and it was convenient to have his wife at the mid-point to cancel stamps.

Within a year, Robert A. Peletier built a house and returned to St. Louis to bring out his wife and other relatives in fall 1861. Within ten years there were fifty families of New Brunswick and Quebec French-Canadian extraction living in the Frenchtown area in houses that were put together in the old French building style of hewn logs joined by dovetail notching.[391] The names preserved in the St. Louis Catholic church register and cemetery—Deschamps, Jacques, Lucier, Boyer, and Hamel—bear striking similarities to those of the Northwest Métis, but there are no readily apparent connections beyond a shared religion.

Louis Broun and his wife had wintered at the head of Flathead Lake in 1847–48, but they stampeded to the California gold strike in company with Antoine Plante, Camille Launcelot, and Francois Finlay. Michquam Finlay and his Kutenai wife were more resistant to temptation and were living in Montana in 1849–50. Nicholas and Patrick Finlay, who fled from the Spokane country at the beginning of the Cayuse War, relocated to the Jocko Agency when it was established.[392] The returning forty-niners in-

Jocko Catholic Church and cemetery at Arlee, Montana, with Mission Mountains in the background. Last resting place of many descendants of the mountain freemen. —Author's photo.

cluded Francois Gravelle, the Revais brothers, Joe Ashley, and a former American mountaineer named Jack Fisher. A native of Savoy, France, Gravelle came from California to marry a Kutenai woman, the sister of Ashley's wife. Their descendants became leaders of the Grasmere Kutenai band.

Joe Ashley was the son of Jean Pierre Ashley. Marriages under that name recorded at St. Ignatius mission include the names Irvine, Finlay, and the Flathead daughter of the former HBC man Francis Ermatinger.[393]

Basil Finlay *dit* Pial ranched near the north end of Flathead Lake, in what was noted as the "Half-Breed Settlement" on the 1864 DeLancy map of Montana Territory. It was his daughter, Emmerence Marengo, who retained much of the folk memory about the northern tribes.

The Finlay family reassembled in the former Flathead country. Abraham, who brought dispatches from the Olympia capital of Washington Territory to the Salish-Kutenai Indian Agency in 1857, settled in the Bitterroot Valley three years later, where Augustin *dit* Koostah and Dominic were living.

It was the Colvile resident George Taylor who took the 1860 United States census for Spokane County, Washington Territory. Between 16 and 25 September he traveled to the lower end of the Bitterroot Valley to count the former trappers and old HBC men who were living near the Jesuit mission and at Hell Gate. Among the numerous "Phinlays" or Finlays, Taylor named Augustine (aged sixty), Francois (forty-five), Abraham (forty-four), Bonaparte (forty-three), Peter (forty-one), Jacob (thirty-seven), Nicholas (thirty-two), James, Joseph (thirty), Baptiste (thirty), Alex (twenty-seven), and Dominic (twenty-seven).

The tribe of Jacco persisted into the next century. On 16 August 1940 the Montana *Missoulian* ran a story under the headline "Indians to Dance in the Blackfoot," which mentioned that eighty-year-old Sam Finlay, Jacco's grandson, participated in the ceremonies.[394]

But it was Francois Finlay *dit* Benetsie who made the greatest impact on that part of the world. After going to the California mines with Antoine Plante, Finlay and his Kutenai wife returned in 1852 to the Deer Lodge Valley, where they found traces of gold.[395] Francois took the nuggets to the Fort Connah trader Angus McDonald, who advised him that as a British citizen he could not prove a claim and that he had better keep his find quiet. That was a forlorn hope because McDonald's teamster, little Joe Morelle, also found gold near Lake Pend Oreille and started the stampede of miners that contributed to the Yakima Indian War of 1855–56. McDonald shipped seventeen pounds of gold dust to Victoria from mines near where the Clark Fork entered the Columbia, but another six years passed before Finlay's Gold Creek discovery attracted the interest of Granville and James Stuart and others. Blessed with good fortune, Finlay made another discovery, on Wild Horse Creek in the upper Kootenay country, in 1863. But this time he took his poke to the HBC trader at the Tobacco Plains.

The Montour brothers were split by their tribal affiliations. Louis Bob and his Mollala wife lived on the Grande Ronde reservation, but his brother George returned to the Flathead country and married a Nez Perce woman. They trafficked with local Indians until George was killed, under mysterious circumstances, during the year of the Nez Perce retreat.[396]

The great southward loop of the Kootenay River and the familiar Tobacco Plains area housed several children of the shadows. David McLoughlin, son of the HBC chief factor John, crowded close to the Canadian border at Porthill, Idaho. After ranging the world and helping open Japan to the west, Archibald McDonald's part-Chinook son, Ranald, returned to the mountain lodge near old Fort Colvile. Others were of the clan of Angus McDonald, whose legacy in western Montana and British Columbia included his daughter, Christina, an Indian trader and astute businesswoman in her own right. Although Forbes Barkley followed his father-in-law, John McLoughlin, to Oregon City, some of his sons went to the Blackfoot reservation in Montana, as did the descendants of the Fort Walla Walla trader Pierre Pambrun.

Fort Victoria, on Vancouver Island, became the HBC fallback point after George Simpson recognized the appetite of the Columbia River bar for HBC shipping. The governor had personally learned the impracticality of navigation on the Fraser River. The tight little rock-bound harbor at the tip of Vancouver Island commanded the Strait of Juan de Fuca and seemed a better port for the conduct of maritime business.

James Douglas, the second in command at Fort Vancouver, inherited the job of establishing the new operation. Douglas drew his construction crew from HBC servants at the depot and Fort Nisqually. His assistant was young Joseph William McKay, an educated Rupert's Land Métis from the Red River settlement. His uncle was Charles McKay, who helped form the Oregon provisional government.

After the Oregon boundary decision, Joseph William McKay helped in the construction of Fort Victoria. By 1848 he had earned the rank of postmaster and was second in command the next year, when Douglas negotiated treaties with the local Indians. After exploring the Cowichan and Comox valleys, and establishing a fishery on San Juan Island, McKay went north in 1852 to the recent coal discoveries at Nanaimo. The bastion he ordered built to protect the miners from local Indians still guards that harbor.

As proprietor of a farm at Cadboro Bay near Fort Victoria, McKay was entitled to a seat in the Vancouver Island House of Assembly. When politics and cultural life were upset by the Fraser River gold rush, McKay was sent to take charge of the Thompson River district, and lived at Kamloops for six years. Until 1878 he was in charge of the Kootenay district operations from Fort Yale and earned promotion to chief factor. After extensive private business operations led to his dismissal from the Company, McKay served as Indian agent on the Northwest coast and at the Kamloops and Okanogan agencies. He personally inoculated 1,300 Indians against smallpox. In 1893 he was assistant to the superintendent of British Columbia Indian affairs. Joseph William McKay was one of the few mixed bloods to climb to full partnership in the Hudson's Bay Company and enjoy the status of an officer and gentleman.[397]

Many of the social distinctions that shadowed the lives of Pacific Northwest mixed bloods came from the attitudes expressed by Governor George Simpson and perpetuated by his staff. Simpson was a field superintendent, and his officers plant managers, but their control over the labor force imposed pre-Victorian English social attitudes upon a captive work force.

Due to the wealth of documentary evidence available in the massive collection of HBC business records, Métis studies have fixed on the lives of the officer class as representative of the fur trade population. The Pacific Northwest was different because that cant was modified by the egalitarian input of Yankee associations. Those were old English and New England social values turned wicked. It was racial prejudice rather than social pressure that the western freemen endured from overland pioneers. There is a tortured track of that experience implied in James McMillan's retirement from the trade he had helped develop. In 1817 he "put off" his country wife, Kilakotah, upon the undoubtedly bribed Louis LaBonte, and took furlough in Britain. When McMillan returned to the undemanding job of operating the Red

River experimental farm, he was married to a proper Scottish wife.

The new Mrs. McMillan's young brother, Archibald McKinlay, was taken into Company service about the same time that she came to the Red River, and was sent to York Factory, where he received advice from the aspiring arbiter of the new social order, James Hargraves. After being advised against taking "some petticoat or not petticoat as a playmate," the young clerk was sent west. McKinlay managed to confine his interests to casual relationships until 1836, when he became involved with Sarah Julia Ogden. She was the daughter of the former Snake Brigade leader, now a Thompson river trader, and his Salish wife.

McMillan's cast-off petticoat Kilakotah had a daughter by a previous union with the Astorian Mathews. The attractive daughter of the country was irresistible to another promising young clerk, George Barnston, but their union doomed his career to obscurity in distant places.

The tangled skeins of those fur trade interrelationships raised the social and legal question of the validity of country marriages. It had been nothing for Mathews or McMillan to put off their Chinook companions, or for the governor and McTavish to do the same east of the mountains. But in 1838 new social pretensions arrived at Fort Vancouver when the new post chaplain, the Reverend Henry Beaver, landed with his sternly religious wife. Undoubtedly sent to ensure that the West kept up with the development of Red River society, Beaver soon offended honorable husbands like Chief Factor John McLoughlin and Chief Trader Peter Skene Ogden.

Enraged by aspersions against his half-Ojibwa wife, Marguerite Wadin McKay, McLoughlin authenticated their union with civil and Catholic ceremonies, and gave Beaver a well-deserved caning. By refusing to legalize his marriage to Julia, Ogden created a legal loophole that his Canadian relatives later exploited to cheat her of his estate.

The more placating James Douglas allowed Beaver to confirm his relationship with the Métisse daughter of William Connolly. Amelia Douglas was embarrassed by her lack of English, but she spoke French, her mother's native Cree, and probably the Chinook jargon. Although the legitimacy of her father's country marriage to Susanne Pas de Nom was ultimately upheld in the courts of Canada, Amelia was not spared the aspersions of the Beavers, or the later disapproval of the first minister of the Church of England at Fort Victoria.

Fort St. James, British Columbia, one of the last fur trading posts in its original state.
—Author's photo.

The aptly named West Coast post became a stronghold of transplanted Victorianism. Lady Douglas overcame the embarrassment of her origin, and the Métisse daughters of the trader John Work learned to handle hoop skirts and teacups. Christina McDonald occasionally came to town from the Kootenay country to arrange her business and ride like a proper lady in the governor's carriage.

Victoria was the emphatic period to the final sentence of the Oregon Question, but a transverse relationship persisted. The ports of Portland and Victoria remained closely linked, just as the waters of Puget Sound connected Fort Nisqually and Seattle to New Westminster and Vancouver. Political abstractions aside, under the skin they were all Pacific Northwesterners.

Interior British Columbia preserved another example of Métis persistence. Son of a voyageur and an Iroquois mother, Jean Baptiste Lolo came west about 1817 as a North West Company interpreter; he worked for the HBC at Fort St. James in the New Caledonia district in 1822. Six years later, Lolo became involved in the marital affairs of the Thompson River trader Francis Ermatinger, and was sent in pursuit of his fugitive country wife and her Indian lover. Taking his orders literally, Lolo clipped the

Indian's ears and created a minor scandal that embarrassed Ermatinger's career.[398] When an unjust trader had Lolo flogged at Fort St. James in 1841, local Indians threatened reprisal, and the trader had to appoint him a chief. The next year, Father Demers baptized him as Jean Baptiste Lolo, but he was better known as St. Paul.

Although called a chief around Kamloops, St. Paul had no real authority among the Shuswap Indians, who regarded him as an untrustworthy trader. Lolo balanced power through his command of Indian language, minor authority, and sly manipulation of opportunity. Retiring from Company service in 1845, he became a trader and packer in his own right, with a horse range that was larger than the present Indian reserve. Later, during the gold rush, he ran a store at the mouth of Tranquille Creek. He died in 1868 at the age of seventy.[399] One daughter of his large family became the wife of the HBC trader John Todd and presumably made the transition into Victoria society.

Fuller details of the Métis experience in British Columbia require more pages than are available to this study, but there is one last knot in the buckskin string that plateau tribesmen used to recall past events. Julia, the stepdaughter of old Francois Rivet, became the country wife of Peter Skene Ogden very soon after he took charge of Spokane House in late fall 1818. She has been

Home of Archibald McKinlay and Sarah Julia Ogden, near Newberg, Oregon. —Helen Austin Collection.

described as Spokane, Flathead, or Nez Perce, with some kind of Iroquois kinship, and once told her daughter that her father was half-Crow.[400] When the Ogden family passed through Fort Colvile, they had Father Demers baptize their six-week-old son, Isaac. At that time the mother's name was recorded as Julie Spokane.[401]

After spending winter 1844–45 in England and Scotland, sans Julia, Ogden was sent back to the Columbia with two British undercover agents in tow. Recognizing that the mixed-blood population wasn't going to rise in defense of empire, the secret agents reported to London, and by September 1846 news arrived that the U.S.-Canada boundary was set at 49 degrees north latitude.[402]

Ogden and Douglas drew the unenviable duty of holding Fort Vancouver to the bitter end to salvage as much as possible from the settlement of HBC claims. The old fur trader was living at the McKinlay home overlooking Oregon City when he died on 27 September 1854. One of the foremost defenders of British aspirations is buried in American soil.

Champoeg School students, circa 1859, and teacher Samuel Willard King. —Helen Austin Collection.

Julia kept close to her stepfather's family, and when her step-brother, Joseph Rivet, died of alcoholism in 1852, she looked after his orphan son, Faubien. In a letter to his son-in-law, Archy McKinlay, Ogden wrote, "I hope the Old Lady will take care of his property," but revealed his own feelings by bequeathing the boy £100 to be paid in £20 annual installments.[403]

Because of Ogden's obstinate stand about marriage, his Canadian relatives were able to claim most of the estate. In 1862 the widow Ogden went to live with her daughter Sarah Julia and Archibald McKinlay at Lac la Hache in British Columbia. She is buried there in a quiet graveyard overlooking the lake. Some of her memories are preserved in a musty trunk, but those stretching back to forgotten Montreal parishes, the Missouri River, Spokane and the mountain hunt, the brigade trail, Oregon and French Prairie are mostly forgotten. British Columbia is richer for having her.

Closeup of Faubien Rivet, grandson of Francois Rivet. —Helen Austin Collection.

Gravestone of Julia Rivet Ogden at Lac la Hache, B.C. —Author's photo.

261

~18~

A PERSISTENT HERITAGE

I n listing the dead among the Red River colonists, John Flett
named Mrs. Le Blanc, although she actually came to Oregon
three years earlier under tragic circumstances. Nancy, called
Matooskie, was the Métisse daughter of Roderick McKenzie, and
the niece of Donald McKenzie. She had been the country wife of
John George McTavish, but in the fall of 1830 Governor George
Simpson and McTavish returned from furlough with English
brides. Matooskie was humiliated by being "turned off" without
warning. Outraged old fur traders forced McTavish into a settlement that was attractive to a Red River miller, Pierre Le Blanc,
who married her in the Catholic church on 7 February 1831.
Seven years later, the governor completed the house cleaning by
sending Le Blanc to the Columbia District. That tragic trip claimed
their five-year-old daughter on the Athabaska portage, and as their
boat risked the roiling Dalles des Mort on the upper Columbia
River, an upset drowned Le Blanc and three of the children. The
widow Le Blanc was a dependent of Fort Vancouver, according
to Flett, until she died at the Cowlitz in 1851.[404]

The McKenzie girls were star-crossed. Matooskie's sister
Arabella McKenzie had scandalized the Red River Academy by
seducing a young Indian student and getting pregnant. To quiet
the gossip, the embarrassed Reverend David Jones quietly married her off to John Clark Spence.[405] Arabella and John Clark
Spence arrived in the West with the Red River colonists, and
during the gold rush he became the luckless victim of
Goldsborough Bruff's amateur medicine.

John Calder, a former surgeon at York Factory, and Sarah
Humphrey, a daughter of the country, had a son born at the
Edmonton outpost of Painted Cree in 1806. The dramatic events
of the Napoleonic Wars must have impressed Calder, who named

the child Horatio Nelson.[406] Fifteen-year-old H. O. Calder went to work for the Hudson's Bay Company; he served at Cumberland House and York Factory between 1821 and 1824, but was cut off in the last round of staff reductions. Going to the Red River settlement, he married the widow Reine on 1 November 1830. She was the daughter of an officer named Budd and sister of a young Métis destined to become a notable missionary. Nancy's Swiss husband, Michael Reine, died in Company service, so she was pleased to have her three children under Calder's protection. Two boys, Michael and Charles Wren, came west with them in 1841.

After the disillusioned colonists left Nisqually, the Wrens stayed to work for the Company, under the watchful eye of a family friend. By October 1843, Charles had saved enough of his small salary to send a note for eight shillings to his mother. He eventually acquired a land claim in the Nisqually area, but during the Indian wars was suspected of aiding the hostiles. At the HBC claims hearings, the testimony of Charles Wren and others helped the Company collect $200,000 in compensation for its lost improvements.[407] His descendants persisted in the area, and their memory is preserved in the collections of the archives of British Columbia, Washington State, and St. Martin's College, Olympia.[408]

Michael Wren saved enough from working as a packer on the Cowlitz portage to go to the Tualatin plains and buy a claim. He married Christine, the daughter of his neighbor David Monroe, and settled down in Washington County to raise a family and be a model citizen.[409]

Nancy Calder wrote to her missionary brother on 14 March 1848 that she had already lost four of her children and now feared for the son who was off to the gold mines with Horatio. The family did not lag in developing their donation land claim, and the first surveys show that H. O. Calder had a respectable part under cultivation by 1851. Two years later, they sold half of the attractive property for $1,450. Later, apparently following the example of John Flett, the Horatio Nelson Calder family relocated to Pierce County, Washington Territory, where Horatio died in 1885 and Nancy a year later.

Family ties included Horatio's brothers, Peter and John Calder, who also served the Company in the Pacific Northwest. Sometime in the fall of 1841, John maintained that Governor Simpson gave him permission to locate at Nisqually with the colonists. Captain McNeill queried James Douglas about that because the Company had reinstated the regulation requiring discharged men to return to the place of their enlistment.[410] Obliged to make the long journey to the Red River settlement, Calder met and married Mary McKay, the widow of the murdered John Bird. With his new bride and her sons, Calder recrossed the mountains in 1843 or 1844 and located a claim near Fort Vancouver on the Fourth Plain. Five years later, John Calder was another casualty of the unhealthy California mines.

Wren's neighbor, the Inverness Scot David Monroe, married Nancy Ann Daley at Fort Churchill in 1830. Monroe was working as the York Factory cooper when Nancy died, and he had to find someone to look after his motherless children. He chose the washerwoman Betsy Rendall, who was said to be Indian but was more likely Métisse. She kept Monroe's baby in a "moss bag" or erect Indian cradleboard, according to the wife of the post factor.

In the eyes of Letitia Hargrave, an English woman who assumed the role of social arbitrator of Rupert's Land, Betsy's reputation was compromised by a succession of temporary husbands. Betsy's most recent mate, John Rendall, had abandoned her when his contract expired in the summer 1840. Mrs. Hargrave enjoyed gossiping about the washerwoman's checkered past, unaware that her own husband, James, asked to be remembered to Betsy with a kiss.

Four or five failed relationships led the disillusioned Betsy to suspect that her suitors were only interested in the eighty-eight pounds she had saved by working as a washerwoman. Nevertheless, she yielded to Monroe's proposal of marriage on 11 August 1841, and left with him the next year to make a fresh beginning in the less critical world of western Oregon.[411] She died on 5 December 1851, leaving six children.

Monroe's eldest daughter, Christine, married the substantial young Michael Wren, whose claim adjoined her father's, and her sister Catharine married Ebenezer Pomeroy, the son of a prominent American overlander of 1842. Ellen Monroe became the wife of an American named William E. Cooper. After he died in 1855, Ellen married John Flett and moved with him to Nisqually.

The name Flett also returned to the Colvile area. Nineteen-year-old Scottish-born Thomas Flett joined the HBC in 1833 and three years later was sent to Kootenay Post on the south side of the river, in the middle of the famed Tobacco Plain. Although 400 miles from Colvile, it was still south of the later boundary. There Flett traded furs, buffalo skins, deerskins, and "what was valuable" until he was reassigned to Fort Colvile in 1840, leaving old Berland in charge. Thomas spent another decade at Colvile; then he went to the Willamette Valley in 1851. In taking a place south of present Woodburn he was a bit removed from the center of the French-Canadian community but close enough to be within St. Louis parish.

His deceased Kutenai wife, Nancy, had given him a daughter named Clementia, who was about fifteen when he married Lizette Hubert on 22 June 1851. Six months later, Clementia was baptized so she could marry the widower Oliver Brisbois. An old friend from past times in the mountains, Isabelle Montour McKay must have been gratified to act as godmother. Another young daughter, Marguerite, married Auguste Douillet on 8 July 1856. Having accomplished the task of finding husbands for his daughters, and oppressed by disputes concerning his farm, Thomas Flett was ready to return to the Colvile area and take a land claim twenty-five miles south of the old fort.

In September 1865 Flett traveled to Fort Victoria to give testimony before the joint commission examining the claims of the Hudson's Bay Company and Puget Sound Company. His testimony was more straightforward than that of his old mountain associate, Angus McDonald. When McDonald was questioned about what could possibly justify the States paying a million dollars for the old Fort Hall site, he slid his tongue into the corner of a cheek and suggested its use as a game preserve.[412]

The bare facts of family relationships show how solidly mixed bloods fit into the established pioneer community. After farming until 1883, Monroe turned the place over to his children and moved to the nearby town of Forest Grove. He was a ninety-one-year-old respected member of that community when he died on 5 March 1891.[413]

Family histories also suggest that the Red River settlement continued feeding mixed bloods into the Oregon country between the recorded migrations of 1841 and 1854. Perhaps those settlers were part of what Governor Simpson must have enjoyed calling "the mania to move to the Columbia."

The second immigrant party from the Red River settlement in 1854 lacked political significance but was encouraged by Simpson as a means of eliminating undesirable half-breeds. When fed-up Métis had forced the free trade issue five years earlier, James Sinclair was a leader. Sinclair's trip to the California gold rush allowed Simpson's resentment to cool, and his return through the Oregon settlements suggested that the Walla Walla River landing was destined to become an important outfitting center for the inland empire. Disenchanted Métis from the Willamette Valley were already grazing cattle on those excellent pastures, but

Americans could not hold claims until the Indian title was extinguished. There was a brief window of opportunity for a British subject. Through some carefully circumspect arrangements with Simpson, Sinclair traded an appointment to Fort Walla Walla for his promise to bleed off more Red River half-breeds.[414]

About 100 persons—twenty-eight adult men, eleven married women, several unmarried women, and a goodly number of children and infants—assembled on the White Horse Plain at the end of May 1854. Sinclair's list included the names Bird, Birston, Brown, Campbell, Flett, Gibson, Hudson, Moar, Rowland, Sutherland, Taylor, and Whitford, but was noticeably lacking French immigrants.

After seven months on the trail, the travelers reached Fort Walla Walla on 16 December and split up. Some went north to Colvile or Spokane, and others descended the Columbia to join old friends and relatives on the Tualatin plains. Two of the new arrivals, William Gibson and William Rowland, were married to Elizabeth and Nancy Flett, and Roderick Sutherland was the husband of Letitia McKay's stepsister.[415]

There was a countermovement east of some well-known children of the fur trade. When Captain Cornoyer took over the command of Company K of the First Regiment of Mounted Volunteers, Antoine Rivais inherited the mixed-blood company and saw it through the end of the Yakima/Walla Walla War. He was a son of the Oregon country, born in 1816, who had settled on the French Prairie. After the Indian wars, Rivais settled at Ravalli, Montana, and died among his mother's Flathead tribesmen on 23 February 1886.[416]

Tom McKay's eastern-educated son, William, also climbed to respectability through the reservation system. During the American Civil War, Billy served as the agency physician at Warm Springs reservation, and from 1869 until his death on 2 January 1893 he conducted a private practice on the Umatilla reservation. The McKay brothers were warriors. One-eyed Alex was more like their father and earned a fleeting notoriety at the end of the Spokane Indian War. William and his younger brother Donal led scouts during the Modoc War. Afterward, billed as "Daring Donald McKay," Donal followed the theatrical circuit with a traveling medicine show.[417]

The most sophisticated son of the country returned to Oregon just in time to die. The life of Jean Baptiste Charbonneau bracketed the pioneer history of the region from the first exploration to the frontier decline. According to a knowledgeable Mandan trader, his mother, Sacagawea, died in 1812, and the baby who had crossed the continent on her back was taken to St. Louis for education. He was living in the traders' village at the mouth of the Kansas River in 1823 when a visiting German scientific traveler, Prince Paul of Wurttemburg, recognized the baby who figured in the journals of Lewis and Clark.

> Here I also found a youth of sixteen, whose mother, a member of the tribe of Sho-sho-nes, or Snake Indians, had accompanied the Messrs. Lewis and Clarke, as an interpreter, to the Pacific Ocean in 1804 to 1806. This Indian woman married the French interpreter of the expedition, Toussaint Charbonneau, who later served me in the capacity of interpreter. Baptiste, his son, whom I mentioned above, joined me on my return, followed me to Europe, and has since then been with me.[418]

Six years later, Baptiste, now a finished gentleman proficient in several languages, returned from Europe with his indulgent patron. It is uncertain why he engaged with the American Fur Company brigade of 1829, but during the years Charbonneau spent in the mountains, he acquired a full sack of adventures. At one time he was lost in Cache Valley above the Great Salt Lake for eleven days. In 1842 the explorer John Charles Frémont found him on an island in the South Platte River, guarding a stranded cargo of buffalo hides for Louis Vasquez and Andrew Sublette. Frémont was pleased to find that he could construct "a very good mint julep." The next summer Baptiste was driving one of the carts in the large hunting party fielded by the Scots sportsman William Drummond Stewart. The excursion paralleled the first great overland migration to the Oregon country.

As the mountain trade closed down, Baptiste Charbonneau marched to California with the Mormon Battalion. A year later, he was appointed alcalde for the Indian community near the mission of San Luis Rey. Baptiste was in good position for an early jump on the gold discovery, and he mined near Murderer's Bar, where Oregon mixed bloods soon appeared. Unsuccessful as a miner, Baptiste worked as a clerk at the Orleans Hotel in Auburn, California, in 1861. Five years later, he decided to leave California to try his luck in the recently discovered Montana mines. Traveling with two companions, Baptiste fell sick in southeastern Oregon and died at the small settlement of Inskip's ranch in Jordan Valley.[419]

These capsule biographies are meant to demonstrate the interlocked and lasting relationships between the Northwest mixed bloods. More important, genealogical tracking shows how hu-

Major N. A. Cornoyer, Adams, Oregon, veteran of Indian wars. —Elwood Evans, *History of the Pacific Northwest: Oregon and Washington* (Portland: North Pacific Publishing, 1889).

man bonds knitted the new Northwest together. It is unfortunate that the lineages of Americans with mixed ancestry are not so easily traced. Those first arrivals from the old French settlements of the Mississippi Valley were not that much different from their Canadian cousins. The upper Missouri River, like the north Saskatchewan, funnelled them to the passes through the mountains.

Later mixed bloods were swept in with the tide of overland immigrants. Perhaps one of them who came from the old coureur-de-bois retreats on the Illinois side of the Mississippi River can represent those unnamed. After working for the American Fur Company, Narcisse A. Cornoyer went to the California gold rush. Drifting into the Willamette Valley in 1851, he found French-speaking settlers and perhaps some distant relatives. Cornoyer was held in such high regard at the outbreak of the Yakima war that he was elected captain of Marion County Company K of the First Regiment of Oregon Mounted Volunteers. The returning war hero was a Marion County law officer until he shifted to the Indian service in eastern Oregon. From farming superintendent at the Umatilla Agency, Cornoyer rose to the position of agent and held that post from 1871 until 1880. His appreciative wards granted him 160 acres of land, and Narcisse continued farming on the reservation until his death on 31 March 1909.

By the end of the Civil War, the children of the shadows found it more and more difficult to apply their peculiar talents to a constricting world. Eastern critics and western frontiersmen made cruel references to "squaw men," white males with Indian wives. Arrangements tolerable on the frontier became laden with implications of miscegenation no longer acceptable to polite society. Like the term *half-breed,* which was no longer a proud designation, *squaw man* implied a slur. Wise men did not use the term face-to-face with the likes of the retired mountaineers Craig, Meek, or Newell, who were touchy about the honor of their Nez Perce wives.

After settling among his wife's people, William Craig performed useful services as an intermediary between government and tribe. Robert Newell and Joseph L. Meek were active in the pioneer community and provisional government, which sheltered their mates from a good deal of criticism. It was a later overlander, Nathan Olney, who made the error of taking a middle Columbia River Indian companion too late in the pioneer period to escape public criticism. Worse, he planted their home on the last miles of the Oregon Trail, where strangers could not miss his arrangement.

Olney's handy location earned him appointment as an Indian subagent to the Walla Walla Indians at the beginning of the plateau Indian wars. In conjunction with James Sinclair, he shared responsibility for expanding the hostilities. In his brief moment of saloon fame, Olney threw over the Tenino woman and formed a brief, disastrous relationship with Sinclair's widow.

Recognizing that his appointee had turned into a loose cannon, the Indian superintendent, Palmer, shunted Olney off to an obscure post on the southern Oregon coast, where his scandalous behavior finally resulted in complete dismissal. Olney returned to his Indian wife and eventually drifted to the Yakima reservation, where his descendants earned well-deserved respectability.

The reverse experience is shown in the career of Spokane Jackson. John W. Jackson rode in from Fort Hall in 1846 in company with one of ol' Daniel's grandsons, A. D. Boone. He gave his place of birth as Connecticut or New York. Perhaps he had become acquainted on the overland trail with Horace Hart, who was coming to visit his brother-in-law, the Presbyterian missionary Henry Spalding. The next year Jackson was packing for the Clearwater mission but left the doomed Whitmans three days before the killings began. Trapped by hostiles at Lapwai, Jackson and Hart considered fleeing across the mountains to the Missouri River but were rescued with the other survivors. Hart and Jackson joined Captain Maxon's company to help punish the murderers. When the army returned, Jackson tried unsuccessfully to collect $4,400 from Spalding for the work he had done at Lapwai and the loss of his pack train.[420]

Some time during those eventful years, Jackson formed a country arrangement with a daughter of the Spokanes called Jane. It must have been a rewarding relationship, as he told Elkanah Walker in 1850 that he was willing to give $100 toward reestablishment of the Spokane mission and the education of his wife's tribesmen.

After living in Clackamas County and near Salem, the family settled south of The Dalles in remote Moad Hollow. A son, John, was born in 1849, followed by Charles in 1852; Pierre, who was baptized two years later, failed to survive. Jackson, who legitimized his relationship with Jane on April Fool's Day 1860, was developing as a substantial citizen. He worked with a partner named Todd to construct a bridge at the Deschutes River crossing. When it was carried away, the determined men rebuilt it the next year; it eventually passed into the hands of a man named Sherer. Locally known as Spokane Jackson because of his marriage, John spent time away at the British Columbia mines or in a cinnabar mining adventure in Douglas County.[421]

Jane apparently returned to her people and lived on Moran Prairie west of the growing town of Spokane. The return was difficult: one of her sons was killed while shooting up the streets of Cheney. Her youngest, Billy, was also a hell-raiser. When he was reprimanded by Chief Three Mountains, he shot the old man and fled. Wounded trying to escape, he died unrepentant. When Spokane Jackson died intestate in 1873, only his sons John and Charles were still living. Intimate details of the relationship are not known, but it appears that Jackson was a responsible citizen in a difficult social position, who did as well as most pioneers. But when his mixed-blood children tried to return to their mother's people, they no longer fit into tribal life.[422]

Other squaw men were drawn to the southern coast by a brief gold rush. Perhaps they were out-of-date echoes of lone hunters, unadjusted frontiersmen, or former miners, natural loners who could not accept the world as it was turning out and had to find mates desperate enough to endure their peculiarity. The dark lonely canyons and dripping forests were safely removed from the socially critical valley settlements, but there was the potential for eccentricity and the occasional realization of madness in those retreats.[423]

Those grim images contrast with the deliberate withdrawal of the country sons of former gentleman officers of the British fur trade. From Fort Colvile, Archibald McDonald wrote to friends expressing the dilemma of staying in the country with socially unacceptable wives and families or of abandoning them to start over in a proper marriage. In the end, McDonald took Jane and the family to Ontario where, with the exception of the wanderer Ranald, they made a reasonably successful adaptation.

Scandal-loving and secretly scandalous Victorians created the romantic myths about half-breeds. It proved the failure of the natural world, and the dramatic last line of that social lesson, delivered over flickering gas footlights in a stage whisper, was, "There is no going back."

But even myths must have exceptions. More than has been realized of the significance of the Pacific Northwest mixed bloods may have been implied in the theatrical commitment. To fix an accurate image of a unique people, it is necessary to get beyond the stereotype and recover something of real lives. In the shady,

Gravestone of Ranald McDonald, who helped open Japan, on Sanpoil River near Curlew, Washington.
—Author's photo.

serene churchyard, or the dusty Indian cemeteries decorated with fading plastic flowers, the children of the fur trade are finally at rest. It doesn't matter that suburban sprawl and composition-board castles have crowded out the forgotten ghosts, that the interstate blacktops the old brigade trails, or that most of the man-eating rapids have been drowned by hydroelectric dams.

These abbreviated life histories and vignettes are a way of recovering the lost experiences of the mixed bloods and of showing them as an overlooked but persistent ethnic minority. The first half of the nineteenth century was the Métis period in the Pacific Northwest. During those years they were hunters, explorers, and useful links to the native peoples, and the commodity that the beaver trappers produced was the basis of the economy. Trappers supported the commercial operations and political pretensions of the two national interests that competed for the region until the enticements of free land forced a final resolution of the Oregon Question.

Those aging hunters and their crop of mixed-blood children were pawns of international politics, but what might have been a substantial British population were poor representatives of

Serene resting place of the Cowlitz pioneers, St. Francis Xavier churchyard, Toledo, Washington. —Author's photo.

empire. They preferred to risk the uncertainties of a republican frontier. The rapid expansion of the American population diluted the influence of the mixed bloods and masked their legacy. Those developments forced them to make grave adjustments. In many ways the collective experience of the Northwest Métis paralleled that of other marginal peoples. They stood between opposing cultures, interpreting and mediating, but never completely at home in either faction. Too long on the cutting edge, they purposefully grew dull in retirement and, like Ulysses' boatmen, were satisfied to rest from wandering and rust in disuse.

I like to think that those social and political concerns passed without disturbing the last days of the placid old Chinook woman Kilakotah. During her life, she had been the companion to a defeated Astorian, a Nor'wester in retreat, and finally a retired trapper who settled on the French Prairie. The lack of English shielded her from the slurs of American neighbors, and few strangers understood enough of the Chinook jargon to intrude on her serenity.

Notes

Chapter 1–Parents of the Mixed Bloods

1. To minimize the derogatory racial implications in such terms as *mixed bloods, half-breeds, bois brules,* or *chicots,* this study uses the word *Métis* as a broad description of the blending of Old and New World racial elements. The fur traders used the term *half-breed* without negative implications, as the late Lily McAuley, a daughter of the trade, proudly reaffirmed at the Michilimackinac fur trade conference in 1991. For further discussion, see Jacqueline Peterson and Jennifer S. H. Brown, eds., *The New Peoples: Being and Becoming Métis in North America* (Lincoln: University of Nebraska Press, 1985), 3–6; and John E. Foster, "Some Questions and Perspectives on the Problems of Métis Roots," in Peterson and Brown, *New Peoples,* 73.

2. Alexander Henry, "Report of Northwest Population, 1805," in Elliott Coues, ed., *New Light on the Early History of the Greater Northwest: The Manuscript Journals of Alexander Henry, Fur Trader of the Northwest Company and of David Thompson, Official Geographer and Explorer of the Same Company, 1799-1814* (1897; reprint, Minneapolis: Ross & Haines, 1965), 1:282.

3. W. S. Wallace, *Documents Relating to the North West Company* (Toronto: Champlain Society, 1934), 210–11; Walter O'Meara, *Daughters of the Country: The Women of the Fur Traders and Mountain Men* (New York: Harcourt, Brace & World, 1968), 244.

4. Coues, *New Light,* 2:768; Edgar I. Stewart and Jane R. Stewart, eds., *The Columbia River, by Ross Cox* (Norman: University of Oklahoma Press, 1957), 151; Reuben Gold Thwaites, ed., *Original Journals of the Lewis and Clark Expedition, 1804-1806,* 8 vols. (1904–5; reprint, New York: Antiquarian Press, 1959) 3:301.

5. J. Nelson Barry, "Astorians Who Became Permanent Settlers," *Washington Historical Quarterly* 24 (October 1933): 297–301. The Ramsey story is also the subject of a historical novel by John Seeley White, *The Spells of Lamazi: A Historical Novel of the Pacific Northwest Coast* (Portland: Breitenbush Publications, 1982).

6. Gary Moulton, in his recent editing of the Lewis and Clark journals, argues that the Ramseys' supposed genetic heritage was impossible unless there was an even earlier European connection. See Gary E. Moulton, ed., *The Journals of the Lewis and Clark Expedition*, vol. 6, November 2, 1805–March 22, 1806, (Lincoln: University of Nebraska Press, 1990), 147, 148 n. 3, and vol. 3, August 25, 1804–April 6, 1805 (Lincoln: University of Nebraska Press, 1987), 183 n. 2.

7. M. O. Skarsten, *George Drouillard . . .* (Glendale: Arthur H. Clark, 1964); *Journals of Congress* vol. 30, 210–11, 234–36, 401–2.

8. Coues, *New Light*, 1:35–36. British traders on the north Saskatchewan who received Drouillard's property from the killers were told that he had been extensively tattooed on his lower body, a northeastern Indian practice. The two men killed with him were Shawnee.

9. Several boatmen of Métis heritage accompanied Lewis and Clark as far as the Mandan villages on the Missouri but were sent back to St. Louis in spring 1805. Others remained with the Indians and probably filtered into the mountain trade.

10. "William Pink's Journal," in Arthur S. Morton, "Nipawi, on the Saskatchewan River, and Its Historic Sites," *Transactions of the Royal Society of Canada* (1944): 121.

11. The most recent treatment of the Lewis and Clark journals identifies Grenyea as Francois Fleury *dit* Grenier. This young man appears to have been a former engagé of British traders absconding from debt. In 1830 Pierre Grenier was a boatman and trapper with Peter Skene Ogden's Snake hunting brigade; he drowned at The Dalles of the Columbia. His widow was Therese Spokane, whose daughter, Marie Anne, had been born in 1829. See Moulton, *The Journals of Lewis and Clark*, vol. 8, June 10–September 26, 1806 (Lincoln: University of Nebraska Press, 1993), 311, 316 n. 1.

12. Rivet remained in the mountains and was with Thompson in the Flathead country. On 21 January 1839, when the eighty-year-old trapper married a twenty-five-year-old woman at Fort Vancouver, he gave his home parish as St. Sulpice, District of Montreal, and her name as Therese Teteplatte. Two of Rivet's sons married at the same time. Antoine, age twenty-five, wed Emilie Pend d'Oreille, and Joseph, age twenty-three, married Rose Lacourse. Rivet's wife had a daughter by an earlier marriage, Julia, who married Peter Skene Ogden.

13. These speculations are based on several studies to determine the identity and activities of the fascinating McClellan. See J. B. Tyrrell, "Letter of Roseman and Perch, July 10th, 1807," *Oregon Historical Quarterly* 38 (December 1937): 191–97; T. C. Elliott, "The Strange Case of David Thompson and Jeremy Pinch," *Oregon Historical Quarterly* 40 (June 1939): 188–99; "Discussion Notes," in Alvin M. Josephy, Jr.,

The Nez Perce Indians and the Opening of the Northwest (New Haven: Yale University Press, 1965), 658–63; Harry M. Majors, "John McClellan in the Montana Rockies 1807," *Northwest Discovery: The Journal of Northwest History and Natural History* 2 (November–December 1981): 554–630.

14. The 1796 census of the River Raisin near Detroit shows an interesting catalog of names later recognizable in the West: LaBonte, Drouillard, Bellerre, Rivard, Bissonet, and Laframboise. Michel Bourdeaux (Bourdon), who had a white wife and small black child, apparently married Genevieve Plesses *dit* Belair before their daughter was born in 1792. Charles Courtin was the son of Charles Denis Courtois *dit* Marin, a physician in the area. See 1796 Census of Wayne County, Winthrop Sargeant Papers, Ohio Historical Society; Christian Denissen, *Genealogy of the French Families of the Detroit River Region 1701–1911* (Detroit: Detroit Society for Genealogical Research, 1976), 141, 304.

15. M. Catharine White, trans. and ed., *David Thompson's Journals Relating to Montana and Adjacent Regions, 1808–12* (Missoula: Montana State University Press, 1950), 88. Some time after 1763, the Green Bay trader Pierre Grignon had a son by a Menomenee wife known as Pierrche, and in 1777 he had another son named Pierre Antoine by Langlade's daughter. Pierre Grignon was with the North West Company at Rocky Mountain House in 1806 but seems to have become a freeman by 1 November 1809.

16. Milo Milton Quaife, ed., *Gabriel Franchere: A Voyage to the Northwest Coast of America* (1854; reprint, New York: Citadel Press, 1968), 91, 101, 218.

17. White, *David Thompson's Journals*, 208–13 nn. 107, 109.

18. Merle Wells, "Michael Bourdon," in *The Mountain Men and Fur Trade of the Far West*, ed. LeRoy R. Hafen, 10 vols. (Glendale: Arthur H. Clark, 1965–72), 3:55–60; K. G. Davies and Alice M. Johnson, eds., *Peter Skene Ogden's Snake Country Journal 1826–7* (London: Hudson's Bay Record Society, 1961), 92. In tracing Bourdon's descendants among the Oregon country Métis, one finds the name at Fort Laramie and at the Frenchtown cemetery near Missoula. On the Flathead Indian reservation in 1908 there were nine individuals named Bourdon. National Archives, RG 75, boxes 106, 107, Flathead Agency Rolls, FRC, Seattle.

19. Coues, *New Light*, 2:776, 780.

20. See Harriet D. Munnick, "Pierre Dorion," in *The Mountain Men*, 8:107–12.

21. Jacqueline Peterson, "Many Roads to Red River: Métis Genesis in the Great Lakes Region, 1680–1815," in Peterson and Brown, *New Peoples*; Elizabeth Mason and Adele Rahn, "Web of Power in the Fur Trade of the Old South West: A Genealogical Approach," Paper presented to the Fifth North American Fur Trade Conference, Montreal, 1 June 1985.

22. Kenneth W. Porter, "Roll of the Overland Astorians, 1810–1812," *Oregon Historical Quarterly* 34 (January 1933): 105–12; "List of people in the Columbia for Winter 1813/14," Hudson's Bay Company Archives (hereafter HBCA) F4/61, 6–7d, in B. C. Payette, comp., *The Oregon Country under the Union Jack: Postscript Edition* (Montreal: Payette Radio, 1962), 189–90.

23. Carson, St. Michel, Delauny, Cannon, Hoback, Reznor, Robinson, Cass, Miller, Dubrieul, Turcotte, LaChappelle, and Landire.

24. This is an appropriate place to provide a full list of biographies to be found in LeRoy R. Hafen, ed., *The Mountain Men and the Fur Trade of the Far West,* 10 vols. (Glendale: Arthur H. Clark, 1965–72).

    "Michel Bourdon," by Merle Wells, 3:55–60.

    "Jean Baptiste Charbonneau," by Ann W. Hafen, 1:205–24.

    "Toussaint Charbonneau," by LeRoy R. Hafen, 9:52–62.

    "Charles Compo," by Clifford M. Drury, 8:87–93.

    "William Craig," by Frederick Merk, 2:99–116.

    "James Craigie," by Merle Wells, 6:133–37.

    "Pierre Dorion," by Harriet D. Munnick, 8:107–12.

    "George Drouillard," by M. O. Skarsten, 4:69–82.

    "George Wood Ebberts," by Harvey E. Tobie, 4:83–96.

    "Francis Ermatinger," by Harriet D. Munnick, 8:157–280.

    "Jean Baptiste Gervais," by Harriet D. Munnick, 7:121–29.

    "Joseph Gervais," by Kenneth L. Holmes, 7:131–45.

    "Antoine Godin," by Aubrey L. Haines, 2:175–78.

    "Richard Grant," by Merle Wells, 9:165–86.

    "Ignace Hatchiorauquasha (John Grey)," by Merle Wells, 7:161–75.

    "William Kittson," by Gloria Griffen Cline, 9:245–50.

    "Louis Labonte," by Harriet D. Munnick, 7:191–99.

    "Michel Laframboise," by Doyce B. Nunis, Jr., 5:145–70.

    "Etienne Lucier," by Harriet D. Munnick, 6:247–58.

    "Jean Baptiste Lucier *dit* Gardipee," by Harriet D. Munnick, 8:211–19.

    "Thomas McKay," by David Lavender, 6:259–77.

    "John McLoughlin," by Kenneth W. Holmes, 8:235–45.

    "Joseph McLoughlin," by Ruth Stoller, 9:269–77.

    "Finan MacDonald," by Merle Wells, 5:207–16.

    "Donald Manson," by Harriet D. Munnick, 7:217–25.

    "Joseph L. Meek," by Harvey E. Tobie, 1:313–35.

    "Robert Newell," by LeRoy R. Hafen, 8:251–76.

    "Peter Skene Ogden," by Ted J. Warner, 3:213–38.

    "Pierre Chrysologue Pambrun," by Kenneth W. Holmes, 3:239–47.

    "Pierre Pariseau," by Harriet D. Munnick, 6:319–23.

    "Francois Payette," by Kenneth W. Holmes, 6:325–52.

"Simon Plamondon," by Harriet D. Munnick, 9:321-30.

"Antoine Plante," by Jerome Peltier, 5:291-96.

"Francois Rivet," by Harriet D. Munnick, 7:237-43.

"Jim Swanock and the Delaware Hunters," by Harvey L. Carter, 7:293-300.

"Pierre Tevanitagon (Old Pierre)," by Merle Wells, 4:351-57.

"Elbridge Trask," by Jo Tuthill, 4:369-80.

"Caleb Wilkins," by Harvey E. Tobie, 3:385-95.

"John Work," by Ray M. Reeder, 2:363-78.

The index in volume 10 also contains scattered references to other individuals associated with the mixed bloods of the Pacific Northest.

Chapter 2–The Steel Trappers

25. Henry, "Report of Northwest Population," 1:282.

26. Thomas James, *Three Years among the Indians and Mexicans* (1846; reprint, New York: Lippencott, 1962), 46, 53.

27. For Jim Delaware, see Adolf and Beverly Hungry Wolf, *Indian Tribes of the Northern Rockies* (Skookumchuck, B.C.: Good Medicine Books, 1989), 93-94.

28. Soon after the British conquest of New France in 1760, the British superintendent of western Indians, Sir William Johnson, asked that fox and beaver traps be sent to the Indian trade at Detroit. In 1764 he ordered 5,000 beaver traps, which were valued at ten shillings each, and sold them to the Indians for two middle-sized beaver or two bucks (buckskins). Baltizer Geere, a Philadelphia merchant, sent 100 steel traps down the Ohio River to the trading firm of Baynton, Wharton & Morgan in 1767. See Carl P. Russell, *Firearms, Traps, and Tools of the Mountain Men* (New York: Alfred A. Knopf, 1967), 125, citing James Sullivan, et al., eds., *The Papers of Sir William Johnson*, vol. 3 (Albany: University of the State of New York, 1921-65), 335, 388; *Illinois Historical Collections*, vol. 10, 339, 403; and "Bayton, Wharton, and Morgan Account Book," Pennsylvania Historical Commission, Harrisburg MS, 200. See also, Richard Gerstill, *The Steel Trap in North America: The Illustrated Story of Its Design, Production, and Use with Fur Bearing and Predatory Animals from Its Colorful Past to the Present Century* (Harrisburg, Penn.: Stackpole Books, 1985).

29. Edwin James, ed., *A Narrative of the Captivity and Adventures of John Tanner during Thirty Years Residence among the Indians in the Interior of North America* (1830; reprint, Minneapolis: Ross & Haines, 1956), 17-40; Arthur S. Morton, ed., *The Journal of Duncan M'Gillivray of the North West Company at Fort George on the Saskatchewan, 1794-1795* (1929; reprint, Fairfield, Wash.: Ye Galleon Press, 1989), 48.

30. Richard Glover, ed., *David Thompson's Narrative, 1784-1812* (Toronto: Champlain Society, 1962), 156-57.

31. Calvin Martin, *Keepers of the Game: Indian-Animal Relationships and the Fur Trade* (Berkeley: University of California Press, 1978), 16-17,

citing Robin F. Wells, "Castoreum and Steel Traps in Eastern North America," *American Anthropologist* 74, (June 1972): 479–83.

32. Alice M. Johnson, ed., *Saskatchewan Journals and Correspondence, 1795-1802* (London: Hudson's Bay Record Society, 1967), 130.

33. Johnson, *Saskatchewan Journals*, xci–xcii; J. B. Tyrrell, ed., *David Thompson's Narrative of His Explorations in Western America, 1784-1812* (Toronto: Champlain Society, 1916), 205, 312, 314–16; Jack A. Frisch, "Iroquois in the West," *Handbook of North American Indians,* vol. 15, *Northwest* (Washington, D.C.: Smithsonian Institution, 1978), 544.

34. Tomison to HBC, Cumberland House, 6 June 1802, HBCA B239/b/67, 18, in Johnson, *Saskatchewan Journals*, xci–xcii; Payette, *The Oregon Country*, 569–95. There appear to have been eight Iroquois employed by the XY Company in November 1801. Two individuals are named in engagements of 1 July 1801: Pierre Tegarahoute and Ignace Tegarahoute, as well as Jean Bapt. Giasson, who may have been Iroquois. Payments were made in April 1803 to the returning hivernauts: J. Bte. Iroquois, L. Neyahraza, Michel Iroquois, Jacques Iroquois, Sawatis Iroquois, Jacques Montour, J. B. Eno, and Ant. Godin. Engagements at that time named Pierre Bostonnais ("The Iroquois"), Joseph Finterzruwalt, Pierre the Iroquois, and Pierre Tagaueatare.

35. "General Return of the Departments and Posts occupied by the North West Company in the Indian Country, 30 October 1802," in Gordon Charles Davidson, *The North West Company* (1918; reprint, New York: Russell & Russell, 1967) 281; also in B. C. Payette, comp., *The Northwest* (Montreal: Payette Radio, 1964), 227.

36. "Journey to Bow River and R. Mts in Nov. 1800," in Coues, *New Light,* 2:704.

37. Johnson, *Saskatchewan Journals*, 311n, 312n, 313n, 317.

38. Donald Jackson, *Thomas Jefferson and the Stoney Mountains* (Urbana: University of Illinois Press, 1981), 111. This story raises an intriguing question: Did other Iroquois return home with stories of their mountain experiences?

39. Quaife, *Gabriel Franchere*, 91.

40. Information from genealogical charts prepared by Trudy Nicks, Royal Ontario Museum.

41. Frisch, "Iroquois in the West," 544–45. The reference to hair color suggests an earlier Métis heritage, probably deriving from captives adopted by the Iroquois during the colonial wars. Blondness still prevails at Kanawake.

42. Selkirk to Bird, Montreal, 24 April 1818, HBCA B49/b/1, 42d-4.

43. Selkirk to Dickson, 22 May 1818, British Columbia Provincial Archives, Selkirk Papers microfilm, 20429.

44. Cumberland House Correspondence, HBCA B49/b/2, 2d-3, 27d, 30d.

45. Lamb, W. Kaye, ed., *Sixteen Years in the Indian Country: The Journal of Daniel Williams Harmon, 1800-1816* (Toronto: Macmillan of Canada, 1957), 193.

46. Iroquois Accounts, 1818-21, HBCA F4/35.

47. White, *David Thompson's Journals.* Thompson's steersman, Thomas the Iroquois *dit* Big Knife, married a Kutenai woman named Ahn-Akahi, and their son, Eneas Paul Big Knife, served as Kutenai chief from 1870 to 1900. The chieftainship was inherited by Isaac Big Knife, who led from 1901 to 1903; his brother Koostahtah was the leader from 1904 to 1942. Their monument is in the Dayton, Montana, cemetery. Interview with P. H. Shea, 17 January 1973, in Rowland Bond, *Early Birds of the Northwest: 100 Years of Western History From Jacques Raphael Finlay to Dutch Jake Goetz* (Nine Mile Falls, Wash.: Spokane House Enterprises, 1971-72), 21.

48. Coues, *New Light*, 2:734-36.

49. HBCA F4/61, fols. 6-7d, in Payette, *The Oregon Country*, 191-94. Compare to the list Alex Henry made of seventy-six persons who departed Fort George on the Columbia 4 April 1814, including Jacques Thathaine, Ignace Saliahone, M. Picard, Thomas Canaswarel, A. Cayalle. Among the fifty men who planned to summer with Henry were Louis Pocquin, Joseph Paquia, and Jean Baptiste Sakanakie. Coues, *New Light*, 2:868-75.

50. If this is pronounced "Monicue," it resembles a Detroit Wyandot name for the person also known as Between the Logs, who was often associated with the Eno trading family and the Ohio Valley Montours.

51. Eno *dit* Canada was associated with the Montour clan. In his later association with the HBC, Piccard was called Iroquois. HBC records referring to twenty Iroquois engagés are in HBCA F4/35, Iroquois Accounts 1819 (1818-1821).

52. Stewart and Stewart, *The Columbia River*, 364-66.

53. Edmonton House Journal, 1 March 1814, HBCA B60/a/12, 11.

54. Edmonton House Journal, 1814-15, HBCA B60/a/13, 2d, 3, 4d.

55. Stewart and Stewart, *The Columbia River*, 119 n. 3, 321. Joseph Larocque (1787-1866) served the North West Company on Churchill River before coming to the Columbia.

56. "4 Feb 1819, [Engagement of] Francis Obonisawin et all of St. Francis to MTF&Co, comme chasseurs dans les dependences du Columbia," Antoine Roy, "Repertoire des engagements pour l'ouest, 1805-1821," *Report L'Archivist de la Province de Quebec pour 1945-1946*, 338. See also, Gordon M. Day, The Identity of the St. Francis Indians (Ottawa: National Museum of Man, 1981).

57. Kenneth A. Spaulding, ed., *Alexander Ross: The Fur Hunters of the Far West* (1855; reprint, Norman: University of Oklahoma Press, 1956), 109.

58. Ibid., 194. Ross wrote this years later but had not forgotten how difficulties with the Iroquois had spoiled his career.

59. Ibid., 127-29. Alexander Ross recalled that a conscience-stricken Iroquois named Oskononton, who brought the disagreeable news, was reassigned to the Cowlitz, where he was killed.

60. J. G. McTavish to Agents and Proprietors of the North West Company, Fort William, 22 April 1821, in Davidson, *North West Company*, 304, and in Payette, *The Oregon Country*, 503.

61. Spokane District Report 1822-23, HBCA B208/e/1. In fur trade usage, Ojibwa from around Sault Ste. Marie were often called Saulteurs.

62. Frederick Merk, *Fur Trade and Empire* (Cambridge: Harvard University Press, 1931), 36.

63. Simpson to McLoughlin, 10 April 1824, HBCA D4/5, fols. 40-61.

64. Merk, *Fur Trade and Empire*, 135, 143-44. No one named Isaac appears in Ross's list, but the man may have been Ignace L'Iroquois, who came down the Columbia with Thompson in 1811 and was still around Fort George in March 1814. When the boat brigade left, Ignace Salihone was paddling with Maurice Picard and Thomas Canaswarel. Saliahone left his family at Fort George, where they were mistreated by Mr. McDougall's Indian wife and had to be relocated outside the fort with the Nipissings. Coues, *New Light*, 2:860, 891, 908.

65. Savoie Lottinville, ed., *Duke of Wurttemberg: Travels in North America, 1822-1824*, by Paul Wilhelm, trans. Robert W. Nitske (Norman: University of Oklahoma Press, 1974), 328, 376; Dale L. Morgan, ed., *The West of William H.Ashley . . . , 1822-1838* (Denver: Old West Publishing Company, 1964), 51, 252.

66. Thomas Donaldson, *Extra Census Bulletin: Indians of the Six Nations of New York* (Washington, D.C.: United States Census Publishing Office, 1892), 39-41, 76. The three leaders of the St. Regis Indians in 1797 and 1802 traced descent to captives taken from colonial settlements during the Indian wars.

67. Warren A. Ferris, *Life in the Rocky Mountains: A Diary of Wanderings on the Sources of the Rivers Missouri, Columbia, and Colorado from February 1830 to November 1835*, ed. Paul C. Phillips, (Denver: Old West Publishing Company, 1940). The yarns were also picked up by the sportsman William Drummond Stewart and recast into his fictionalized account, *Edward Warren* (1854; reprint, Missoula: Mountain Press Publishing Company, 1986).

68. T. C. Elliott, ed., "Journal of John Work,"*Washington Historical Quarterly* 3 (July 1912): 200.

69. Ferris, 113-16; Roy, "Repertoire des engagement," 339. "7 May 1819, Paul Fraser du Glengarry to MTF&Cie as commis for six years in the northwest." The name does not appear in the lists of Nor'westers taken over by the HBC in 1821. There was also another rough trader named Paul Fraser who operated in the Kamloops area in 1860s.

70. Mikell De Lores Wormell Warner and Harriet Duncan Munnick, trans. and eds., *The Catholic Church Records of the Pacific Northwest: Vancouver* (vols. 1-2) *and Stellamaris Mission* (St. Paul, Oreg.: French Prairie Press, 1972), A. 40.

The multivolume Catholic Church Records of the Pacific Northwest (hereafter CCRPNW) is an invaluable resource for northwestern researchers. For further information, see: Harriet Duncan Munnick, comp., in collaboration with Mikell Delores Warner, *CCRPNW: St. Paul, Oregon, 1839-1898*, vols. 1-3, (Portland: Binford & Mort, 1979); Harriet Duncan Munnick, comp., *CCRPNW: St. Louis Register I, 1845-1868; St. Louis Register II, 1869-1900; Gervais Register, 1875-1893; Brooks Register, 1893-1909* (Portland: Binford & Mort, 1982); Harriet Duncan Munnick, comp., *CCRPNW: Oregon City Register, 1842-1890; Salem Register, 1864-1885: Jacksonville Register, 1854-1885* (Portland: Binford & Mort, 1984); Harriet Duncan Munnick and Steven Dow Beckham, eds., *CCRPNW: Grand Ronde Register I, 1860-1885; Grand Ronde Register II, 1886-1898; St. Michael the Archangel Parish, Grand Ronde Indian Reservation, Grand Ronde, Oregon; St. Patrick's Parish, Muddy Valley, Oregon* (Portland: Binford & Mort , 1987); Harriet Duncan Munnick and Adrian R. Munnick, comps., *CCRPNW: Missions of St. Ann and St. Rose of the Cayouse, 1847-1888; Walla Walla and Frenchtown, 1859-1872; Frenchtown 1872-1888* (Portland: Binford & Mort, 1989).

71. Stewart and Stewart, *The Columbia River*, 142. Merle Wells points out that Finan McDonald had already married Peggy Pend d'Oreille.

72. Spokane District Report, 1822-23, HBCA B208/e/1, 5; John C. Jackson, *Shadow on the Tetons: David E. Jackson and the Claiming of the American West* (Missoula: Mountain Press Publishing Company, 1993), 116-17.

73. The Grey family settled there and received the attention of the former trader David E. Jackson. "1 March 1832, To amt paid Grove Cook for Board Louis Gray from 1st Oct 1831 to 1st Oct 1832, 52.00; Clothing for Louis Gray, 12.50. 20 July 1833, Smith, Jackson & Sublette note to Martin Iroquois for 484.14." "D E Jackson's act with Jackson & Sublette," Missouri Historical Society, Sublette Papers, in David Jackson Collection, 9997, American Heritage Center, University of Wyoming, Laramie. Jackson appears to have supported young Grey's schooling in western Missouri.

74. Gloria Ricci Lothrop, ed., *Recollections of the Flathead Mission by Fr. Gregory Mengarini, S.J.* (Glendale: Arthur H. Clark, 1977), 32-33.

75. When the Detroit Wyandot William Walker visited eastern Kansas to scout sites for relocation, he passed through St. Louis and made a copy of William Clark's drawing of a Chinook Indian. This was forwarded to a gullible missionary supporter and helped generate interest in the West. Walker may have been related to Manicque, Montour, or Enos, who were on the Columbia in 1814.

76. Donald R. Johnson, ed., *William H. Gray: Journal of His Journey East, 1836-1837* (Fairfield, Wash.: Ye Galleon Press, 1980), 67-70.

77. Lothrop, *Recollections of the Flathead Mission*, 35. "Creole" in this sense meant a native of the country.

78. See Jacqueline Peterson, with Laura Peers, *Sacred Encounters: Father De Smet and the Indians of the Rocky Mountain West* (Norman: University of Oklahoma Press, 1993), 89.

79. Winona Adams, ed., "An Indian Girl's Story of a Trading Expedition to the Southwest About 1841 [1840]," *Frontier Omnibus* (Missoula: Montana State University Press, 1962), 122. The Delaware had been under the influence of Moravian missionaries for a long time, and Hill's alma mater developed from Eleazar Wheelock's Indian School. Also bear in mind that the story was filtered through the memory of Angus McDonald.

80. See Burt Brown Barker, ed., *Letters of Dr. John McLoughlin Written at Fort Vancouver, 1829-1832* (Portland: Oregon Historical Society, 1948); Warner and Munnick, *CCRPNW: Vancouver*, A. 39; Munnick, *CCRPNW: St.Paul*, A. 39; John A. Brown and Robert H. Ruby, *The Cayuse Indians: Imperial Tribesmen of Old Oregon* (Norman: University of Oklahoma Press, 1972), 81, 129.

81. Warner and Munnick, *CCRPNW: Vancouver*, 47; Munnick and Beckham, *CCRPNW: Grand Ronde*, 83-84.

82. Warner and Munnick, *CCRPNW: Vancouver*, 47; Munnick, *CCRPNW: St. Paul*, A. 90.

Chapter 3—Jacco

83. Bond, *Early Birds of the Northwest*, 13-27. This study includes information on living descendants such as Mrs. Pearl M. Wood and Mr. Walter Goodman of Chewelah, Washington, Mrs. P. H. Shea of Spokane Valley, and Mrs. W. A. Whitford of Spokane. Bond states that Jacco's first wife was Cree and the third Spokane. Among the children named are Francois *dit* Benetsee, who may have been born in Rupert's Land about 1805, Nicolas, Xavier, Patrick, and Augustus *dit* Koostah.

84. James Finlay engraved 1766 on his Beaver Club medal to mark his first winter in the Northwest. That was the same year his Montreal wife gave birth to their first son.

85. Douglas MacKay, *The Honourable Company: A History of the Hudson's Bay Company* (Toronto: McClelland and Stewart, 1966), 94-95.

86. Harold A. Innis, *The Fur Trade in Canada: An Introduction to Canadian Economic History* (1930; reprint, New Haven: Yale University Press, 1964), 189.

87. Charles M. Gates, ed., *Five Fur Traders of the Northwest* (1965; reprint, St. Paul: Minnesota Historical Society, 1971), 136-38, 154, 156.

88. Reminiscences of Roderick McKenzie are found in L. R. Mason, ed., *Les Bourgeois de la Compagne du Nord-Ouest Récits de Voyages et Rapports Indits Relatif au Nord-Ouest Canadian*, 2 vols. (Quebec: A. Cote

et Compagnie, 1889–90; reprint, New York: Antiquarian Press, 1960), 1:63.

89. Edmonton House Journal, HBCA B60/a/6, 6.

90. Ibid., 22 October 1807, HBCA B60/a/7, 4d.

91. Irene M. Spry, "Routes Through the Rockies," *Beaver* (Autumn 1963): 29.

92. Coues, *New Light*, 2:582.

93. White, *David Thompson's Journals*, 94, 103.

94. The two experienced western hands who guided the HBC officer Howse appear to have been Joseph and Louis Pacquin, sometimes called the Grand and Petite Nipissing.

95. Thompson's Narrative in J. A. Meyers, "Jacques Raphael Finlay," *Washington Historical Quarterly* 10 (July 1919): 165.

96. Spaulding, *Alexander Ross*, 12.

97. Edmonton House Journal, 1814–15, HBCA B60/a/13, 4d, 7d.

98. Ibid., October 1814, HBCA B60/a/13, 3.

99. Eric J. Holmgren, "Jacques-Raphael Finlay," *Dictionary of Canadian Biography*, vol. 6 (Toronto: University of Toronto Press, 1987), 253.

100. Merk, *Fur Trade and Empire*, 31.

101. David Lavender, ed., *The Oregon Journals of David Douglas . . . during the years 1825, 1826, and 1827*, vol. 1 (Ashland: Oregon Book Society, 1972), 78–81.

102. T. C. Elliott, ed.,"The Journal of John Work, July 5–September 15, 1826," *Washington Historical Quarterly* 6 (January 1915): 37.

103. Edmonton House Journal, October 1828, HBCA B60/a/26, 14d.

104. Warner and Munnick, *CCRPNW: Vancouver*, A. 26.

105. Clifford M. Drury, *Nine Years with the Spokane Indians: The Diary of Elkanah Walker, 1838–1848* (Glendale: Arthur H. Clark, 1976), 429 n. 91.

106. Clifford M. Drury, *Marcus and Narcissa Whitman and the Opening of Old Oregon* (Glendale: Arthur H. Clark, 1973), 201–2.

107. Flathead Agency Enrollment Correspondence and Downs Index, National Archives, RG 75, boxes 106, 107, FRC, Seattle.

Chapter 4–New Ways to Play an Old Game

108. Stewart and Stewart, *The Columbia River*, 111–12 n. 14.

109. Glover, *David Thompson's Narrative*, 165; Stewart and Stewart, *The Columbia River*, 192–93.

110. National Archives, RG 76, boxes 106, 107, FRC, Seattle.

111. A disgruntled Spokane buffalo hunter said in winter 1814–15 that the post was established three snows earlier.

112. Milo Milton Quaife, ed., *Adventures of the First Settlers on the Oregon or Columbia River, by Alexander Ross* (1849; reprint, New York: Citadel Press, 1969), 228–29.

113. Stewart and Stewart, *The Columbia River*, 209–11, 213.

114. Spaulding, *Alexander Ross*, 96.

115. Quaife, *Adventures of the First Settlers*, 155, 163.

116. These lines of descent are fully explored by Juliet Pollard in her Ph.D. dissertation tracing the children educated at Fort Vancouver, "The Making of the Métis: Race, Class, and Gender in the Nineteenth Century Pacific Northwest" (University of British Columbia, 1989).

117. Merk, *Fur Trade and Empire*, 104–105.

118. Carl Landerholm, trans., *Notices and Voyages of the Famed Quebec Mission to the Pacific Northwest* (Portland: Oregon Historical Society, 1956).

119. Munnick, *CCRPNW: St.Paul*, A. 30, A. 34–35, A. 36, A. 40, A. 52, A. 54, A. 73, A. 75.

120. Munnick, *CCRPNW: Vancouver*, A. 54.

Chapter 5–Snake Country Hunters

121. Quaife, *Adventures of the First Settlers*, 209–14, 237, 262–64, 297; Spaulding, *Alexander Ross*, 57, 68–71.

122. The Spokane House journalist's description of Bourdon as "a young man who was employed by the Company to conduct them" must have been a sly joke, as he would have been around fifty years old at the time of the coalition, and a son born after 1807 would have been too young for such responsibility.

123. Spokane District Report, 1822–23, HBCA B208/e/1, 4–5. The list of men who did not come out of the Snake country the previous fall (those who left the Snake Brigade of Michel Bourdon) included: "1. Joseph St. Armand, 2. Pierre Cassawasa, 3. Francois H. Frenetorosue, 4. J. Gardipee, 5. Francois Wm. Hodgens, 6. J. McLeod (survived to return 1825), 7. Francois Method (survived to return 1825), 8. Thos. Nakarsheta, 9. Patrick O'Conner (killed returning), 10. Ignace Sokhonie, 11. Ignace Sokhonie's stepson, 12. Louis St. Michael, 13. Ignace Tahekeurate, 14. Lazard Teycaleyecourigi (survived to return 1825)."

124. Lottinville, *Duke of Wurttemberg*, 328. "By a strange adventure, a party of hunters from Montreal in Canada, mostly Iroquois and half-bloods, had, after a hunting expedition to the western regions, come to the Council Bluffs to seek the aid and protection of the American government. These hunters . . . had left their home on

the St. Lawrence some years ago in a party of about thirty with their families." See also Jackson, *Shadow on the Tetons*, 49, 54, 62.

125. Spokane District Report, 1822-23, HBCA B208/e/1, 4-5. "The men who accompanied Mr. McDonald this spring [presumably older Columbia Freemen, included:] 26. Jean B. Bouchard, 27. Alex Carson, 28. Ignace Dehodionwasse, 29. Charles Groslui, 30. Jean Bpt. Grandriau, 31. Antoine Godin, 32. Ignace Katcheiorongueshe, 33. Louis Kanota, 34. Louis Konitagen (Kanitagan, killed 6 Feb 1825), 35. Ignace Konitagen, 36. Lazard Hayaiguarelita, 37. Charles Loyer, 38. Charles LaGasse, 39. Martin Miaquin, 40. Antoine Paget, 41. Jos. Perrault, 42. Francois Sansfacon, 43. Sauteau St.Germain, 44. Fran. Sasanirie, 45. Baptise Sowenge, 46. Pierre Tavenitogen & two sons, 47. Pierre Tennotiessin, 48. Jacque Thataracton, 49. Laurent Karowtowshow, 50. Jacques Osistericha (remains with the Kutenai)."

126. Merle Wells points out that this fight was west of Lemhi Pass rather than east, as other sources have erroneously reported.

127. Spaulding, *Alexander Ross*, 208-9.

128. Spokane District Report, 1822-23, HBCA B208/e/1, 3d."The custom of giving debts has not yet been introduced in this district. Furs are paid for as presented. We are in the habit of advancing large supplies to freemen who are old Canadians and Iroquois, many of them having large families, wander about like Indians and adopt their manner of life. These people generally summer in the Snake Country well stored in some parts with beaver and near the buffalo."

129. Merk, *Fur Trade and Empire*, 38.

130. Stuart to HBC, Fort Edmonton, 7 January 1827, John Stuart Letterbooks microfilm, Oregon Historical Society MS 1502; Glyndwr Williams, ed., *Peter Skene Ogden's Snake Country Journals 1827-28 and 1828-29* (London: Hudson's Bay Record Society, 1971), 36 n. 1, 122 n. 3.

131. Edward Roberts memo, 19 March 1837, cited in Pelly to Smith, 20 March 1837, HBCA A10/4, in John S. Galbraith, *The Hudson's Bay Company as an Imperial Factor, 1821-1869* (Berkeley: University of California Press, 1957), 21.

132. "Copy of a Document Found among the Private Papers of the Late Dr. John McLoughlin," Transactions of the Oregon Pioneer Association (Salem, 1880), 48-51.

133. Warner and Munnick, *CCRPNW: Vancouver*, A. 18-21.

134. Pollard, "The Making of the Métis."

135. John A. Hussey, *Champoeg, Place of Transition: A Disputed History* (Portland: Oregon Historical Society, 1967), 46-55.

136. *Told by the Pioneers: Reminiscences of Pioneer Life in Washington*, vol. 2 (Olympia: Washington Pioneer Project, 1938), 115. A. H. Roundtree, a Lewis County pioneer of 1852, knew of the donation land claim of a Frenchman named Pershell, Pierre Charles.

137. Cecelia Svinth Carpenter, *Fort Nisqually: A Documented History of Indian and British Interaction* (Tacoma: Tahoma Research Service, 1986), 39; James R. Gibson, *Farming the Frontier: The Agricultural Opening of the Oregon Country, 1786-1846* (Seattle: University of Washington Press, 1985), 92.

138. Galbraith, *Hudson's Bay Company*, 202-4, 214-15.

Chapter 6–Thomas McKay, Fur Trader

139. Innis, *The Fur Trade in Canada*, 192.

140. The life of Thomas McKay has been treated in Fred Lockley, "Reminiscences of Leila McKay," *Oregon Journal* 7 (October 1927): 16-21, and was reprinted in Lockley, *History of the Columbia River from The Dalles to the Sea* (Chicago: S. J. Clarke Publishing Company, 1928), 64-75; Annie Laurie Bird,"Thomas McKay," *Oregon Historical Quarterly* 40 (June 1939): 1-18; Annie Laurie Bird, *Thomas McKay* (Caldwell, Ida.: Caxton Printers, 1972); David Lavender, "Thomas McKay," in *The Mountain Men*, 6:258-77.

141. Hussey, *Champoeg*, 24-26.

142. "Certificate of inditements found at Montreal, No. 3, The King vs. Thomas McKay, for murder of Captain Rogers, 19 June 1816," British Columbia Provencial Archives, Selkirk Papers microfilm, 4554.

143. Ross Cox, a former associate in the West, met McKay returning to the interior on 15 July 1817. He was then identified with such Nor'wester cut-throats as Samuel Black and Peter Skene Odgen, also exiled to the West for their excesses in the Athabaska country.

144. Merk, *Fur Trade and Empire*, 62, 124.

145. London Office Records, HBCA A34/1, 65d, and Records of Governors of Rupert's Land, HBCA D4/5, 25d-27d, in Glyndwr Williams, ed., *Hudson's Bay Miscellany, 1670-1870* (Winnipeg: Hudson's Bay Record Society, 1975), 222.

146. Ibid., 221-22.

147. "Jason Lee Diary," *Oregon Historical Quarterly* 17 (September 1916): 249.

148. Gustavus Hines, *Oregon: Its History, Condition, and Prospects* (1850; reprint, New York: Arno Press, 1973). The Cayuse wife lived for many years on the Umatilla reservation.

149. "George Roberts," *Oregon Historical Quarterly* 63 (June 1962): 208.

150. Howard I. Mitchell, ed., *The Journals of William Fraser Tolmie, Physician and Fur Trader* (Vancouver, B.C.: Mitchell Press, 1963), 176.

151. Warner and Munnick, *CCRPNW: Vancouver*.

152. "White's Law of the Nez Perce," in Brown and Ruby, *The Cayuse Indians*, 86-92, 297-98.

153. See Portland Genealogical Forum publications of abstracts for Provisional and Territorial Government Donation Land Claims, Portland, Oregon.

154. Munnick and Munnick, comps., *CCRPNW: Missions of St. Ann and St. Rose of the Cayouse*, baptism 20, 2.

155. Edward J. Kowrach, ed., *Journal of a Catholic Bishop on the Oregon Trail: The Overland Crossing of Rt. Rev. A. M. A. Blanchet, Bishop of Walla Walla, from Montreal to Oregon Territory, March 23, 1847, to January 23, 1851* (Fairfield: Ye Galleon Press, 1978).

156. Theodore T. Johnson, *California and Oregon, or Sights in the Gold Region* (Philadelphia: J. B. Lippencotte, 1857), 185.

157. W. C. McKay papers, Pendleton Public Library, Oregon Historical Society microfilm 413, reel 2.

Chapter 7–The Oregon Question

158. Adams, "An Indian Girl's Story," 122.

159. Lois Halliday McDonald, *Fur Trade Letters of Francis Ermatinger* (Glendale: Arthur H. Clark, 1980), 124.

160. Gibson, *Farming the Frontier*, 82–87.

161. Statement of John McLean in John S. Galbraith, *The Little Emperor: Governor Simpson of the Hudson's Bay Company* (Toronto: Macmillan, 1976), 122. Simpson's character and attitudes are explored more fully in Jennifer S. H. Brown, *Strangers in Blood: Fur Trade Company Families in Indian Country* (Vancouver: University of British Columbia Press, 1980), and Sylvia Van Kirk, *"Many Tender Ties": Women in Fur Trade Society in Western Canada, 1670-1870* (Winnipeg: Watson & Dwyer Publishing, 1980).

162. Williams, *Peter Skene Ogden*, 36 n. 1, 122 n. 3.

163. Pelly to Glenelg, 10 February 1837, HBCA A8/2, in John S. Galbraith, "The Early History of the Puget's Sound Agricultural Company," *Oregon Historical Quarterly* 55 (September 1954): 237, 239.

164. For the HBC officers' reaction, see Galbraith, "Early History of the PSAC," 242-43, and scattered comments in G. P. de T. Glazebrook, ed., *The Hargrave Correspondence, 1821-1843* (Toronto: Champlain Society, 1938).

165. Governor and Committee to Finlayson, 4 March 1840, HBCA A6/25, in Galbraith, "Early History of the PSAC," 252.

166. Simpson to Finlayson, 10 September 1840, and Simpson to McLoughlin, 11 September 1840, HBCA D4/25, 103v.

167. Simpson correspondence, HBCA D4/25, 105-105d, in Gibson, *Farming the Frontier*, 111-12.

168. Finlayson to Simpson, 1 May 1841, HBCA D5/6, fol. 137, in Glyndwr Williams, ed., *London Correspondence Inward from Sir George*

Simpson, 1841–41 (London: Hudson's Bay Record Society, 1973), 35 n. 4.

169. Agreement at Fort Garry, 31 May 1841, HBCA F16/2, fol. 194a. Half of the produce went to the farmer and half to the Company.

170. Signatories of the letter to Governor C. F. Alexander Christie, 29 August 1845, in Irene M. Spry, "The Métis and Mixed-Bloods of Rupert's Land before 1870," in Peterson and Brown, *New Peoples*, 110.

171. "List of Emigrants for the Columbia," undated on paper watermarked 1835, Puget's Sound Agricultural Company Miscellaneous Papers, HBCA F26/1, fol. 2.

Chapter 8–Overland to the Columbia

172. John Flett, "Interesting Local History: A Sketch of the Emigration from Selkirk's Settlement to Puget Sound in 1841," *Tacoma Daily Ledger*, 18 February 1885. Flett had previously published another version, "Oregon Reminiscences, 1841," in the *Olympia Washington Standard*, 25 August 1882.

173. Earl of Southesk, *Saskatchewan and the Rocky Mountains* (Rutland, Vt.: Charles Tuttle Company, 1969), 44.

174. R. C. Russell, *The Carlton Trail: A Broad Highway into the Saskatchewan Country from the Red River Settlement, 1840–1880* (Saskatoon: Modern Press, 1955), 1, 8.

175. Mitchell, *The Journals of William Fraser Tolmie*, 347; George T. Allen, "Journal of a Voyage from Fort Vancouver, Columbia River, to York Factory, Hudson's Bay, 1841," Transactions of the Oregon Pioneer Association (Salem, 1881).

176. Allen, "Journal of a Voyage from Fort Vancouver," 53; Mitchell, *Journals of William Fraser Tolmie*, 338–40.

177. Andrew Pambrun, "The Story of His Life as He Tells It," Eastern Washington College of Education, Hargraves Library MS, in print as Andrew Dominique Pambrun, *Sixty Years on the Frontier in the Pacific Northwest* (Fairfield, Wash.: Ye Galleon Press, 1978), 63, 69, 94.

178. The main sources on the Bidwell-Bartleson party are John Bidwell, *Echos of the Past about California* (Chicago, 1928); Joseph Williams, *Narrative of a Tour from the State of Indiana to Oregon Territory in the Years 1841-2* (New York: Cadmus Bookshop, 1921); H. M. Chittenden and A. D. Richardson, eds., *Life, Letters, and Travels of Father Pierre Jean De Smet* (New York: Francis P. Harper, 1905).

179. Flett, "Interesting Local History."

180. Ibid.

181. Sir George Simpson, *Narrative of a Journey Round the World During the Years 1841 and 1842* (London: Coburn, 1847), 60.

182. Ibid., 62.

183. Simpson commented on the old woman, but this approximation is drawn from the Brown and Van Kirk studies of Indian wives.

184. The hunt is described by several observers; one graphic picture is in J. Russell Harper, ed., *Paul Kane's Frontier: Including Wanderings of a Artist among the Indians of North America*, by Paul Kane (Fort Worth: University of Texas Press, 1971), 69, 71–72.

185. Simpson, *Narrative*, 81.

186. Harper, *Paul Kane's Frontier*, 138.

187. Simpson to Sinclair, 26 July 1841, HBCA D4/591, in D. Geneva Lent, *West of the Mountains: James Sinclair and the Hudson's Bay Company* (Seattle: University of Washington Press, 1963), 130. "I leave three of my people here to assist in getting the boats up from Fort Assiniboine [on the Athabaska River to the north] in the mountains, and it will be necessary that six or seven of your people should be separated from our party, as with the three men left by me to bring the boats back to Fort Assiniboine in time to transport the Columbians going from York Factory who may be expected there by the latter end of August. It is the utmost importance that every exertion should be used to get your people up to Jasper's House in order that the boats may be available in time for Mr. Manson and his party. Your blacksmiths should be set to work in nail-making immediately upon their arrival here, and they remain a day or two after their families taken their departure from Fort Assiniboine, so as to complete their work as they may easily overtake the main party before they get to the Athabaska River, and immediately on landing at Jasper's House, Bernier, Spence, and other handy men you may have should be dispatched with all expedition to the Boat Encampment to prepare wood and build boats by the time they reach the Boat Encampment."

188. They may have suspected that Simpson was on a record-breaking circumnavigation of the world, which would benefit from such a geographic contribution as the discovery of a new pass. To be followed by a herd of emigrants might lessen the dramatic effect.

189. Flett, "Interesting Local History."

190. Simpson, *Narrative*, 76. The rhetoric comes from the Governor's ghost writer, the inexperienced Judge Thom.

191. Flett, "Interesting Local History."

192. Ibid.

193. Ibid.

194. Simpson, *Narrative*, 81.

195. Flett, "Interesting Local History."

196. "Archibald McDonald, Fort Colvile Correspondence Outward," British Columbia Provencial Archives MS.

197. Edward C. Robbins interview with Mary McKay Elliott, "Evolution of County from the Primitive State," unidentifiable newspaper clipping in Grace Rafferty family scrapbook, probably from the *Hillsboro Argus*, n.d. This study has depended, in part, upon information and photographs held in private family collections. Out of respect for their privacy, additional information has not been released for publication.

198. Clifford M. Drury, *First Women over the Rockies: The Diary of Mrs. Elkanhah Walker II* (Glendale: Arthur H. Clark, 1963), 220.

199. John M. Canse, ed., "Log of the *Lausanne*, IV, Henry Bridgemen Brewer," *Oregon Historical Quarterly* 30 (March 1929): 112.

Chapter 9–Betrayal on the Columbia

200. Simpson to HBC, Fort Vancouver, 25 November 1841, HBCA D4/110, fols. 1–38d, in Williams, *London Correspondence Inward*, 74–78.

201. For background, see Drew Crooks, "The Story of John Edgar," *Occurrences: The Journal of the Fort Nisqually Historic Site* 11 (Spring 1993): 3–9.

202. Fort Nisqually Miscellaneous Papers, Oregon Historical Society microcopy of Henry Huntington Library Collection.

203. McLoughlin to McDonald, 12 November 1842, Coe Collection, Yale University, in Katharine Marie Troxel, "Fort Nisqually and the Puget Sount Agricultural Company," Ph.D. dissertation (University of Indiana, 1950), 359.

204. Henry Buxton Jr. to E. E. Dye, Forest Grove, 28 September 1892, E. E. Dye Collection, Oregon Historical Society.

205. Flett, "Interesting Local History."

206. Letitia McKay to T. A. Wood, Veterans Pension File, Oregon Historical Society MS.

207. Buxton to Dye, 13 October 1892, E. E. Dye Collection, Oregon Historical Society.

208. Joseph Schafer, "Dispatch from Simpson to Governor, Deputy Governor, and Committee, Fort Vancouver, 25 November 1841," *American Historical Review* 14 (October 1908): 79.

209. Williams, *London Correspondence Inward*, 99.

210. John C. Jackson, "Red River Settlers vs. Puget Sound Agricultural Company, 1854-55," *Oregon Historical Quarterly* 85 (Fall 1984): 280–81.

211. When Simpson said fourteen, he was counting the three new families but left out Klyne and the two families that stayed at Spokane.

212. Buxton to Dye, 28 September 1892, E. E. Dye Collection, Oregon Historical Society.

213. Van Kirk, *Many Tender Ties,* 45; information about the estate of John McKay and annuities paid to Charles McKay is in HBCA to author, 5 July 1971.

214. Robbins, "Evolution of County from the Primitive State."

215. Williams, *London Correspondence Inward,* 92–94.

216. "Diary of Wilkes in the Northwest," *Pacific Northwest Quarterly* 17 (April 1926): 131; Charles Wilkes, *Narrative of the United States Exploring Expedition during the Years 1838, 1839, 1840, 1841, 1842,* 5 vols. (London, 1845), 4:305–7.

217. Recent excavations at the Fort Nisqually site were reported by Guy F. Moura, "Fort Nisqually, Columbia District: Palisades, Transfer Prints, and Bone Marrow" (paper presented at the Sixth North American Fur Trade Conference, Mackinac Island, Michigan, September 1991).

218. Simpson, *Narrative,* 110.

219. McNeill to Douglas, 12 January 1842, Fort Nisqually Correspondence Outward, British Columbia Provencial Archives MS.

220. Williams, *London Correspondence Inward,* 76–77, 100.

221. Ibid., xxxii, 107–8.

222. Ibid., 101–2, 106–7.

223. Ibid., 107–8.

224. London Correspondence Outward, HBCA A6/26. fols.14–14d; HBC to Finlayson, 1 June 1842, in Lent, *West of the Mountains,* 163.

225. A. C. Anderson memo on Fort Nisqually, circa 1841, British Columbia Provencial Archives MS.

226. Dugald McTavish to Hargrave, Fort Vancouver, 2 April 1842, in Glazebrook, *Hargrave Correspondence,* 385.

227. McNeill to Douglas, Fort Nisqually, 19 December 1841, Fort Nisqually Correspondence Outward, British Columbia Provencial Archives.

228. McNeill to Douglas, Fort Nisqually, 12 January 1842, Fort Nisqually Correspondence Outward, British Columbia Provencial Archives.

229. Fort Nisqually Advances to Settlers 41/42 and Sales to Settlers Outfit 1842, Fort Nisqually Miscellaneous Papers, Oregon Historical Society microcopy of Henry Huntington Library Collection.

230. L. McKay to Wood, and Buxton to Dye, Nisqually Correspondence Book.

231. McNeill to Douglas, Fort Nisqually, 28 February 1842, Fort Nisqually Correspondence Outward, British Columbia Provencial Archives. This quotation is the first reference to the mill that was later relocated on the north Tualatin Plains by Charles McKay.

232. E. E. Rich, ed., *The Letters of John McLoughlin from Fort Vancouver to the Governor and Committee,* 3 vols. Second Series, 1839–44 (London: Hudson's Bay Record Society, 1943), 2:77.

233. Ibid., 2:120.

234. Ibid., 2:79.

235. Simpson to Aberdeen, 29 March 1845, HBCA D4/66 in Joseph Schafer, ed., "Documents Relative to the Ware and Vavasour Military Reconnaissance in Oregon, 1845-6," *Oregon Historical Quarterly* 10 (March 1909): 13–16; also discussed in Galbraith, *HBC as an Imperial Factor*, 236–37, 458 n. 11.

236. Galbraith, *Little Emperor*, 156–57.

Chapter 10–Strangers in Paradise

237. Munnick, *CCRPNW: St. Paul*, A. 60–62.

238. Ibid., A. 49–50. The name Louis LaBonte also appears among the names recorded on the River Raisin south of Detroit in mid-July 1796.

239. Joseph Gervais of Maskonge, Quebec, left his home in 1797, when he went to the Arkansas River to hunt buffalo for the New Orleans market. Thomas Vaughn and Martin Winch, *Joseph Gervais: A Familiar Mystery Man* (Portland: Oregon Historical Society, n.d.; reprint, *Oregon Historical Quarterly* 64 [December 1965]). In an interesting coincidence of names, in 1803 Joseph Gervais led Pawnee Indians to a meeting with the governor of Santa Fe to conclude a peace treaty that opened the way for Jacques D'Eglise and Laurent Durucher to try the Santa Fe trade. After the United States takeover in 1804, army officers reported Spanish traders on the headwaters of the Platte who were trading with the Americans. Two men backed by the Kaskaskia merchant William Morrison left St. Louis in July 1804 to join Gervais who was waiting for them "in the [Indian] nations." Perhaps this was the same Joseph Gerbais who was employed at Kaskaskia to trade with the Indians along the Missouri. Annie Heloise Abel, ed., *Tabeau's Narrative of Loisel's Expedition to the Upper Missouri* (Norman: University of Oklahoma Press, 1939), 241. Spanish authorities were concerned about the intentions of the Lewis and Clark party, and on 13 October 1805, Jaoquim del Real Alencaster, governor of New Mexico, ordered Pedro Vial to investigate and arrest the members of the corps of discovery. Vial took Jacques D'Eglise, Juan Chabert, and Jarvey as his interpreters. See Abraham P. Nasatir, *Borderland in Retreat: From Spanish Louisiana to the Far Southwest* (Albuquerque: University of New Mexico Press, 1976), 139.

240. Vaughn and Winch, *Joseph Gervais*, 334–38.

241. Munnick, *CCRPNW: St. Paul*, A. 1, A. 28–29; Lucy Ball, Kate Ball Powers, and Flora Ball Hopkins, comps., *Born to Wander: Autobiography of John Ball, 1794-1884* (1925; reprint, Grand Rapids: Grand Rapids Historical Commission, 1994), 61.

242. See "Copy of a Document Found among the Private Papers of the late Dr. John McLoughlin," Transactions of the Oregon Pioneer Association (Salem, 1880), 50, and Rich, *Letters of John McLoughlin*, 1:173–74, both in Gibson, *Farming the Frontier*, 130–31.

243. Ibid., 131.

244. Ibid., 131-32.

245. Harvey L. Carter, "Ewing Young," in *Trappers of the Far West* (Lincoln: University of Nebraska Press, 1983; reprinted from Hafen, *The Mountain Men*), 63-65.

246. "Mr. Slacum's Report," Reports Committees, vol. 1 (1838-39), 25th Cong. 3rd Sess, and "Memorial of William A. Slacum . . . ," Senate Document 24, 25th Cong. 2nd Sess., both in Gibson, *Farming the Frontier*, 131, 132 (for a table naming the settlers).

247. Ibid., 92, apparently citing the Joint Claims Commission, or Carpenter, *Fort Nisqually*, 96, citing Meany, *History of the State of Washington*, 99; Williams, *London Correspondence Inward*, 43.

248. George F. Plamondon, *The Plamondon Family*, cited in Warner and Munnick, *CCRPNW: Vancouver*, A. 80. Another source calls Plamondon the first French Canadian to explore the Cowlitz River to the Big Bottom country, where he became acquainted with Chief Scarrewa and married one of his daughters. After this wife, Veronica, died in 1827, Plamondon married a northern Indian woman, and then Emelie Finlay Bernier. She is called the part-Cowlitz daughter of Pierre Bernier. After her death, Plamondon married Louise Pelletier, niece of Father Blanchet. See Darleen Ann Fitzpatrick, "We Are Cowlitz: Traditional and Emergent Ethnicity," Ph.D. dissertation (University of Washington, 1986), 149-52.

249. Williams, *London Correspondence Inward*, 93-94.

250. Undated list of emigrants for the Columbia, Puget's Sound Agricultural Company Miscellaneous Papers, HBCA F26/1, fol. 2.

251. Flett, "Interesting Local History"; *Tacoma News*; Washington State Library Donation Land Claims file, Julien, Marcel Bernier statements in Donation Land Claims applications; Marcel Bernier testimony taken at Victoria, 1 August 1865, *British and American Joint Commission for the Final Settlement of the Claims of the Hudson's Bay Company and Puget Sound Agricultural Company*, vol. 2 (Washington, D.C.: Government Printing Office, 1867).

252. Warner and Munnick, *CCRPNW: Vancouver*, A. 66.

253. C. Stuart Houston, "Pierre St. Germain," The Artic Institute of North America (September-December 1986). Comparison of notes with this noted arctic specialist has led to a satisfactory identification.

254. It is possible that his son and namesake, born in 1817 returned to the Red River farm where he signed a petition in 1869 opposing the formation of a provisional government by Louis Riel.

255. Oregon Provisional Land Claims Book, vol. 4, 299; Washington State Library Donation Land Claims file, Joseph St. Germain application papers.

256. Washington State Library, Donation Land Claims, file of John Baptist Reille; Lewis County Tax Roll, 1847; 1850 and 1860 Federal Census, Lewis County.

257. *Oregon Spectator*, 8 July 1847.

258. Statements about the various Larocque families, or speculations about their relationship, are loosely derived from Munnick, *CCRPNW: St. Paul*, passim, and Annotations, A. 55–56.

259. Lottie LeGett Gurly, comp., *Genealogical Material in Oregon Provisional Land Claims*, abstracted, vols. 1–8 (Portland: Portland Genealogical Forum, 1982), 64, 68, 82; Munnick, *CCRPNW: St. Paul*, A. 32. Munnick suggests that Francois, Luc, and Joseph Gagnon may have been brothers. Luc and his wife, Julie Gregoire, were recorded as natives of Canada. According to the 1860 census, eighty-year-old Luc was born in Canada, sixty-year-old Julie was born in the Oregon country and called an Indian, as was their thirty-year-old son, Antonio.

260. "Reminiscences of Hugh Cosgrove," *Oregon Historical Quarterly* 1 (September 1900): 261.

261. Oregon Historical Society Newspapers microfilm, *Oregon American and Evangelical Unionist*.

262. 1850 U.S. Census for Oregon, and mortality schedule.

263. Thomas W. Prosch, *McCarver and Tacoma* (Seattle: Lowman & Hanford, 1906), 133.

264. Munnick, *CCRPNW: St. Paul*, A. 69–70; the author's collection of historical documentation relating to seven generations of the Montour family.

265. Copies of papers relating to this interesting case collected by Harriet Duncan Munnick are now administered by the St. Paul Historical Society, St. Paul, Oregon.

Chapter 11–Rawhide Knots

266. Frances Fuller Victor, *The River of the West: Life and Adventure in the Rocky Mountains and Oregon* . . . . (1870; reprint, Columbus, Ohio: Long's College Book Company, 1950), 175–76, 238, 256.

267. "Memoirs of Virginia Meek," MS then in possession of Mrs. John Gates, in Dorothy O. Johansen, ed., *Robert Newell's Memoranda: Travles in the Teritory of Missourie; Travle to the Kayuse War; together with A Report on the Indians South of the Columbia River* (Portland: Champoeg Press, 1959), 10, 28.

268. Judy Gates Goldman, Portland Genealogical Forum Bulletin (January 1965).

269. Leslie M. Scott, "First Taxes in Oregon, 1844," *Oregon Historical Quarterly* 31 (March 1930): 1–24.

270. Through the courtesy of Judy Gates Goldman, from the manuscript of Gertie Pasley Meek.

271. Victor, *River of the West*, 443.

272. Ibid., 457–58.

273. Ibid., 496.

274. Alvin M. Josephy, Jr., *The Nez Perce Indians and the Opening of the Northwest* (New Haven: Yale University Press, 1965), 413.

275. Ibid., 245.

276. Ibid., 430 n. 44.

277. Heirship Register, p. 4, Nez Perce, Bureau of Indian Affairs, Northern Idaho Agency, National Archives, RG 75, Box 0084, FRC, Seattle.

278. Josephy, *Nez Perce Indians*, 427–28.

Chapter 12–The New Republicans

279. Williams, *London Correspondence Inward*, 82.

280. Robert J. Loewenberg, *Equality on the Oregon Frontier: Jason Lee and the Methodist Mission, 1834–43* (Seattle: University of Washington Press, 1976), 140–68, 195–228.

281. The French Canadians/Métis voting for organization were Charles Campo, Etienne Lucier, Francois X. Mattieu, and Charles McKay.

282. Samuel Parker, *Journal of an Exploring Tour beyond the Rocky Mountains under the direction of the A. B. C. F. M. performed in the years 1835, '36 and '37* (1838; reprint; Minneapolis: Ross & Haines, 1967), 116; Drury, *Nine Years with the Spokane Indians*, 101.

283. Oregon Provisional and Territorial Government Papers, Oregon Historical Society microfilm; George H. Himes, *Souvenir of the Eighty-fourth Anniversary of the Organization of the First American Civil Government West of the Rocky Mountains . . . .* (Portland: Oregon Historical Society, 1927). This list of "French settlers who voted against the organization of the Provisional Government at Champoeg, May 2, 1843," included:

Louis Aucent	David Dompierre	Augustin Lambert
Amable Arquoit	Andre Dubois	Alexis La Prate
Cyfois Bargeau	Jean B. Ducharme	Andre Longtain
Pierre Beleque	Antoine Felice	Moyse Lore
Pascal Biscornais	Louis Forcier	Joseph Matte
Louis Boivers	Luc Gagnon	Fabien Maloin
Antoine Bonenfant	Pierre Gauthier	David Mongrain
Alexis Brisebois	Joseph Gervais	Pierre Papin
Oliver Brisebois	Jean Gingras	Pierre Pariseau
Joseph Brunelle	Etienne Gregoire	Augustin Remon
Andre Chalifoux	Andre La Chapelle	Thomas Rio
Adolph Chamberlain	Louis La Bonte	Charles Rondeau
Joseph Cornoyer	Xavier Laderout	Andre Sanders
Joseph Delard	Michel Laferty	Gideon Senecalle
Pierre Depot	Michel La Frambois	Jacques Servant
Joseph Despart	Jean B. Lalcoure	Louis B. Van Dalle

284. "Recollections of George B. Roberts," Bancroft Library MS; "Recollection of a Chief Trader in the HBC, Statement of Joseph William McKay, Agent of the HBC at Fort Simpson, B.C., 1844–1856," Bancroft Library MS. McKay was the mixed-blood nephew of Charles McKay.

285. David C. Duniway and Neil R. Riggs, eds., *The Oregon Archives, 1841–1843* (Portland: Oregon Historical Society, n.d.), reprint of *Oregon Historical Quarterly* 60 (1959): 211–80.

286. Frances Fuller Victor, *The Early Indian Wars of Oregon and Washington, Compiled from the Oregon Archives and Other Sources with Muster Rolls* (Salem: F. C. Baker, 1894), 555–57.

287. Jackson, "Red River Settlers vs. Puget Sound Agricultural Company," 289.

Chapter 13–Charles McKay: A Public Man

288. For a record of John McKay's service at Brandon House, see HBCA B22/a/5, B22/a/9–13, and B22/a/15–18a. Mary Favel was the daughter of the HBC trader John Favel of the lower Albany River.

289. See Brandon House Journal, HBCA B22/a/17, fol. 19d, and B22/a/18a, fol. 3. See also, T. R. McCloy, "John Richards McKay," in *The Dictionary of Canadian Biography*, vol. 8 (Toronto: University of Toronto Press, 1985).

290. Peter Fidler's Brandon House Journal describes its capture by the Métis, HBCA B2/a/19.

291. McCloy, "John Richards McKay," 10:475.

292. Register of Marriages, HBCA E4/1b, fol. 220, no. 130; Red River Census, 1831–35, 1838–40, HBCA E5/5–10.

293. Robbins, "Evolution of County from the Primitive State."

294. Alvin T. Smith Diaries, Oregon Historical Society MS.

295. They were J. W. Baily and George Gay, who came from California in 1835; Francis Fletcher and Joseph Holman, who arrived in 1840 with the Peoria overland party; William Johnson, an old fur trapper who had been in the West since 1835; John Pickerell (later Edmunds), since 1839; and John L. Morrison, who arrived the previous year.

296. Hussey, *Champoeg*, 150–53.

297. Duniway and Riggs, *Oregon Archives*, 211–80.

298. Oregon Archives, doc. 1582, Oregon Historical Society microfilm.

299. Oregon Provisional and Territorial Government Papers 908 and 12186, Oregon Historical Society microfilm.

300. Johansen, *Robert Newell's Memoranda*, 93–94.

301. Alvin T. Smith Diaries, Oregon Historical Society MS; Private Journal of Thomas Lowe, Fort Vancouver, June 15, 1843–45, January

1846, British Columbia Provencial Archives MS; Oregon Provisional and Territorial Government Papers 41, 1183, Oregon Historical Society microfilm; Jonas A. Jonasson, "Local Road Legislation in Oregon," *Oregon Historical Quarterly* 42 (June 1941): 164.

302. Oregon Provisional and Territorial Government Papers 1710, Oregon Historical Society microfilm. Columbia later became Hillsboro.

303. *Oregon City Spectator* (June 1846).

304. Oregon Provisional and Territorial Government Papers 1711, Oregon Historical Society microfilm; T. M. Ramsdell, "Reminiscences," Transactions of the Oregon Pioneer Association (Salem, 1896), 109.

305. Peter H. Burnett, *Recollections of an Old Pioneer* (New York: Appleton & Company, 1888), 181; Alvin T. Smith Diaries, Oregon Historical Society MS; Ramsdell "Reminiscences," 110.

306. McNeill to Douglas, 28 February 1842, Fort Nisqually Correspondence, British Columbia Provencial Archives; *Oregon Spectator*, 29 October 1846; Overton Johnson and William H. Winter, "Route Across the Rocky Mountains, 1843," *Oregon Historical Quarterly* 7 (June 1906): 167.

307. Private Journal of Thomas Lowe, Fort Vancouver, British Columbia Provencial Archives MS; Alvin T. Smith Diaries, Oregon Historical Society MS.

308. Victor, *Early Indian Wars of Oregon*, 504; Johansen, *Newell's Memoranda*, 105-6, 115-16. Variations on this spelling include Kawiniha, Conniah, Cownish.

309. *Oregon Spectator*, 20 January 1848. Company D, The Fifth Company. Captain Thomas McKay, 1st Lt. Charles McKay, 2nd Lt. Alex McKay, Orderly Sgt. Edward Dupois, 1st Sgt. George Montour, 2nd Sgt. Baptist Dorio [Dorion], 3rd Sgt. David Crawford, 4th Sgt. Gideon Pion; Privates: Ampreville [Umfreville], C. Beauchman, N. Bird, A. Bonapaus, J. Cunningham, C. Coweniah, J. A. Delard, F. Dupre, N. English, J. Gervais, F. Gravelle, J. Gustonis, A. Lafaste, O. Lafaste, L. Laplante, R. Linkletter, L. Montour, J. Paine, A. Pearce, A. Plante, A. Poisier, A. Russie, J. Sinegratte, J. Spence, Wm. Towses, A. Vatrais, B. Landeriste, P. Lacourse.

310. Bird, *Thomas McKay*, 81.

311. Ashby Pearce narrative quoted in address of Judge Charles E. Wolverton, Transactions of the Oregon Pioneer Association (Salem, 1898), 67; Johansen, *Newell's Memoranda*, 108-9.

312. Brown and Ruby, *The Cayuse Indians*, 128-31.

313. *Oregon Spectator*, 23 March 1848.

314. Jackson family scrapbooks and recollections.

315. Robbins, "Evolution of County from the Primitive State."

316. Fred Lockley, "Interview with Alice Redmond," *Oregon Journal* 12 (December 1932).

317. "J. O. Fry's Trip Across the Plains and Early Days in the West," *Cosmopolis [Washington] Enterprise*, 29 October 1930, Oregon Historical Society MS 427.

318. *Oregon Spectator*, 17 October 1850.

319. Washington County District (Circuit) Court Record Book, September 1849–June 1852, item 59.

320. Thomas E. Jessett, "Episcopalian Origins," *Oregon Historical Quarterly* 48 (December 1947): 299.

321. Thomas Fraser to John Richards McKay, London, circa 1764, HBCA A10/60, fol. 63, and A6/39, fol. 265–265d.

322. See John C. Jackson, *A Little War of Destiny* (Fairfield, Wash.: Ye Galleon Press, in press).

323. Washington County Probate File 383; Horse Claims "futures" were expected payments for losses in the Indian war.

324. A. J. Splawn, *Ka-mi-akin, Last Hero of the Yakimas* (Portland: Binford & Mort, 1944), 134.

Chapter 14–A Transplanted Sisterhood

325. Statement of Archibald C. MacDonell of Williamstown, Ontario, a great-great-grandnephew, in Bond, *Early Birds of the Northwest*, 29–30. According to Bond, Marguerite returned to Charlottenburgh, Ontario, with Finan in 1827, and on 5 September 1828 they purchased land from the fur trader Peter Grant. Six more children were born to the family, making ten in all. Marguerite died in 1843, Finan in 1851, and both were buried in St. Raphael's cemetery, Glengarry County.

326. Spaulding, *Alexander Ross*, 96.

327. Victor, *The River of the West*, 176.

328. Simpson, *Narrative*, 62.

329. Georgia Willis Read and Ruth Louise Gaines, eds., *Gold Rush: The Journals, Drawings, and Other Papers of J. Goldsborough Bruff, Captain Washington City and Californai Mining Association, April 2, 1849–July 20, 1851* (New York: Columbia University Press, 1949), 372–73.

330. Ulysses Jackson Estate Papers, Washington County Probate Court Records, Hillsboro, Oregon; *Oregon Reports*, vol. 9, 275.

331. Fred Lockely interview with James C. McKay, *Oregon Journal*, 4 March 1932.

332. Governor Abernathy, a representative of the mission party, brought up the liquor issue in 1846, but the provisional legislature only provided for a licensing system, which he refused to sign, and which passed over his veto. Next year the issue was approved by the people by a margin of seventeen votes. On 12 June 1848 prohibition was approved by a vote of 700 to 683. In Twality, 119 voted for it, 95 against.

333. Avery Sylvester, "Voyages of the Pallas and Cheminus," *Oregon Historical Quarterly* 34 (December 1933): 366.

334. Barry M. Gough, *The Royal Navy on the Northwest Coast of North America, 1810-1914*, vol. 1 (Vancouver: University of British Columbia Press, 1971), 74-75.

335. Janice K. Duncan, *Minority Without a Champion: Kanakas on the Pacific Coast, 1788-1850* (Portland: Oregon Historical Society, 1972), 1–24; Henry E. Reed, "William Johnson," *Oregon Historical Quarterly* 34 (December 1933): 314-23.

336. *Oregon Spectator*, 14 May 1846.

337. Robbins, , "Evolution of County from the Primitive State."

338. Fred Lockley, "Mary Alpin Interview," in *History of the Columbia River from The Dalles to the Sea*, 699; William Burris Estate File, Washington County Probate Court, Hillsboro, Oregon.

339. F. X. Mathieu, Sunday *Oregonian*, August 1886, in S. A. Clark, *Pioneer Days in Oregon History* (Portland: J. K. Gill Company, 1905), 470.

340. Read and Gaines, *Gold Rush*, 359-60.

341. Veterans Pension File, Oregon Historical Society.

Chapter 15–Half-Indian Troubles

342. Portland Public Library photocopy of Margaret Jewett Baily, *The Grains or Passages from the Life of Ruth Rover* (Portland: Carter Austin, 1854). The author was more inclined to find sympathy for the beleaguered Indians than for her unhappy husband, Doctor William Bailey, whose attempt to get out of their miserable marriage through divorce generated this response.

343. Loewenberg, *Equality on the Oregon Frontier*, 90-91, 237-38.

344. Ibid., 62.

345. Frederick Merk, *The Oregon Question: Essays in Anglo-American Diplomacy and Politics* (Cambridge: Belknap Press of Harvard University Press, 1946), 248.

346. George Wilkes, *The History of Oregon: Geographical and Political* (New York: William H. Colyer, 1845), 102.

347. J. M. Bacon, "Mercantile Life in Oregon City," copy of Bancroft Library MS in Multnomah County Library, Portland.

348. McLoughlin to HBC, 28 March 1845, in Rich, *McLoughlin's Fort Vancouver Letters*, Third Series, 73.

349. McLoughlin to Simpson, 3 March 1845, in Robert Carlton Clark, *History of the Willamette Valley* (Chicago: S. J. Clark, 1927), appendix 7, 804-6.

350. Schafer, "Documents Relative to the Warre and Vavasour Military Reconnaissance," 72.

351. W. H. Gray, *History of Oregon, 1792-1849, Drawn from Personal Observation and Authentic Information* (Portland: Harris & Holman; New York: American News Company, 1870), 343. Bear in mind that Gray and Newell were philosophical opponets at this writing and there may have been an intention to embarrass the outspoken mountaineer.

352. Janice K. Duncan, *Minority without a Champion: Kanankas on the Pacific Coast, 1788-1850* (Portland: Oregon Historical Society, 1972), 17–18.

353. James Taylor Papers, Oregon Historical Society MS 1006.

354. Gray, *History of Oregon*, 544.

355. J. Quinn Thorton, "History of the Provisional Government," *Oregon Pioneer Transactions, 1874*, 43; Gray, *History of Oregon*, 544.

356. M. V. Havard, "The French Half-breeds of the Northwest," *Annual Report of the Smithsonian Institution, 1879* (Washington, D.C.:, Government Printing Office, 1879), 313–14.

357. Sicade, Henry, "A paper read to the Research Club of Tacoma on 10 April 1917," in Washington State Historical Society, *Building a State, Washington 1889-1939* (Tacoma: Pioneer Incorporated, 1940), 491–92.

Chapter 16–John Flett: A Man Between

358. Johansen, *Newell's Memoranda*, 94; Brown and Ruby, *The Cayuse Indians*, 81, 129.

359. E. E. Rich, ed., *Colin Robertson's Correspondence Book, September 1817 to September 1822* (Toronto: Champlain Society, 1939), 213. The country marriage was legalized 7 December 1823, the same time that five sons were baptized.

360. "Narrative of the Reverend George Flett," *Manitoba Free Press*, 12 March 1887, from a photostat furnished by C. A. Kipling, of Calgary, whose genealogical material is now in the Kipling Genealogy Collection, Glenbow Institute.

361. E. S. Rogers, "Southeastern Ojibwa," *Handbook of North American Indians*, vol. 15, *Northeast* (Washington, D.C.: Smithsonian Institution, 1978), 764–65.

362. "Narrative of the Reverend George Flett."

363. Thomas Simpson to Hargrave, 9 December 1835 and 11 August 1836, in Glazebrook, *Hargrave Correspondence*.

364. On 22 January 1842, Chloe Bird Flett died in childbirth on the north Tualatin plains; her husband, James, died the following year. Their four children were thrown upon the kindness of the community. Mary E. Flett was adopted by the Archibald McKinlay family, Charlotte by the Thomas Smith family, and Jemmima by the McKay and John Flett families. The joint land holding of James and David Flett was purchased by the American immigrant Jacob Hoover, and part

of the money was used to clear James's debt for two cows acquired from the HBC after he left Nisqually. See Kipling Genealogy Collection, Glenbow Institute; *Hillsboro Argus*, 24 February 1972, 6; Mrs. Robert A. Palmer to author, Myrtle Creek, 7 August 1982.

David Flett moved to Wapato Lake, near his brother John, where he died on 5 September 1846. His widow married the Indiana pioneer J. B. Rogers. On her death, one son, John B. Flett, disposed of his inheritance for a good horse. The other son, William G. Flett, became a ward of his uncle John and married Lydia, a daughter of neighbor William Dougherty; in later years William proposed to collect the portraits of the Red River folk "to commemorate the facial appearance of the noblest body of men since Columbus." See Alvin T. Smith Diaries, Oregon Historical Society MS; E. E. Dye Collection, Oregon Historical Society; Flett to Steel, 4 January 1892, Oregon Historical Society MS 335; *Oregon Journal*, 2 February 1939 and 8 November 1942.

365. W. A. Slacum, "Slacum's Report on Oregon," *Oregon Historical Quarterly* 13 (June 1912): 175–224; Charles Wilkes, "Report on the Territory of Oregon (1832–42)," *Oregon Historical Quarterly* 12 (September 1911): 269–99.

366. A. J. Allen, comp., *Ten Years in Oregon: Travels and Adventures of Doctor E. White and Lady West of the Rocky Mountains* (Ithaca: Andrews & Company, 1848), 189–90, also in Brown and Ruby, *The Cayuse Indians*, Appendix A.

367. National Archives, Bureau of Indian Affairs, Oregon Superintendency of Indian Affairs, 1842–1880, in Harold Mackey, *The Kalapuyans* (Salem: Mission Mill Museum Association, 1974), 83–84.

368. Photocopy of a letter collected by historical dealer W. H. Murray, purported to be the in hand of Robert Newell, 19 August 1846, Multnomah County Public Library MS, also in Johansen, *Robert Newell's Memoranda.*.

369. Alvin T. Smith Diaries, Oregon Historical Society MS.

370. Read and Gains, *Gold Rush*, 826, 1073 n. 107.

371. Mackey, *The Kalapuyans*, 84–85.

372. Terence O'Donnell, *An Arrow in the Earth: General Joel Palmer and the Indians of Oregon.*(Portland: Oregon Historical Society, 1991).

373. Copy of a treaty with the Tualatin Indians, Oregon Historical Society MS 144.

374. *Tacoma Daily Ledger*, 13 December 1892, Flett folder, Washington State Historical Society; Official Proceedings of U.S. Commissioners to treat with the tribes common to the two territories begun 29 May 1855, Oregon Historical Society; Lawrence Kip, "The Indian Council at Walla Walla, May and June 1855," in *Contributions of the Department of Economics and History, University of Oregon, Sources of the History of Oregon*, vol. 1, (Eugene: Star Job Office, 1897), 2.

375. Copy of a pocket diary of Joel Palmer for the year 1854, Oregon Historical Society MS 114; photocopy of Wasco treaty, Oregon Historical Society MS 144.

376. Extracted from *Treaties and Agreements of the Indian Tribes of the Pacific Northwest* (Washington, D.C.: Institute for the Development of Indian Law, n.d).

377. John S. Reason to citizens of Tualatin Plains, 18 October 1855, Oregon Provisional and Territorial Government Papers 6502, Oregon Historical Society microfilm.

378. John Flett, "The Removal of the Oregon Indians," *Tacoma Daily Ledger*, 11 September 1892, Flett folder, Washington Historical Society.

379. Ells to Reverend S. B. Treat, 3 October 1857, *Letters and Papers of the American Board of Commissioners for Foreign Missions*, 248.

380. The Tshimakain mission of Cushing and Myra Eells failed to gain a single Spokane Indian convert, and they had to retreat during the Cayuse War. Their son Edwin, who was born there in July 1841, later became an Indian agent on the coast. See George P. Castile, "Edwin Eells, U.S. Indian Agent, 1871–1895," *Pacific Northwest Quarterly* 72 (April 1981): 61–62.

381. Washington County, Oregon, Deed Book H, 267.

382. George M. Guilmet and David Whited, "Incontenence and Biomedicine: Examples of Puyallup Indian Medical Ethnohistory," paper presented at the Third Biennial Meeting of the Society for Philosophy and Technology, Enschele, The Netherlands, 14–16 August 1985, copy in Puyallup Indian Reservation folders, National Archives, FRC, Seattle.

383. Information concerning the Puyallup Reservation is abstracted from Marshall Helsa and Ann Kennedy, comps., "Preliminary Inventory of Puyallup Indian Agency," 1974, National Archives, FRC, Seattle.

384. John Flett to *Tacoma News*, 2 February 1884.

Chapter 17–A Dispersed Community

385. John'Francis Grant, a son by an earlier marriage born at Fort des Prairies in 1831 and educated at Quebec, returned to join his father at Fort Hall in 1845. The killing of his brother James by jealous Blackfoot relatives in August 1883 touched off tragic circumstances for those tribesmen.

386. Paul C. Phillips, ed., *Granville Stuart: The Montana Frontier, 1852–1864* (1925; reprint, Lincoln: University of Nebraska Press, 1977), 125–26, 129.

387. Marie Cuffe Shea, *Early Flathead and Tobacco Plains: A Narrative History of Northwestern Montana* (Author, 1977), 20.

388. Carroll Van West, *A Traveler's Companion to Montana History* (Helena: Montana Historical Society Press, 1986), 175. Merle Wells names

Louis Seymore Grant as a descendent doing graduate studies on a proud heritage.

389. Phillips, *Granville Stuart*, 197–98.

390. Shea, *Early Flathead and Tobacco Plains*, 30.

391. Van West, *Traveler's Companion*, 135.

392. Catharine, a daughter of Patrick Finlay and Rosalie Ashley, married a man named Couture. Among her sisters, Rosalie married Alexander Morigeau, Angelic married Palin, Mary Ellen married John Mullen and then Jones, Julia married Courville, and Mary Ann married Peter King. Mrs. Wood said Marie Gaspar (from Sault Ste. Marie) was also a wife of Patrick Finlay. Bond, *Early Birds of the Northwest*, 26–27.

393. Shea, *Early Flathead and Tobacco Plains*, 38–39.

394. White, *David Thompson's Journals*, 83 n. 53.

395. Phillips, *Granville Stuart*, 137–40.

396. Roxanne DeMarce, ed., *Blackfoot Heritage: 1907–1908* (Browning: Blackfoot Heritage Program, n.d.); author's private collection of materials concerning the Montour family.

397. Richard Mackie, "Joseph William McKay," in *Dictionary of Canadian Biography*, 12:641–43.

398. Barker, *Letters of Dr. John McLoughlin*, 185.

399. Mary Balf, *Kamloops: A History of the District* (Kamloops, n.d.), 10–11.

400. Sarah McKinlay to E. E. Dye, 20 May 1892, in E. E. Dye Collection, Oregon Historical Society.

401. Warner and Munnick, *CCRPNW: Vancouver*, 52, baptism 114. At that time Julia's stepbrother, Joseph Rivet, also was traveling with them and baptized his two-year-old son, Charles, by a Spokane woman. Julia's daughter Sarah Julia Ogden McKinlay does not help the mystery in statements she made to the historian Eva Emery Dye. She wrote that her mother came from the Flatheads, but in another letter indicated that her mother's father, a Flathead chief, was half-Crow and that her mother met a Crow brother near Salt Lake when she was traveling with the Snake Brigade. McKinlay to Dye, Savona, 30 December 1891, 20 May 1892, E. E. Dye Collection, Oregon Historical Society.

402. Gloria Griffin Cline, *Peter Skene Ogden and the Hudson's Bay Company* (Norman: University of Oklahoma Press, 1974), 145, 156, 164, 176–77.

403. Warner and Munnick, *CCRPNW: Vancouver*, A. 70; Cline, *Peter Skene Ogden*, 215.

Chapter 18–A Persistent Heritage

404. Van Kirk, *Tender Ties*, 187–88, 278 n. 41; Munnick, *CCRPNW: St. Paul*, A. 58.

405. HBCA E4/1b, fol. 235 in Van Kirk, *Tender Ties*, 148, 273 n. 11.

406. *Genealogical Material in Oregon Donation Land Claims* (Portland: Portland Genealogical Forum), 2:78.

407. *Evidence for the United States in the Matter of the Claim of the Hudson's Bay Company pending before the British and American Joint Commission* (Washington, D.C.: M'Gill & Witherow, 1867), 64. Testimony of Richard Flandeau that Charles Wren, a half-breed Indian, was long in the service of the Company. He caught calves and yearlings belonging to the Company and killed up to a hundred head of cattle.

408. Wren Family correspondence and papers, British Columbia Provincial Archives.

409. H. K. Himes, *History of Oregon* (Chicago: Lewis Publishing Company, 1893), 131; *Genealogical Material in Oregon*, 1:92.

410. McNeill to Douglas, 8 February 1842 and 7 March 1842, Fort Nisqually Correspondence Outward, British Columbia Provincial Archives.

411. Margaret A. MacLeod, *The Letters of Letitia Hargrave* (Toronto: Champlain Society, 1947), xliii, 36n, 72, 77, 85n, 127, 213; also in Van Kirk, *Many Tender Ties*, 88–89.

412. *British and American Joint Commission for the Settlement of Claim of the Hudson's Bay and Puget Sound Agricultural Companies* (Montreal: John Lovell, 1868), 113–15; Munnick, *CCRPNW: St. Louis*, 37, 91, A. 4.

413. Washington County, Oregon, Deed Book H; Washington County, Oregon, Probate File 970, Estate of David Munro.

414. Sinclair to Simpson, San Francisco, 19 March 1851; Sinclair to Simpson, Red River, 28 August 1853; Simpson to Sinclair, Lachine, 8 October 1853; Sinclair to Simpson, Red River, 1 November 1853; Simpson to Sinclair, Lachine, 22 December 1853; Simpson to Sinclair, Lachine, February 1854, all in Lent, *West of the Mountains*, 225–27, 231–34.

415. "John V. Campbell Narrative," *Washington Historical Quarterly* 7 (July 1916): 187–201.

416. Biographical sketches in William N. Bischoff, S.J., *We Were Not Summer Soldiers: The Indian War Diary of Plympton J. Kelly, 1855–1856* (Tacoma: Washington State Historical Society, 1976), 144, 161–62, 167–68.

417. Keith Clark and Donna Clark, *Daring Donald McKay or The Last War Trail of the Modocs* (Portland: Oregon Historical Society, 1971), xiii–xix.

418. Lottinville, *Duke of Wurttemberg*, 271 n. 43.

419. Irving W. Anderson, "J. B. Charbonneau, Son of Sacajawea," *Oregon Historical Quarterly* 71 (September 1970): 247-64; "J. B. Charbonneau to Date," *Oregon Historical Quarterly* 72 (March 1971): 78-79; Ann Hafen, "Baptiste Charbonneau," *The Mountain Men*; vol. 1; Helen Addison Howard, *American Frontier Tales* (Missoula: Mountain Press Publishing Company, 1982), 44-47, 49-51. Particular thanks to Merle Wells for keeping alive the memory of a unique personality.

420. A. D. Boone to E. E. Dye, 8 December 1904, in E. E. Dye Collection, Oregon Historical Society; Spalding Collection, Penrose Memorial Library, Whitman College; Spalding to Ogden, Clearwater, 25 December 1847, in *Oregon Spectator*, 20 January 1847.

421. U. S. Census, 1850, 1860; *Oregon Statesman*, 10 April 1860; Vital Statistics File, Oregon Historical Society; William A. McNeal, *A Brief History of Old Wasco County* (The Dalles: McNeal, 1975).

422. Lloyd Brown, comp., *Index of Clackamus County Probate Records, 1845-1900* (Mount Hood Genealogical Forum, n.d.), 57; Bond, *Early Birds of the Northwest*, 136-37.

423. For background on the southern coast, see Beverly H. Ward, *White Moccasins* (Myrtle Point: Author, 1986).

Selected Bibliography

Manuscript Sources

Bancroft Library, Berkeley, California
    George B. Roberts Recollections
    Joseph William McKay Recollections

British Columbia Provincial Archives, Victoria
    Fort Colvile Correspondence
    Fort Nisqually Correspondence
    Lowe Papers
    Selkirk Papers Microfilm
    Wren Family Correspondence and Papers

Hudson's Bay Company Archives,
Manitoba Provincial Archives, Winnipeg
    Brandon House Journals
    Flatheads Post Journals
    Fort Edmonton Journals, Correspondence and Accounts
    Fort George, Columbia River Journal
    Fort Vancouver Correspondence Outward and Accounts
    Peter Fidler Exploration, Journals and Maps
    Spokane House Journals and Reports
    Snake Hunting Expedition Field Journals
    North West Company Records
    Red River Settlement, Register of Marriages and Census

Missouri Historical Society, St.Louis
    Ashley Papers
    Campbell Collection
    Chouteau Collection
    Fur Trade Collection
    Sublette Papers
    Waldo Papers

Oregon Historical Society, Portland
> Fort Nisqually Miscellaneous Papers (microcopy of Henry
> Huntington Library Collection)
> Indian War Veterans Pension File
> Newspapers microfilm
> Provisional and Territorial Papers microcopy
> Provisional Land Claims Insurance microcopy
> Scrapbooks
> A. T. Smith Diaries
> John Stuart Letterbooks microcopy
> Eva Emory Due Collection

Pendleton Public Library, Pendleton, Oregon
> W. C. McKay Papers

United States National Archives, Federal Records Center,
> Seattle, Washington
> Indian Reservation Files

Washington County Court and Probate Court Records, Hillsboro, Oregon

Washington State Library, Olympia
> Donation Land Claims File
> County Tax Rolls
> Pioneer Interviews Collection

Printed Sources

Abel, Annie Heloise, ed. *Tabeau's Narrative of Loisel's Expedition to the Upper Missouri.* Norman: University of Oklahoma Press, 1939.

Adams, Winona, ed. "An Indian Girl's Story of a Trading Expedition to the Southwest About 1841 [1840]." In *Frontier Omnibus*, edited by John W. Hakola. Missoula: Montana State University Press, 1962.

Ball, Lucy, Kate Ball Powers, and Flora Ball Hopkins, comps. *Born to Wander: Autobiography of John Ball, 1794-1884.* 1925. Reprint, Grand Rapids: Grand Rapids Historical Commission, 1994.

Barry, J. Nelson, "Astorians Who Became Permanent Settlers." *Washington Historical Quarterly* 24 (July 1933): 221-31 and (October 1933): 282-301.

Bird, Annie Laurie. Thomas McKay. Caldwell, Ida.: Caxton Printers, 1972.

———. "Thomas Mckay." *Oregon Historical Quarterly* 40 (June 1939): 1-18.

Bond, Rowland. *Early Birds of the Northwest: 100 Years of Western History from Jacques Raphael Finlay to Dutch Jake Goetz.* Nine Mile Falls, Wash.: Spokane House Enterprises, 1971-72.

Brackenridge, Henry Marie. *Views of Louisiana.* Pittsburgh, 1814. Reprint, Chicago: Quadrangle Books, 1962.

British and American Joint Commission for the Final Settlement of the Claims of the Hudson's Bay and Puget's Sound Agricultural Companies [Proceedings]. Montreal: J. Lovell, 1868.

Brown, Jennifer S. H. *Strangers in Blood: Fur Trade Company Families in Indian Country.* Vancouver: University of British Columbia Press, 1980.

Carpenter, Cecelia Svinth. *Fort Nisqually: A Documented History of Indian and British Interaction.* Tacoma: Tahoma Research Service, 1986.

Chittenden, Hiram Martin, and Alfred Talbot Richardson, eds. *Life, Letters and Travels of Father Pierre-Jean De Smet, S.J., 1801-1873.* 4 vols. New York: Francis P. Harper, 1905.

Cline, Gloria Griffin. *Peter Skene Ogden and the Hudson's Bay Company.* Norman: University of Oklahoma Press, 1974.

"Copy of a Document Found among the Private Papers of the Late Dr. John Mcloughlin." *Serial Transactions of the Oregon Pioneer Association for 1880.* Salem, Oregon, 1881.

Coues, Elliott, ed. *New Light on the Early History of the Greater Northwest: The Manuscript Journals of Alexander Henry, Fur Trader of the Northwest Company, and of David Thompson, Official Geographer and Explorer of the same Company, 1799-1814.* 2 vols. Minneapolis: Ross & Haines, 1897. Reprint, Minneapolis: Ross & Haines, 1965.

Davidson, Gordon Charles. *The North West Company.* 1918. Reprint, New York: Russell & Russell, 1967.

Davies, K. G., and Alice M. Johnson, eds. *Peter Skene Ogden's Snake Country Journal 1826-7.* London: Hudson's Bay Record Society, 1961.

DeMarce, Roxanne, ed. *Blackfoot Heritage. 1907-1908.* Browning, Mont.: Blackfoot Heritage Program, n.d.

Donaldson, Thomas. *Extra Census Bulletin: Indians of the Six Nations of New York.* Washington, D.C.: United States Census Publishing Office, 1892.

Donnelly, Joseph P., ed. *Wilderness Kingdom: Indian Life in the Rocky Mountains, 1840-1847, the Journals and Paintings of Nicolas Point, S.J.* New York: Holt, Rinehart & Winston, 1967.

Drury, Clifford M. *Marcus and Narcissa Whitman and the Opening of Old Oregon.* Glendale: Arthur H. Clark, 1973.

———. *Nine Years with the Spokane Indians: The Diary of Elkanah Walker, 1838-1848.* Glendale: Arthur H. Clark, 1976.

Elliott, T. C. "Journal of Alexander Ross—Snake Country Expedition." *Oregon Historical Quarterly* 14 (December 1913): 366-88.

——. "The Journal of John Work, July 5–September 15, 1826." *Washington Historical Quarterly* 6 (January 1915): 26–49.

——. "The Strange Case of David Thompson and Jeremy Pinch." *Oregon Historical Quarterly* 40 (June 1939): 188–99.

Ferris, Warren A. *Life in the Rocky Mountains: A Diary of Wanderings on the Sources of the Rivers Missouri, Columbia, and Colorado, from February 1830 to November 1835.* Edited by Paul C. Phillips. Denver: Old West Publishing Company, 1940.

Foster, John E. "Some Questions and Perspectives on the Problems of Metis Roots." In *The New Peoples: Being and Becoming Metis in North America,* edited by Jacqueline Peterson and Jennifer S. H. Brown. Lincoln: University of Nebraska Press, 1985.

Franchere, Hoyt C., trans. and ed. *The Overland Journal Diary of Wilson Price Hunt.* Ashland: Oregon Book Society, 1973.

Frisch, Jack A., "Iroquois in the West." In *Handbook of North American Indians.* Vol. 15, *Northwest.* Washington, D.C.: Smithsonian Institution, 1978.

Galbraith, John S. "The Early History of the Puget's Sound Agricultural Company." *Oregon Historical Quarterly* 55 (September 1954): 234–59.

——. *The Hudson's Bay Company as an Imperial Factor, 1821–1869.* Berkeley: University of California Press, 1957.

——. *The Little Emperor: Governor Simpson of the Hudson's Bay Company.* Toronto: Macmillan of Canada, 1976.

Gates, Charles M., ed. *Five Fur Traders of the Northwest.* St. Paul: Minnesota Historical Society, 1965.

Gerstill, Richard. *The Steel Trap in North America: The Illustrated Story of Its Design, Production, and Use with Fur Bearing and Predatory Animals from Its Colorful Past to the Present Century.* Harrisburg, Penn.: Stackpole Books, 1985.

Gibson, James R. *Farming the Frontier: The Agricultural Opening of the Oregon Country, 1786–1846.* Seattle: University of Washington Press, 1985.

Giraud, Marcel. *Le métis canadien.* Paris: Institut d'Ethnologie, Museum National d'Histoire Naturelle, 1945. Reprint, translated by George Woodcock, *The Metis of the Canadian West.* 2 vols. Lincoln: University of Nebraska Press, 1986.

Glazebrook, G. P. de T., ed. *The Hargrave Correspondence, 1821–1843.* Toronto: Champlain Society, 1938.

Glover, Richard, ed. *David Thompson's Narrative, 1784–1812.* Toronto: Champlain Society, 1962.

Gough, Barry. *The Journal of Alexander Henry the Younger, 1799–1814.* 2 vols. Toronto: Champlain Society, 1992.

Gray, William H. *A History of Oregon, 1792–1849: Drawn from Personal Observations and Authentic Information.* Portland: Harris & Holman, N.d. Reprint, New York: The American News Company, 1870.

Hafen, LeRoy R., ed. *The Mountain Men and the Fur Trade of the Far West.* 10 vols. Glendale: Arthur H. Clark, 1965–72.

Haines, Francis D., ed. *The Snake Country Expediton of 1830–1831: John Work's Field Journal.* Norman: University of Oklahoma Press, 1971.

Hines, Rev. Gustavus. *Oregon: Its History, Condition, and Prospects.* New York: George H. Derby & Company, 1850. Reprint, New York: Arno Press, 1973.

Holmes, Kenneth L. *Ewing Young: Master Trapper.* Portland: Binford & Mort, 1967.

Holmgren, Eric J. "Jacques-Raphael Finlay." In *Dictionary of Canadian Biography.* Vol. 6. Toronto: University of Toronto Press, 1987.

Hungry Wolf, Adolf, and Beverly Hungry Wolf. *Indian Tribes of the Northern Rockies.* Skookumchuck, B.C.: Good Medicine Books, 1989.

Hussey, John A. *Champoeg, Place of Transition: A Disputed History.* Portland: Oregon Historical Society, 1967.

Innis, Harold A. *The Fur Trade in Canada: An Introduction to Canadian Economic History.* New Haven: Yale University Press, 1930. Reprint, New Haven: Yale University Press, 1964.

Jackson, Donald. *Thomas Jefferson and the Stoney Mountains.* Urbana: University of Illinois Press, 1981.

James, Edwin, ed. *A Narrative of the Captivity and Adventures of John Tanner during Thirty Years Residence among the Indians in the Interior of North America.* 1830. Reprint, Minneapolis: Ross & Haines, 1956.

James, Thomas. *Three Years among the Indians and Mexicans.* Waterloo, Ill., 1846. Reprint, New York: Lippincott, 1962.

"Jason Lee Diary." *Oregon Historical Quarterly* 17 (September 1916).

Johansen, Dorothy O., ed. *Robert Newell's Memoranda: Travles in the Territory of Missourie; Travle to the Kayuse War; together with a Report on the Indians South of the Columbia River,* Portland: Champoeg Press, 1959.

Johnson, Alice M., ed. *Saskatchewan Journals and Correspondence, 1795–1802.* London: Hudson's Bay Record Society, 1967.

Johnson, Donald R., ed. *William H. Gray: Journal of His Journey East, 1836–1837.* Fairfield, Wash.: Ye Galleon Press, 1980.

Johnson, Theodore T. *California and Oregon, or Sights in the Gold Region.* Philadelphia: J. B. Lippencotte, 1857.

Josephy, Alvin M., Jr. *The Nez Perce Indians and the Opening of the Northwest.* New Haven: Yale University Press, 1965.

Kowrach, Edward J., ed. *Journal of a Catholic Bishop on the Oregon Trail: The Overland Crossing of Rt. Rev. A. M. A. Blanchet, Bishop of Walla Walla, from Montreal to Oregon Territory, March 23, 1847, to January 23, 1851.* Fairfield, Wash.: Ye Galleon Press, 1978.

Lamb, W. Kaye, ed. *Sixteen Years in the Indian Country: The Journal of Daniel Williams Harmon, 1800-1816.* Toronto: Macmillan of Canada, 1957.

Landerholm, Carl, trans. *Notices and Voyages of the Famed Quebec Mission to the Pacific Northwest.* Portland: Oregon Historical Society, 1956.

Lavender, David, ed. *The Oregon Journals of David Douglas . . . during the Years 1825, 1826, and 1827.* Vol. 1. Ashland: Oregon Book Society, 1972.

Lent, D. Geneva. *West of the Mountains: James Sinclair and the Hudson's Bay Company.* Seattle: University of Washington Press, 1963.

Lewis, William S., and Paul C. Phillips, eds.*The Journal of John Work.* Cleveland: Arthur H. Clark, 1923.

Lockley, Fred. "Reminiscences of Leila McKay." *Oregon Journal* (16 October 1927).

Lothrop, Gloria Ricci Lothrop, ed. *Recollections of the Flathead Mission by Fr. Gregory Mengarini, S.J.* Glendale: Arthur H. Clark, 1977.

Lottinville, Savoie, ed., *Duke of Wurttemberg: Travels in North America, 1822-1824,* by Paul Wilhelm, translated by Robert W. Nitske. Norman: University of Oklahoma Press, 1974.

McDonald, Lois Halliday, ed. *Fur Trade Letters of Francis Ermatinger.* Glendale: Arthur H. Clark, 1980.

Mackay, Douglas. *The Honourable Company: A History of the Hudson's Bay Company.* Toronto: McClelland and Stewart, 1966.

MacLeod, Margaret A., ed. *The Letters of Letitia Hargrave.* Toronto: Champlain Society, 1947.

Majors, Harry M. "John McClellan in the Montana Rockies, 1807: The First American after Lewis and Clark." *Northwest Discovery: The Journal of Northwest History and Natural History* 2 (November-December 1981).

Mason, Elizabeth, and Adele Rahn. "Web of Power in the Fur Trade of the Old South West: A Genealogical Approach." Paper presented to the Fifth North American Fur Trade Conference, Montreal, 1 June 1985.

Merk, Frederick. *The Oregon Question: Essays in Anglo-American Diplomacy and Politics.* Cambridge: Belknap Press of Harvard University Press, 1946.

——, ed. *Fur Trade and Empire: George Simpson's Journal 1824–1825*. Cambridge: Harvard University Press, 1931.

Meyers, J. A. "Jacques Raphael Finlay." *Washington Historical Quarterly* 10 (July 1919): 163–67.

Miller, David E., ed. "Peter Skene Ogden's Journal of his Expedition to Utah in 1825." *Utah Historical Quarterly* 22 (April 1952).

Mitchell, Howard I., ed. *The Journals of William Fraser Tolmie, Physician and Fur Trader*. Vancouver, B.C.: Mitchell Press, 1963.

Morgan, Dale L., ed. *The West of William H. Ashley . . . , 1822–1838*. Denver: Old West Publishing Company, 1964.

Morton, Arthur S. "Nipawi, on the Saskatchewan River, and Its Historic Sites." *Transactions of the Royal Society of Canada* (1944).

——, ed. *The Journal of Duncan M'Gillivray of the North West Company at Fort George on the Saskatchewan, 1794–1795*. Toronto: Macmillan, 1929. Reprint, Fairfield, Wash.: Ye Galleon Press, 1989.

Munnick, Harriet Duncan, ed. *Catholic Church Records of the Pacific Northwest*. 6 vols. Portland: Binford & Mort, 1979.

Nasatir, A. P., ed. *Before Lewis and Clark*. 2 vols. St. Louis: St. Louis Historical Documents Foundation, 1952.

O'Meara, Walter. *Daughters of the Country: The Women of the Fur Traders and Mountain Men*. New York: Harcourt, Brace & World, 1968.

Oglesby, Richard. *Manuel Lisa and the Opening of the Missouri Fur Trade*. Norman: University of Oklahoma Press, 1963.

Oregon Archives including the Journals, Governor's Messages, and Public Papers of Oregon. Salem: Asahel Bush, 1853.

Owens, Nancy Jean. "Indian Reservations and Bordertowns: The Metropolis-Satellite Model Applied to the Northwestern Navahos and the Umatillas." Ph.D. diss., University of Oregon, 1976.

Park, Robert E. "Human Migration and the Marginal Man." *American Journal of Sociology* 33 (May 1928): 881–93.

Partoll, Albert J., ed. "Mengarinni's Narrative of the Rockies." In *Frontier Omnibus* Missoula: Montana State University Press, 1962.

Payette, B. C., comp. *The Northwest*. Montreal: Payette Radio, 1964.

——, comp. *The Oregon Country Under the Union Jack: Postscript Edition*. Montreal: Payette Radio, 1962.

Peterson, Ethel M. "Oregon Indians and Indian Policy, 1849–1871." Master's thesis. University of Oregon, 1933.

Peterson, Jacqueline, and Jennifer S. H. Brown, eds. *The New Peoples: Being and Becoming Métis in North America*. Lincoln: University of Nebraska Press, 1985.

Pike, C. J. "Petitions of Oregon Settlers: Being a Compilation of Those Documents Addressed to the Congress of the United States from Oregon Settlers during the Decade 1838-1848." Master's thesis, University of Oregon, 1933.

Pollard, Juliet. "The Making of the Métis: Race, Class, and Gender in the Nineteenth Century Pacific Northwest." Ph.D. diss., University of British Columbia, 1989.

Porter, Kenneth W. "Roll of the Overland Astorians, 1810-1812." *Oregon Historical Quarterly* 34 (January 1933): 105-12.

Quaife, Milo Milton, ed., *Adventures of the First Settlers on the Oregon or Columbia River, by Alexander Ross*. London: Smith Elder & Company, 1849. Reprint, New York: Citadel Press, 1969.

———, ed., *Gabriel Franchere: A Voyage to the Northwest Coast of America.* 1854. Reprint, New York: Citadel Press, 1968.

Ray, Arthur J. *Indians in the Fur Trade: Their Role as Trappers, Hunters, and Middlemen in the Lands Southwest of Hudson Bay, 1660-1870.* Toronto: University of Toronto Press, 1974.

Records of the Oregon Supreme Court [Oregon Reports 9]. Portland: Stevens Ness, 1938.

Rich, E. E. *The History of the Hudson's Bay Company.* London: Hudson's Bay Record Society, 1928-29.

———. *Part of Dispatch From George Simpson, Esgr., Governor of Ruperts Land, to the Governor and Committee of the Hudson's Bay Company, London.* London: Hudson's Bay Record Society, 1947.

———, ed. *The Letters of John McLoughlin from Fort Vancouver to the Governor and Committee.* 3 vols. Second Series, 1839-44. London: Hudson's Bay Record Society, 1943.

———, ed. *Peter Skene Ogden's Snake Country Journals, 1824-25 and 1825-26.* London: Hudson's Bay Record Society, 1950.

Rollins, Philip Ashton, ed. *The Discovery of the Oregon Trail: Robert Stuart's Narratives.* New York: Charles Scribner's Sons, 1935.

Roy, Antoine. "Repertoire des engagements pour l'ouest, 1805-1821." In *Raport L'Archivist de la Province de Quebec pour 1945-1946.* Quebec, 1946.

Sicade, Henry. "A Paper Read to the [Washington State Historical Society] Research Club of Tacoma on 10 April 1917." In *Building a State: Washington, 1889-1939.* Tacoma: Pioneer Incorporated, 1940.

Skarsten, M. O. *George Drouillard. . . .* Glendale: Arthur H. Clark, 1964.

Spaulding, Kenneth A., ed. *Alexander Ross: The Fur Hunters of the Far West.* London, 1855. Reprint, Norman: University of Oklahoma Press, 1956.

Spry, Irene M. "The Métis and Mixed Bloods of Rupert's Land before 1870." In *The New Peoples: Being and Becoming Métis in North America,* edited by Jacqueline Peterson and Jennifer S. H. Brown. Lincoln: University of Nebraska Press, 1985.

———. "Routes Through the Rockies." *Beaver* (Autumn 1963): 27–33.

Stewart, Edgar I., and Jane R. Stewart, eds., *The Columbia River, by Ross Cox* Norman: University of Oklahoma Press, 1957.

Stewart, William Drummond. *Edward Warren.* London: G. Walker, 1854; Missoula: Mountain Press Publishing Company, 1986.

Stonequist, Everett V. *The Marginal Man: A Study of Personality and Culture Conflict.* New York: Scribner's Sons, 1937. Reprint, New York: Russel & Russel, 1961.

Thwaites, Reuben Gold, ed. *Original Journals of the Lewis and Clark Expedition, 1804–1806.* 8 vols. New York: Dodd, Mead, 1904–5. Reprint, New York: Antiquarian Press, 1959

———, ed. "P. J. De Smett, S.J., Letters and Sketches, with a Narrative of a Year's Residence among the Indian Tribes of the Rocky Mountains." In *Early Western Travels, 1748–1846.* Vol 27. Cleveland: Arthur H. Clark, 1906.

Tolhrop, Gloria Ricci, trans. and ed. *Recollections of the Flathead Mission by Fr. Gregory Mengarinni, S.J.* Glendale: Arthur H. Clark, 1947.

Treaties and Agreements of the Indian Tribes of the Pacific Northwest. Washington, D.C.: Institute for the Development of Indian Law, n.d.

Tyrrell, J. B. "Letter of Roseman and Perch, July 10th, 1807." *Oregon Historical Quarterly* 38 (December 1937): 191–97.

———, ed. *David Thompson's Narrative of His Explorations in Western America, 1784–1812.* Toronto: Champlain Society, 1916.

Van Kirk, Sylvia. *"Many Tender Ties": Women in Fur Trade Society in Western Canada, 1670–1870.* Winnipeg: Watson & Dwyer Publishing, 1980.

Victor, Frances Fuller. *River of the West: Life and Adventure in the Rocky Mountains and Oregon. . . .* Hartford: R. W. Bliss & Company, 1870. Reprint, Columbus, Ohio: Long's College Book Company, 1950.

Vincens, Simone. *Madame Montour et son temps.* Montreal: Quebec/Amerique, 1979.

Wallace, W. S. *Documents Relating to the North West Company.* Toronto: Champlain Society, 1934.

Wells, Merle. "Michael Bourdon." In *The Mountain Men and Fur Trade of the Far West,* edited by LeRoy R. Hafen. Vol. 3. Glendale: Arthur H. Clark, 1966.

White, John Seeley. *The Spells of Lamazi: A Historical Novel of the Pacific*

Northwest Coast. Portland: Breitenbush Publications, 1982.

White, M. Catharine, ed. *David Thompson's Journals Relating to Montana and Adjacent Regions, 1808-12*. Missoula: Montana State University Press, 1950.

Williams, Glyndwr, ed. *Hudson's Bay Miscellany, 1670-1870*. Winnipeg: Hudson's Bay Record Society, 1975.

——, ed. *Peter Skene Ogden's Snake Country Journals, 1827-28 and 1828-29*. London: Hudson's Bay Record Society, 1971.

——, ed. *London Correspondence Inward from Sir George Simpson, 1841-42*. London: Hudson's Bay Record Society, 1973.

Wood, W. Raymond. "Plains Trade in Prehistoric and Protohistoric Intertribal Relations." In *Anthropology in the Great Plains*. Lincoln: University of Nebraska Press, 1980.

Wood, W. Raymond, and Thomas D. Thiessen, eds. *Early Fur Trade on the Northern Plains: Canadian Traders Among the Mandan and Hidatsa Indians, 1738-1818*. Norman: University of Oklahoma Press, 1985.

Index